Peace, Security and Conflict Prevention

SIPRI–UNESCO Handbook

CW00953303

sipri

Stockholm International Peace Research Institute
Frösunda, S-169 70 Solna, Sweden
Cable: SIPRI
Telephone: 46 8/655 97 00
Telefax: 46 8/655 97 33
Email: sipri@sipri.se
Internet URL: http://www.sipri.se

Peace, Security and Conflict Prevention
SIPRI–UNESCO Handbook

Introduction by
Adam Daniel Rotfeld and Janusz Symonides

OXFORD UNIVERSITY PRESS
1998

Oxford University Press, Great Clarendon Street, Oxford OX2 6DP
Oxford New York
Athens Auckland Bangkok Bagotá Bombay Buenos Aires
Calcutta Cape Town Dar es Salaam Delhi Florence Hong Kong Istanbul
Karachi Kuala Lumpur Madras Madrid Melbourne Mexico City
Nairobi Paris Singapore Taipei Tokyo Toronto Warsaw
and associated companies in
Berlin Ibadan

Oxford is a registered trade mark of Oxford University Press

Published in the United States
by Oxford University Press Inc., New York

British Library Cataloguing in Publication Data
Data available

Library of Congress Cataloging-in-Publication Data
Data available

ISBN 0–19–829429–8
ISBN 0–19–829435–2 (pbk.)

Typeset and originated by Stockholm International Peace Research Institute
Printed in Great Britain on acid-free paper by
Biddles Ltd., Guildford and King's Lynn

Contents

Panels

Maps

SIPRI Yearbooks **referred to in the handbook:**

SIPRI Yearbook 1992: World Armaments and Disarmament (Oxford University Press: Oxford, 1992)

SIPRI Yearbook 1993: World Armaments and Disarmament (Oxford University Press: Oxford, 1993)

SIPRI Yearbook 1994 (Oxford University Press: Oxford, 1994)

SIPRI Yearbook 1995: Armaments, Disarmament and International Security (Oxford University Press: Oxford, 1995)

SIPRI Yearbook 1996: Armaments, Disarmament and International Security (Oxford University Press: Oxford, 1996)

SIPRI Yearbook 1997: Armaments, Disarmament and International Security (Oxford University Press: Oxford, 1997)

Preface

This handbook was undertaken as a joint project of the Stockholm International Peace Research Institute (SIPRI) and the United Nations Educational, Scientific, and Cultural Organization (UNESCO) in 1995. It is a comprehensive, concise compendium of the facts, figures and developments in the field of security and arms control.

In 1989 the International Congress on Peace in the Minds of Men, convened by UNESCO in Yamoussoukro, Côte d'Ivoire, invited states, intergovernmental and non-governmental organizations, and the scientific, educational and cultural communities of the world to help construct a new vision of peace by developing a peace culture. In response, UNESCO has put forward a programme to promote a culture of peace. This concept is anchored in the Constitution of UNESCO, which in its preamble underlines that 'the education of humanity for justice and liberty and peace are indispensable to the dignity of man and constitute a sacred duty which all the nations must fulfil'.

The UNESCO General Conference, during its 28th session in 1995, adopted Resolution 5.3—Transdisciplinary project: Towards a Culture of Peace—by which it invited *inter alia* the Director-General to support the adoption of educational policies, plans and programmes, as well as the design and dissemination of manuals, textbooks and teaching aids for education for peace, human rights and democracy.

On 22 December 1995 and 12 December 1996, the United Nations General Assembly adopted Resolutions 50/173 and 51/101, respectively, which welcome the UNESCO programme and encourage countries, regional organizations and non-governmental organizations to take all necessary action to ensure education for peace, human rights, democracy, international understanding and tolerance. This volume is a response to this request and a contribution to the UNESCO project.

The basic outline of the book was prepared at SIPRI by Ragnhild Ferm, Elisabeth Sköns and Connie Wall. The data in the handbook cover the period 1992–96 and the discussions in the chapters take into account events up to mid-1997. Bradley Feasey, Canada, was commissioned to write the book, based on published SIPRI material. He worked closely with SIPRI in Stockholm and completed his work in 1996. SIPRI updated the information on a number of significant events which occurred in 1996 and early 1997—such as the signing of the Comprehensive Nuclear Test-Ban Treaty, the entry into force of the Chemical Weapons Convention, and finalization of the NATO decision to enlarge its membership.

The chapters are based on research published by SIPRI, chiefly in the *SIPRI Yearbooks* (see page x). The reader is referred to the *Yearbooks* for further information as well as for the original sources that were consulted.

The members of the SIPRI research staff who reviewed material from their fields of expertise for this volume are: Ian Anthony (the arms trade and export controls); Eric Arnett (the comprehensive nuclear test ban); Vladimir Baranovsky (the war in Chechnya); Ragnhild Ferm (the UN Organization, arms control treaties, the chronology, and the glossary, with Connie Wall); Trevor Findlay and Olga Hardardóttir (conflict prevention, management and resolution); Paul George, Agnès Courades Allebeck and Evamaria Loose-Weintraub (military expenditure); Bates Gill (security in the Asia–Pacific region); Shannon Kile (nuclear weapons and arms control); Zdzislaw Lachowski (European security and the ban on land-mines); Adam Daniel Rotfeld (European security); Elisabeth Sköns (arms production); and Jean Pascal Zanders (chemical and biological weapons and arms control). Ragnhild Ferm also acted as the research consultant for the entire volume. Chapter 1 is based on the work of the Uppsala Conflict Data Project which is commissioned annually by SIPRI and contributed by Margareta Sollenberg and Peter Wallensteen of the Department for Peace and Conflict Research, Uppsala University, Sweden. Janusz Symonides, UNESCO, reviewed the material in chapter 6 on the United Nations.

Material was also drawn from work previously commissioned by SIPRI from many other researchers throughout the world, too numerous to mention here; their names appear in the *SIPRI Yearbooks* given as references in the footnotes.

Special thanks go to the editors of this volume, Connie Wall, head of the SIPRI Editorial Department, and Billie Bielckus, who prepared the maps and diagrams, for advice throughout the project, for editing and updating the material, and for setting the book in camera-ready format.

The index was prepared by Peter Rea, UK.

The handbook has been produced to help promote education for peace in universities, teachers' colleges and secondary schools, in particular for UNESCO Chairs and Associated Schools. Although it is mainly an educational aid, it will also be useful for all those interested in the issues of peace, security, arms control and conflict resolution.

Dr Adam Daniel Rotfeld
Director
SIPRI

Professor Janusz Symonides
Director
Division of Human Rights,
Democracy and Peace
UNESCO

November 1997

Introduction

A cooperative security system and a culture of peace

Adam Daniel Rotfeld and Janusz Symonides

1 New threats and challenges

The era of the cold war was marked by both high stability and high military threat, while the post-cold war world of the 1990s is characterized by low military threat and a low level of stability. The bipolar system, based on mutual deterrence between the two global superpowers, is a thing of the past, but a new world order has not yet emerged.

The end of bipolarism triggered global structural change as well as multilateralism. The international system predicated on the principles of interaction between sovereign states is eroding. The world is witnessing not only the globalization and multilateralization of international relations and the growing role of transnational bodies but also the breakup of the international system based on an unswerving respect for the sovereign independence of states. That system functioned, albeit with both successes and failures, since the Westphalia Peace of 1648 which ended the Thirty Years' War. International security was contingent on the balance of power among the large states, with the underlying assumption that individual states are guarantors of security, prosperity and development.

In the post-cold war period, new threats and risks have emerged, at the same time as some of the old ones continue to exist. For example, the risk of an outbreak of global nuclear war has been greatly diminished with the political marginalization of nuclear weapons, but the danger of the proliferation of nuclear and other weapons of mass destruction remains and has in fact increased.

Today, the most likely menace is civil wars and regional conflicts. Indeed, major armed conflicts have one common denominator: they are internal in nature. According to the SIPRI criteria (see chapter 1), the sole interstate major armed conflict in 1996 was that between India and Pakistan.

Another serious threat is posed by the loss of control of developments by the great powers, the multilateral security organizations and the states on whose territories conflicts have broken out. As central governments in some multi-ethnic states are losing control of developments, these states are sliding into anarchy and ungovernability.[1]

The deterioration of the environment now also presents a global threat. Ecological problems often have a trans-boundary effect and even the most sophisticated weapons cannot protect a state from ecological threats. Deforestation, desertification, gradual loss of biodiversity, climate changes, thinning of the zone layer, water and air pollution, and the growing contamination of the planet all create threats to the very survival of humankind. The environmental problem is proof that, if in the past a threat to the security of a state could be repulsed by the action undertaken by this state, either alone or in conjunction with other states, now such threats, because of their global dimension, can only be dealt with effectively through a planetary effort.

The main elements of normal human activity—trade, communications, culture, finance—not to mention society's scourges—drugs, crime, disease, terrorism—increasingly transcend national boundaries and national sovereignty. There is a steady globalisation of institutions in these fields. In *political* life, however, nationalism, and also ethno-nationalism, has re-emerged as a strong and intransigent force. This constitutes a major challenge to internationalism and multilateralism which seemed to be the most sensible course for the nations to pursue after the second world war.[2]

The criterion by which to judge the effectiveness of international security structures, both global and regional, is whether or to what extent they are adequate to meet the new types of threat. Security organizations have proven incapable of preventing or solving such conflicts, and the big powers seem to have lost interest in controlling developments in the areas that in the past were considered their 'zones of influence', especially in Africa. Threats which today undermine stability and may tomorrow threaten world security are 'ripening' on the peripheries of great-power global politics. Conflicts which might be headed off are often played down or ignored so long as they do not escalate into open wars in which tens or hundreds of thousands of lives are endangered. None the less, people's expectations with regard

[1] Kaplan R. D., 'The coming anarchy', *Atlantic Monthly*, Feb. 1994, p. 54.
[2] Urquhart, B., 'The future security agenda', Keynote speech delivered at SIPRI's 30th Anniversary Conference, Stockholm, 3 Oct. 1996.

to ensuring security and prosperity are addressed not only to individual states but also to global and regional transnational organizations.

The fact that present-day conflicts are of an intra-state nature points to the need for an adjustment of the structure of the United Nations. In this context, it is first of all important to note that the effectiveness of UN action is primarily determined by the will of the member states.

An adjustment of the UN inevitably raises the question of the acceptance of the limitation of state sovereignty. Further development of the concept of domestic jurisdiction, the acceptance of the supremacy of international law and a new interpretation of the principle of non-intervention in internal affairs is needed to increase the possibility of effective UN action in cases of internal conflicts and massive violations of human rights.

2   A cooperative security system and domestic factors

The current strategic environment is often portrayed as one of uncertainty and change. Many observers claim that, in fact, everything has changed but geography. A return to the concept of geopolitics and geo-strategy is an expression of intellectual helplessness in the attempt to understand the new realities rather than a promising future-oriented strategy. It is a truism that geographic location is one of the factors in the security of a state, and this is the one factor that is unchangeable. The political and economic elements of security, however, have undergone fundamental changes. It is enough to recall that in Europe, after the breakup of the Soviet Union and Yugoslavia, the division of Czechoslovakia and German unification, more than 20 new states appeared. This development, together with the process of decolonization, has tripled the number of states-subjects of international law in the past half century.

In this context, the view that the nature of international security must be redefined is gaining in prominence. In the past, a shift in the world was indicated by a change in the answers to three questions: Who are the major players? What can they do to one another? What do they wish to do to one another?

A much more important consideration than geographic location is the system of values by which a state is guided—whether it is of a totalitarian, authoritarian or democratic nature. A new definition of the concept of security should, however, take into account not only these values and interests but also the new premises, including the breakup of the Westphalian international system based on the omnipotence of sovereign states. The political significance of the military dimension of security has diminished, while the role of the economic, social and cultural dimensions is growing.

Today, power is to a great extent determined by which state is ahead in the information revolution, and this will be even more true in the future. The dominant position of the United States in communications and information-processing technologies stems from its huge investments and its open society. Space-based surveillance, direct broadcasting, high-speed computers and an unparalleled ability to integrate complex information systems have shaped an information edge that 'can help deter or defeat traditional military threats at relatively low costs'.[3] This has permitted the United States, the members of the European Union, Japan and other highly industrialized countries to strengthen their security and enables them to enhance international stability through attraction rather than coercion. The obstacles to making use of this potential are traditional, predominantly military, perceptions of security and adherence to traditional parameters of security, such as gross national product (GNP), population, energy, land, minerals, and so on, as well as an unawareness of what the information revolution has already contributed and can offer to security efforts.

The evolution of a global security system is not linear but takes place on many planes. Since the threats which the security system was to meet in the past have changed fundamentally, the driving forces, dimensions, forms, procedures and mechanisms of operation of the process must change as well. In the bipolar system, the great powers claimed to be 'international security wardens'; the options were limited and the middle powers had to reconcile themselves to the existing state of affairs. In the multipolar world, small and medium-size states are gaining in significance.

The foundation of security is both the common values that are the product of history, culture, civilization, religion or common institutions and the community of political, economic, military and other

---

[3] Nye, J. S., Jr and Owens, W. A., 'America's information edge', *Foreign Affairs*, vol. 75, no. 2 (Mar./Apr. 1996), p. 20.

vital interests. It is these vital interests that largely determine the rules of conduct of states.

3 An international security system and the interdependence of states

Establishing a new international security order will be a long-term process of accommodating the existing institutions to new tasks rather than one of creating new organizational structures.

The new security system will express the political philosophy of a pluralistic community rather than a specific model or set of abstract assumptions. The comprehensive nature of such a system should reflect three fundamental objectives of peace:

- security;
- social and economic welfare; and
- respect for human rights, justice and organization of society based on democratic principles and the rule of law.

Indivisible international security cannot be identified with equal security. Moreover, the often declared principle of equal security does not exist in practice. Great powers, by definition, have a greater ability to independently ensure their own security than do the small and medium-size states, which see their admission to multilateral structures as an 'insurance policy' against worst-case scenarios.

In search of a new security system, states will increasingly be involved in integration processes and seek to take advantage of multilateral institutions to manage international interdependence. Thus the first item on a future security agenda must be 'to preserve, rationalize and strengthen the international and multilateral framework that has been built up over the last fifty years'.[4] The point is that institutions, by their very nature, are static, while security processes, particularly in the course of a fundamental restructuring of the international system as a whole, are dynamic. The conclusion to be drawn from this is as follows: the multilateral security structures which were created after World War II, such as the United Nations, or during the cold war, such as the North Atlantic Treaty Organization (NATO) and the Western European Union (WEU), require reforms that will adapt them to the radically altered security environment. Thus transformed,

[4] Urquhart (note 2).

they must respond to the new requirements, new policy areas, new competences, and new instruments and decision-making procedures 'for a functional and politically adequate and effective handling of the institutions' list of tasks'.[5]

An important constituent part of the security process is the tangible progress in arms control, limitation and reduction and in disarmament, on the one hand, and, on the other, the diminishing significance of military factors. The priority has become armed conflict prevention, crisis management, peaceful settlement of disputes and conflict resolution.

4   From a culture of violence to a culture of peace

In a world where many regions suffer from increasing tensions, conflicts and violence, making peace a tangible reality is of critical importance. Ethno-nationalism, xenophobia, racism and discrimination against minority groups, religious extremism and violations of human rights are increasingly the cause of local and regional conflicts. Violence fuelled by hatred and directed against non-nationals, refugees, asylum seekers and immigrant workers is a serious threat to domestic security and the very fabric of states themselves. At the same time, exclusion, poverty, urban decay, mass migration, environmental degradation and new pandemic diseases, as well as terrorism and the traffic in drugs, create very real threats to internal and international security.

The current culture of violence—based on distrust, suspicion, intolerance and hatred and on the inability to interact constructively with all those who are different—must be replaced by a new culture— based on non-violence, tolerance, mutual understanding and solidarity and on the ability to solve disputes and conflicts peacefully. The world is in need of such a new culture and a common system of values and new behavioural patterns for individuals, groups and nations because, without them, the major problems of international and internal peace and security cannot be solved.[6]

---

[5] Peters, I., 'New security challenges and institutional change', ed. I. Peters, *New Security Challenges: The Adaptation of International Institutions: Reforming the UN, NATO, EU and CSCE since 1989* (St. Martin's Press: New York, N.Y., 1996), pp. 11–17.

[6] See more in Symonides, J. and Singh, K., 'Constructing a culture of peace: challenges and perspectives—an introductory note', in *UNESCO Peace and Conflict Issues Series: From a Culture of Violence to a Culture of Peace* (UNESCO: Paris, 1996), pp. 9–30.

An analysis of the current situation leads to the conclusion that the main objective formulated in UNESCO's Constitution half a century ago, namely, the construction of the defence of peace in the minds of men and women, is more valid than ever before. Indeed, 'a peace based exclusively upon the political and economic arrangements of governments would not be a peace which could secure the unanimous, lasting and sincere support of the peoples of the world . . . and peace must therefore be founded, if it is not to fail, upon the intellectual and moral solidarity of mankind'.[7]

The end of the cold war created new possibilities for the United Nations system and for the whole of the international community to move towards a culture of peace. Not only has the threat of a global nuclear war been removed to a great extent but the role of the military factor in international relations is decreasing. This, in consequence, paves the way towards disarmament and demilitarization both internationally and internally and towards the elimination of enemy images, distrust and suspicion. Moreover, the sharp divisions and theoretical debates on the concept of human rights are being replaced by recognition that the promotion and protection of all human rights is an important element of peace and development and, as such, is a major concern of the international community as well as a priority objective of the United Nations.

The process of transition towards democracy is another factor conducive to the construction of a culture of peace. Democracies, as proved by historical experience, not only do not make war against each other but also through their systems of governance—rule of law, participation, transparency and accountability—diminish considerably recourse to violence.

The term 'culture' may be used in both a wide and a restricted sense. In the wider meaning, 'culture' concerns the sum of human activities, the totality of knowledge and practice, whereas in the restricted meaning 'culture' is understood mainly as the result of creative activities and the highest intellectual achievements, such as music, literature, art or architecture.

A culture of peace should be understood in the broader sense. 'Culture' is not only a knowledge of certain values but also an adherence to them and a readiness to defend and follow them in everyday

---

[7] See UNESCO's Constitution at URL <http://www.unesco.org>.

life. Thus a culture of peace should be understood as the creation of peaceful, non-violent behavioural patterns and skills.[8]

A fundamental question concerning human nature is pertinent. Are human beings capable of peace? The view that man is the source of all evil, including war, has a long tradition. Its advocates include, among others, St Augustine, Hobbes, Luther, Spinoza, Malthus and Freud. Contemporary research does not confirm the thesis of man's unappeased and irresistible drive for war. A group of well-known scientists challenge the biological pessimism based on alleged human aggressiveness which is so frequently used to explain or even justify war. Violence does not appear either as part of our evolutionary legacy or in our genes; it is in our sociological and cultural roots. Moreover, there is nothing in the neurophysiology of human beings which compels them to react violently and it is possible to create a culture of peace founded on their natural pacific behaviour patterns.

Aggressive behaviour does not stem from human nature but is either a result of a process of education or a response to a painful stimulus. Individuals are normally ready to adapt to their environment and, under normal circumstances, prefer cooperation to aggressiveness. They are also capable of self-control, love, friendship and tolerance. And these dispositions can be developed.

There is a need to elucidate this notion of a culture of peace. In general there are two understandings of peace:

• the 'negative', narrow understanding, which reduces peace to the mere absence of war; and
• the 'positive' understanding, which defines peace as the absence of armed conflict, often enriched by further elements and guarantees which make peace constructive, just and democratic.

In the second sense, peace is not a static state but a dynamically conceived aim of international and national communities. The main, indispensable values on which a positive peace can be built may be grouped around such key notions as justice, human rights, democracy, development, non-violence and peaceful resolution of conflicts. A culture of peace cannot be built during an arms race or militarization of societies, which unavoidably generates enemy images, suspicions and threats. Therefore, disarmament and demilitarization are absolute

---

[8] Symonides and Singh (note 6).

conditions. Positive peace assumes not only the absence of war but also the absence of the instruments and institutions of war.

The human being must be considered as the central subject and ultimate beneficiary of all efforts aimed at the creation of a common and cooperative system of security. 'Human security' in particular implies the right to live in dignity. This cannot be achieved simply through the implementation of political and civil rights but also through that of economic, social and cultural rights, including the right to development.

A culture of peace is intimately linked with a culture of human rights and democracy. Peace cannot be preserved if the basic rights and fundamental freedoms of individuals or groups are violated and when discrimination and exclusion generate conflict. Therefore, the protection of human rights and the promotion of a culture of democracy, which imply *inter alia* the formation of well-informed, democratically minded and responsible citizens, become important elements in the construction of internal and international peace.

Education is at the heart of any strategy for the construction of a culture of peace. It is through education that the broadest possible introduction can be provided to the values, skills and knowledge which form the basis of respect for peace, human rights and democratic principles. The obligation of states to develop education for peace and human rights is already well established in international law.

A culture of peace includes, by definition, an ethical dimension and principles of solidarity, burden-sharing as well as respect for others' cultures and moral values. This must be recognized as being essential. The normative bases should be complemented and enriched by moral or ethical principles.

5 Conclusions

A profound transformation of the international community, leading to the elimination of the causes of conflict and violence, is by no means an easy task. The replacement of the existing culture of violence by a culture of peace, human rights and democracy can only be achieved in a longer perspective. Experience shows that, although political and economic changes may be rapid, cultural changes, in particular changes in the behavioural patterns of individuals, groups and nations, take time. A culture of peace can be achieved only when all potential partners are fully engaged in its realization.

There is no single organizing principle for global security. Globalization, often referred to and identified with Westernization, neither describes nor explains the problems of the present-day world. The paradox is that in parallel with advancing globalization the emerging international security agenda is more focused on domestic, local and regional issues than was the case under the bipolar system.[9] This leads to the following conclusions:

• Institutional forms and instruments of cooperation in the sphere of security should be adequate to the new realities of a pluralistic world—multipolar, multicultural and multi-civilizational.

• The existing security structures were formed to respond to the threats which are the least prevalent today; for example, they are intended to ensure the inviolability of borders that are no longer disputed. The reforms which have been initiated aim at readjusting security institutions to the new tasks: domestic conflict prevention, crisis settlement, peacemaking and developing the new concept of post-conflict peace-building. In addition, the expectations with regard to security that are addressed to regional and subregional organizations as a rule extend beyond the territories of the member states.

• Shaping a new security system, both globally and regionally, is part of the broader historical process in which neither the great powers nor the security organizations have exclusive rights. If the regime of global and international security that is emerging from trial-and-error processes and new experiences is to adhere to the declared democratic values—the rule of law, pluralistic democracy, respect for human rights and market economy—it cannot be based on the hegemony of one or several powers. The security system should give expression to the interdependence of states, where mutual relations are governed by generally accepted principles of international law.

* * *

Based on the published findings of the Stockholm International Peace Research Institute, this book presents the essential facts and developments that underlie the major changes and challenges to a new security system described above. Chapter 1 presents data on the num-

---

[9] Buzan, B., 'Rethinking security after the cold war', *Cooperation and Conflict*, vol. 32, no. 1 (Mar. 1997), p. 12.

ber, type and location of the major armed conflicts in 1992–96, and chapter 2 focuses on multilateral efforts to deal with armed conflict. Background information on military expenditure and on the production of and trade in major conventional weapons is given in chapter 3, while chapter 4 reviews the world stockpiles of nuclear, chemical and biological weapons. The bodies and processes through which arms control takes place are reviewed in chapter 5, which also presents summaries of the main international arms control treaties. Chapter 6 describes the place of the United Nations in the international security system and examines the major bodies and responsibilities of the organization. Cases studies of Europe and Asia are presented in chapter 7 to illustrate different regional and subregional approaches to contemporary security problems. Major events related to armaments and disarmament during the period 1992–96 are listed in the chronology in chapter 8, and the comprehensive glossary provided in chapter 9 amplifies the descriptions, definitions and explanations given throughout the book.

1. Major armed conflicts

1.1 Introduction

A 'major armed conflict' as defined in this chapter is prolonged combat between the military forces of two or more governments or between the military forces of one government and at least one organized armed group. In either case, the conflict must have resulted in at least 1000 battle-related deaths during its duration to be included in the conflict statistics for any year.

This chapter presents information on the number, type and location of the major armed conflicts in 1992–96. Although five years is a short time-span to judge trends in this aspect of international relations, the discussion points out that almost all the new conflicts since the end of the cold war have been conflicts within states and that they generally claim more civilian than military lives.

Two conflicts, both of which have now ended, are described at greater length—the wars in Chechnya and in the former Yugoslavia. After initially thinking that a military victory would be decisive and swift, Russia became bogged down in a guerrilla war in Chechnya that raged for almost two years. In the former Yugoslavia, the fighting has stopped thanks to the Dayton Agreement, but the future remains uncertain, despite elections in Bosnia and Herzegovina.

1.2 Global patterns in armed conflict in 1992–96

The most striking trend in major armed conflicts has been the gradual disappearance of the 'classical' interstate or international conflict. By 1993 all the major armed conflicts were internal, or intra-state. In 1996 all but one were internal.

In these conflicts, one of two categories of dispute has been the source of war. The first category is disputes over government. This could be the type of political system, a change of central government or a change in the government's make-up. The second category is disputes over territory. This could be a matter of control of territory, secession (separation) or autonomy (state-formation wars).

Map of the locations of the major armed conflicts in 1996

Regional distribution of locations with at least one major armed conflict, 1992–96					
Region[a]	1992	1993	1994	1995	1996
Africa	7	7	6	6	5
Asia	11	9	9	9	10
Central and South America	3	3	3	3	3
Europe	4	5	4	3	2
Middle East	4	4	5	4	4
Total	29	28	27	25	24

[a] Only those regions of the world in which a conflict was recorded for the period 1992–96 are included here.

Source: Uppsala Conflict Data Project.

The internal wars have not been without outside actors. In some of them, foreign troops have been involved. For example, the peacekeeping forces of the ECOWAS[1] Monitoring Group (ECOMOG) have been involved in the war in Liberia. The Commonwealth of Independent States (CIS)—including Russia—has aided government forces in Tajikistan. In 1996 the USA conducted air strikes against Iraq in connection with the Kurdish conflict.

A dramatic change occurred in Europe in the early 1990s, with an increase in the number of conflicts from 1990 until 1993. Two of the new conflicts in this region were on the territory of two former communist federations: the Soviet Union and Yugoslavia (see sections 1.4 and 1.5 on Chechnya and the former Yugoslavia, respectively). By 1996, however, the number of major armed conflicts registered for Europe returned to the level of 1989.

Another observation on the period 1992–96 concerns the role of the major powers in local conflicts. By 1995 it was clear that they were generally not interested in supporting one faction over another in local conflicts. Rather, there was more effort to contain and minimize violence. This is a considerable departure from the period before 1991, when many wars were or became battlegrounds for cold war politics.

[1] ECOWAS is the Economic Community of West African States. For a description of the organization, see chapter 9, section 9.1.

Regional distribution, number and types of contested incompatibilities in major armed conflicts, 1992–96[a]

Region[b]	1992 G	1992 T	1993 G	1993 T	1994 G	1994 T	1995 G	1995 T	1996 G	1996 T
Africa	6	1	6	1	5	1	5	1	4	1
Asia	5	9	4	7	4	7	4	8	4	7
Central and South America	3	–	3	–	3	–	3	–	3	–
Europe	–	4	–	6	–	5	–	3	–	2
Middle East	2	3	2	4	2	4	2	4	2	4
Total	16	17	15	18	14	17	14	16	13	14
Total	33		33		31		30		27	

G = Government and T = Territory, the two types of incompatibility.

[a] The total annual number of conflicts does not necessarily correspond to the number of conflict locations in the other panels in this chapter since there may be more than one major armed conflict in each location.

[b] Only those regions of the world in which a conflict was recorded for the period 1992–96 are included here.

Source: Uppsala Conflict Data Project.

The panel on page 15 shows the regional distribution of the locations of major armed conflicts. A 'location' is the territory of at least one state and can be the site of more than one conflict.

As the figures show, the number of locations of major armed conflicts has declined in Africa over the period 1992–96 and remained relatively unchanged in Asia, Central and South America, and the Middle East. In 1996 Europe experienced the lowest number of conflict locations since the dramatic increase in number in the early 1990s.

The panel above shows the regional distribution of conflicts, broken down according to the dispute which was the source of the conflict— the incompatible positions at the root of the conflict. 'G' designates a conflict over government and 'T' a conflict over territory.

Two noticeable patterns are obvious. First, the number of conflicts has dropped and has been dropping since the end of the cold war. Second, more conflicts are fought over territory than over government control.

1.3   The civilian toll

One of the trends of armed conflict in the 20th century has been the increasing toll on civilians. It is believed that some three-quarters of the war deaths in today's wars are civilian. If the numbers of refugees and wounded are added to the figures for deaths, it is estimated that 90 per cent of the war casualties are civilian. However, it must be pointed out that estimating the number of civilian deaths and casualties in war presents particular difficulties to researchers. Exact figures on civilian deaths are impossible to obtain.

One problem concerns definitions. Once there was a somewhat clearer distinction between the military, who were the combatants, and civilians, who were strictly bystanders. This line has become blurred as sympathetic civilians are playing a greater role in assisting fighting forces. Should these civilians be defined as 'combatants'? This problem of definition is perhaps only a minor one compared to others.

Civilians who have war dead in their midst may not wish to make public the extent of their casualties, preferring to get out of the way of the warring parties as quickly as possible. Sometimes the warring sides are eager to provide estimates on how many civilians were killed by their opponents. International media reports about civilian casualties can be used as propaganda during war. For this reason, these kinds of report cannot be considered reliable unless they are verified by a credible third party. Similarly, relief agencies focus their energies on the living, not the dead. In either case, it is difficult to determine how many civilians may have died or been wounded in an encounter.

Modern arms are increasingly accurate. In theory, this should make it easier to avoid killing civilians. At the same time, however, nearly all of today's wars are conflicts within states, and civilians are often deliberately targeted. A case in point is the conflict in Bosnia and Herzegovina, which involved the targeting of civilian populations. This deliberate strategy is in direct contravention of international humanitarian law.[2] None the less, when one of the war aims is to purge the territory of a particular people—'ethnic cleansing'—civilian deaths are an inherent part of the strategy.

---

[2] For example, the Geneva Conventions of 1949 and the 1977 Protocol (I) Additional to the Geneva Conventions relating to the protection of victims of international armed conflicts.

Locations of at least one major armed conflict, 1992–96

1992	1993	1994	1995	1996
Afghanistan	Afghanistan	Afghanistan	Afghanistan	Afghanistan
	Algeria	Algeria	Algeria	Algeria
Angola	Angola	Angola	Angola	
Azerbaijan	Azerbaijan	Azerbaijan		
Bangladesh	Bangladesh	Bangladesh	Bangladesh	Bangladesh
Bosnia and Herzegovina	Bosnia and Herzegovina	Bosnia and Herzegovina	Bosnia and Herzegovina	
Cambodia	Cambodia	Cambodia	Cambodia	Cambodia
Colombia	Colombia	Colombia	Colombia	Colombia
Croatia	Croatia		Croatia	
	Georgia	Georgia		
Guatemala	Guatemala	Guatemala	Guatemala	Guatemala
India	India	India	India	India
India–Pakistan				India–Pakistan
Indonesia	Indonesia	Indonesia	Indonesia	Indonesia
Iran	Iran	Iran	Iran	Iran
Iraq	Iraq	Iraq	Iraq	Iraq
Israel	Israel	Israel	Israel	Israel
Laos				
Liberia	Liberia	Liberia	Liberia	
Mozambique				
Myanmar	Myanmar	Myanmar	Myanmar	Myanmar
Peru	Peru	Peru	Peru	Peru
Philippines	Philippines	Philippines	Philippines	Philippines
			Russia	Russia
Rwanda	Rwanda	Rwanda		
		Sierra Leone	Sierra Leone	Sierra Leone
Somalia	Somalia	Somalia	Somalia	Somalia
South Africa	South Africa			
Sri Lanka	Sri Lanka	Sri Lanka	Sri Lanka	Sri Lanka
Sudan	Sudan	Sudan	Sudan	Sudan
Tajikistan	Tajikistan	Tajikistan	Tajikistan	Tajikistan
Turkey	Turkey	Turkey	Turkey	Turkey
				Uganda
UK	UK	UK		UK

Sources: Uppsala Conflict Data Project, in *SIPRI Yearbooks 1993–1997*.

Conflict locations with at least one major conflict in 1996

Location	Incompat- ibility[a]	Year formed/ year joined[b]	Warring parties[c]	No. of troops in 1996[d]	Total deaths[e] (incl. 1996)
EUROPE					
Russia	Territory	1991/1994	Govt of Russia *vs.* Republic of Chechnya	1 500 000 5 000–10 000	10 000– 40 000
United Kingdom	Territory	1969/1969	Govt of UK *vs.* Provisional IRA	226 000 ..	1 500*

Notes: Provisional IRA = Provisional Irish Republican Army. * The total number of deaths in political violence in Northern Ireland is *c.* 3200. The figure given here is an estimate of the deaths incurred between the Government of the UK and the Provisional IRA; the remaining deaths were mainly caused by other paramilitary organizations such as the Ulster Volunteer Force (UVF) and the Ulster Freedom Fighters (UFF).

Location	Incompat- ibility[a]	Year formed/ year joined[b]	Warring parties[c]	No. of troops in 1996[d]	Total deaths[e] (incl. 1996)
MIDDLE EAST					
Iran	Govt Territory	1970/1991 1972/1979	Govt of Iran *vs.* Mujahideen e-Khalq *vs.* KDPI	513 000* .. 8 000	..

Notes: KDPI = Kurdish Democratic Party of Iran. * Includes the Revolutionary Guard.

Location	Incompat- ibility[a]	Year formed/ year joined[b]	Warring parties[c]	No. of troops in 1996[d]	Total deaths[e] (incl. 1996)
Iraq	Govt Territory	1980/1991 1977/1980	Govt of Iraq *vs.* SAIRI* *vs.* PUK	350 000–400 000 10 000** ***	..

Notes: SAIRI = Supreme Assembly for the Islamic Revolution in Iraq. PUK = Patriotic Union of Kurdistan. * Most of the Shia rebels belong to this group. ** Total strength of Shia rebels. *** PUK troop strength is possibly some 10 000–12 000.

Location	Incompatibility[a]	Year formed/year joined[b]	Warring parties[c]	No. of troops in 1996[d]	Total deaths[e] (incl. 1996)
Israel	Territory	1964/1964	Govt of Israel vs. PLO groups* vs. Non-PLO groups**	170 000–180 000	1948–: >13 000

Notes: PFLP = Popular Front for the Liberation of Palestine. * The Palestine Liberation Organization (PLO) is an umbrella organization; armed action is carried out by member organizations. Although Al-Fatah, the largest group within the PLO, did not use armed force in 1996, other groups (e.g., PFLP) which reject the 1993 Declaration of Principles on Interim Self-Government Arrangements (Oslo Agreement) did. These groups opposed the PLO leadership but were still part of the PLO in 1996. ** Examples are Hamas, PFLP–GC (Popular Front for the Liberation of Palestine–General Command), Islamic Jihad and Hizbollah.

| Turkey | Territory | 1974/1984 | Govt of Turkey
vs. PKK | 500 000
10 000–12 000 | >19 000 |

Note: PKK = Partiya Karkeren Kurdistan, Kurdish Worker's Party, or Apocus.

ASIA

| Afghanistan | Govt | 1992/1992
1994/1994 | Govt of Afghanistan*
vs. Jumbish-i Milli-ye Islami
vs. Taleban | ..
..
.. | >20 000** |

Notes: * It is unclear whether fighting occurred between the Government of Afghanistan and the Hezb-i-Islami in 1996. ** Includes deaths in the fighting since 1992, in which other parties than those listed above also participated.

| Bangladesh | Territory | 1971/1982 | Govt of Bangladesh
vs. JSS/SB | 117 500
2 000–5 000 | 1975–:
3 000–3 500 |

Note: JSS/SB = Parbatya Chattagram Jana Sanghati Samiti (Chittagong Hill Tracts People's Co-ordination Association/Shanti Bahini [Peace Force]).

Cambodia				
Govt	1979/1979	Govt of Cambodia	130 000*	> 25 500**
		vs. PDK	5 000–10 000	

Notes: PDK = Party of Democratic Kampuchea (Khmer Rouge). * Including all militias. ** For figures for battle-related deaths in this conflict prior to 1979, see *SIPRI Yearbook 1990*, p. 405, and note *p*, p. 418. Regarding battle-related deaths in 1979–89, that is, not only involving the Govt and PDK, the only figure available is from official Vietnamese sources, indicating that 25 300 Vietnamese soldiers died in Cambodia. An estimated figure for the period 1979–89, based on various sources, is > 50 000, and for 1989 >1000. The figures for 1990, 1991 and 1992 were lower.

India				
Territory	../1989	Govt of India	1 145 000	> 20 000*
Territory	../1992	vs. Kashmir insurgents**	..	
	1982/1988	vs BdSF	..	
		vs. ULFA	..	

Notes: BdSF = Bodo Security Force. ULFA = United Liberation Front of Assam. * Only the Kashmir conflict. ** Several groups are active, some of the most important being the Jammu and Kashmir Liberation Front (JKLF), the Hizb-e-Mujahideen and the Harkat-ul-Ansar.

India–Pakistan				
Territory	1947/1996	Govt of India	1 145 000	..
		vs. Govt of Pakistan	587 000	

Indonesia				
Territory	1975/1975	Govt of Indonesia	300 000	15 000–
		vs. Fretilin	100–200	16 000 (mil.)

Note: Fretilin = Frente Revolucionâra Timorense de Libertação e Independência (Revolutionary Front for an Independent East Timor).

Myanmar				
Territory	1948/1948	Govt of Myanmar	300 000	1948–50:
		vs. KNU	4 000	8 000
				1981–88:
				5 000–8 500

Note: KNU = Karen National Union.

Location	Incompatibility[a]	Year formed/ year joined[b]	Warring parties[c]	No. of troops in 1996[d]	Total deaths[e] (incl. 1996)
The Philippines	Govt	1968/1968	Govt of the Philippines vs. NPA	107 000 8 000	21 000– 25 000*

Notes: NPA = New People's Army. * Official military sources claim that 6500 civilians were killed during the period 1985–91.

Sri Lanka	Territory	1976/1983	Govt of Sri Lanka vs. LTTE	120 000 6 000–10 000	> 35 000

Note: LTTE = Liberation Tigers of Tamil Eelam.

Tajikistan	Govt	1991/1992	Govt of Tajikistan, CIS Collective Peacekeeping Force in Tajikistan/ CIS Border Troops* vs. United Tajik Opposition**	5 000–7 000 c. 25 000 ..	20 000– 50 000

Notes: * The CIS operation includes Russian border guards and peacekeeping troops with minor reinforcements from Kazakhstan, Kyrgystan and Uzbekistan. ** The major groups constituting the United Tajik Opposition (formerly recorded as the Popular Democratic Army) are the Islamic Resistance Movement, the Democratic Party of Tajikistan and the Rastokhez People's Movement.

AFRICA					
Algeria	Govt	1992/1992 1993/1993	Govt of Algeria vs. FIS* vs. GIA	150 000	30 000– 50 000

Notes: FIS = Front Islamique du Salut, *Jibhat al-Inqath* (Islamic Salvation Front). GIA = Groupe Islamique Armé (Armed Islamic Group). * The Islamic Salvation Army (Armée Islamique du Salut, AIS) is considered to be the armed wing of the FIS. There are also several other armed Islamic groups under the FIS military command.

Location		Year	Warring parties		
Sierra Leone					
	Govt	1991/1991	Govt of Sierra Leone	12 000–18 000	>3 000
			vs. RUF	2 000–4 000	
Note: RUF = Revolutionary United Front.					
Somalia					
	Govt	1991/1991	Govt of Somalia*	..	
			vs. USC faction (Aideed)	1 000	
Notes: USC = United Somali Congress. * Taken to be the USC faction (Mahdi).					
Sudan					
	Territory	1980/1983	Govt of Sudan	80 000	37 000–
			vs. SPLA (Garang faction)	30 000–50 000	40 000 (mil.)*
Notes: SPLA = Sudanese People's Liberation Army. * Figure for up to 1991.					
Uganda					
	Govt	1993/1994	Govt of Uganda	40 000–50 000	>1 000
			vs. LRA	2 000	
Note: LRA = Lord's Resistance Army.					
CENTRAL AND SOUTH AMERICA					
Colombia					
	Govt	1949/1978	Govt of Colombia	146 400	
		1965/1978	vs. FARC	5 700	..*
			vs. ELN	2 500	
Notes: FARC = Fuerzas Armadas Revolucionarias Colombianas (Revolutionary Armed Forces of Colombia). ELN = Ejército de Liberación Nacional (National Liberation Army). * In the past three decades the civil wars of Colombia have claimed a total of some 30 000 lives.					
Guatemala					
	Govt	1967/1968	Govt of Guatemala	44 200	<2 800 (mil.)
			vs. URNG	800–1 100	<43 500 (civ.)
Note: URNG = Unidad Revolucionaria Nacional Guatemalteca (Guatemalan National Revolutionary Unity). URNG is a coalition of three main groups: Ejército Guerillero de los Pobres (EGP), Fuerzas Armadas Rebeldes (FAR), and Organización del Pueblo en Armas (ORPA).					

Location	Incompatibility[a]	Year formed/ year joined[b]	Warring parties[c]	No. of troops in 1996[d]	Total deaths[e] (incl. 1996)
Peru	Govt	1980/1981 1984/1986	Govt of Peru vs. Sendero Luminoso vs. MRTA	115 000 3 000 500	>28 000

Notes: Sendero Luminoso = Shining Path. MRTA = Movimiento Revolucionario Tupac Amaru (Tupac Amaru Revolutionary Movement).

Note that although some countries are also the location of minor armed conflicts the table lists only the major armed conflicts in those countries.

Notes on the definitions and conventions for the table

[a] 'Govt' and 'Territory' refer to contested incompatibilities concerning government (type of political system, a change of central government or in its composition) and territory (control of territory [interstate conflict], secession or autonomy), respectively.

[b] 'Year formed' is the year in which the incompatibility was stated. 'Year joined' is the year in which use of armed force began or recommenced.

[c] The non-governmental warring parties are listed by the name of the parties using armed force. Only those parties which were active during 1996 are listed in this column.

[d] The figure for 'No. of troops in 1996' is for total armed forces of the government of the conflict location and of non-government parties. For government and non-government parties from outside the location, the figure in this column is for total armed forces within the country that is the location of the armed conflict. Deviations from this method are indicated by a note (*) and explained.

[e] The 'total number of deaths' refers to total battle-related deaths during the conflict. If it is possible to separate military from civilian deaths, military deaths are noted by 'mil' and civilian deaths are noted by 'civ', respectively; where there is no such indication, the figure refers to total military and civilian battle-related deaths in the period or year given. Information which covers a calendar year is necessarily more tentative for the last months of the year.

'. .' indicates that no reliable figures, or no reliable disaggregated figures, were given in the sources consulted.
< = less than; > = more than.

Source: Uppsala Conflict Data Project, in *SIPRI Yearbook 1997*, pp. 25–30. The *Yearbook* should be consulted for a complete presentation.

Another phenomenon is insurgencies which rebel against and overthrow governments only to splinter upon victory. The result is infighting and yet more destruction. An example is Afghanistan. Many of the conflicts since the end of World War II have been guerrilla wars. War at such close quarters often leaves civilians caught between guerrillas and the regular military, each of which suspects civilians of being supporters of the other. An example is the Kurdish conflict in eastern Turkey. All these elements of modern warfare contribute to causing more civilian than military casualties.

1.4   The war in Chechnya

According to the Russian Constitution, Chechnya is one of Russia's 21 constituent republics. None the less, since 1991 Moscow has faced a republic that does not recognize Russian rule and considers itself sovereign and independent. Russia's attempt to defeat the Chechen separatists by force led to bloody conflict and a serious failure and embarrassment for Russian policy.

The North Caucasus region, which includes Chechnya, has a long history of resisting rule from outside. The Russian tsars fought a long war in the 19th century to subdue the region. During the rule of Soviet leader Josef Stalin, the Chechens and other ethnic groups suffered ruthless repression.

Russia's first response to the breakaway republic was political, organizing and promoting political opposition to General Dzhokhar Dudayev (who led the separatist movement) in the hope that the Chechen leader would be removed. This strategy failed.

In November 1994 the opposition to Dudayev led a military march on the capital of Grozny that failed, but not before it had resulted in some 400 casualties. Again, it was revealed that Moscow had been involved, and this angered many people not only in Chechnya but also in Russia. Some two weeks later, after a series of decrees from Moscow and an ultimatum calling for the disarming of 'illegal armed formations' in Chechnya, Russian troops invaded Chechnya and began moving towards Grozny, the capital. Russia's campaign did not go well, for several reasons.

Russia had superior forces when measured by numbers and equipment and was able to take control of Grozny and much of the Chechen

Map showing the location of Chechnya

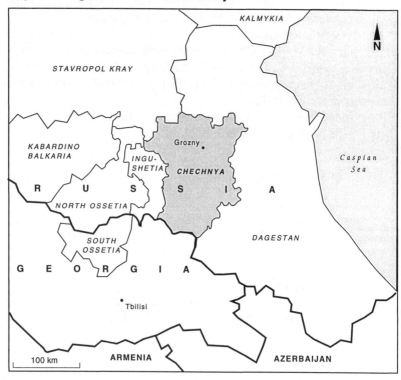

countryside. Defeated in open hostilities, General Dudayev's forces retreated to mountainous areas and adopted guerrilla tactics. With a highly motivated and heavily armed general population, Dudayev was able to draw Russia into a costly local war.

Russia's military performed poorly from the beginning. There was severe criticism in Russia about disorganization, lack of supplies and poor training, strategy and performance. Making matters worse, the serious number of casualties suffered by the Russians weakened morale both in the field and at home. Heavy-handed tactics were used against the Chechens. Tanks, missiles and aircraft were unleashed against Chechen fighters and civilians alike. These methods not only united support behind General Dudayev but also led to condemnation in the Russian media and the Duma, the lower house of the Russian Parliament.

Russian policy was also hampered by electoral considerations. President Boris Yeltsin had to balance public opposition to the war with the cost of defeat in Chechnya and Chechnya's likely independence.

In June 1995 Chechen fighters took dramatic action that forced Russia to open negotiations. The Chechens struck the town of Budennovsk, some 180 km beyond Chechnya's western border, killing several dozen police officers and civilians and taking over 1000 hostages. An attempt to free the hostages failed, with Russia agreeing to peace talks and the safe return of the hostage-takers to Chechnya.

With the assistance of the Organization for Security and Co-operation in Europe (OSCE), an agreement was reached on such issues as a troop withdrawal from the line of contact, an exchange of prisoners and, eventually, the holding of new elections in Chechnya and the appointment of Chechens to the Russian Parliament.

The June agreement was never fully implemented. One of the most important reasons was that the agreement did not deal with the key issue in the conflict—the ultimate status of Chechnya. This gave both sides an interest in preserving their military gains, to give them greater bargaining power when and if discussions were held on Chechnya's political status.

By early October there had been so many violations of the agreement that it was suspended. Elections were held in December 1995, against the wishes of General Dudayev and his allies, and a pro-Moscow puppet government was elected. By the end of the year, Russian armed forces were in control of much of Chechnya but they still faced guerrillas roaming throughout the country, particularly in mountainous areas. President Yeltsin wavered between declaring that military means could not resolve the conflict and calling for strikes against General Dudayev's strongholds.

With presidential elections looming in June 1996, Yeltsin again pressed for an agreement on Chechnya. On 31 March he announced a unilateral cease-fire. However, it failed since it was largely ignored by Chechen fighters and Russian troops alike. In April Dudayev was killed in a rocket attack, and there was some hope that a change in Chechen leadership might bring a new opportunity for peace.

It seemed that peace might be possible when Dudayev's successor, Zelimkhan Yandarbiyev, agreed to a cease-fire in late May. It was not to be. The cease-fire gave way to bloody fighting after President Yeltsin's re-election and a bold rebel attack which retook Grozny in early August.

After the 1996 election, President Yeltsin appointed former General Alexander Lebed as his national security adviser, handing him responsibility for Chechnya. Lebed negotiated a cease-fire on 22 August, which was followed by a draft peace agreement signed by the Chechen leadership on 31 August. Although the agreement is vague on many principles and allows five years before a final settlement of Chechnya's status has to be reached, as of early 1997 fighting had not resumed. All Russian soldiers were officially announced to have left Chechnya by 5 January 1997. Attempts to demilitarize the country were, however, abandoned, and large numbers of weapons were left in the hands of individuals and paramilitary units engaged in criminal and terrorist activities. No Russian laws, institutions or taxes now operate in Chechnya.

The presidential and parliamentary elections in Chechnya of 27 January 1997 were endorsed by Russia and legitimized political power in Chechnya.

The Chechen campaign had a serious impact on Russia. It split the Russian leadership over how to deal with the problem. The Russian public was very negative about the conflict and this feeling of futility and frustration has been shared by Russian soldiers sent to battle. Internationally, the war has undermined Russia's efforts to portray itself as being well on the road to democracy. It has also kept alive fears that Russia still sees itself as an imperial power that will use force to achieve its ends.

For the Chechens, the toll was greater. Unable to defeat their opponent's guerrilla tactics, the Russian military used indiscriminate force, killing thousands and wounding many more.[3] There were also reports of atrocities committed by Russian troops.[4] The economy and infrastructure such as roads, railways and power plants have been heavily damaged and it will take many years to restore Chechnya to even pre-war levels of prosperity.

[3] The estimated number of deaths in the conflict range from 10 000 to 40 000, the majority of which are Chechens. The number of wounded is estimated at over 100 000. The total population of Chechnya was 1 million in 1996. *SIPRI Yearbook 1997*, pp. 25 and 105.
[4] *SIPRI Yearbook 1997*, p. 106.

1.5 Conflict in the former Yugoslavia

The Socialist Federal Republic of Yugoslavia was the creation of Marshal Josip Broz Tito, who led the Yugoslav Communists in the partisan struggle against occupying Nazi German forces in World War II. Tito brought Yugoslavia together as a federal state and ruled until his death in 1980. Without the force of his personality and leadership, the country began to lose cohesion as a political and economic unit. During the 1980s, relations began to break down between the various Yugoslav republics.

In 1990 talks began on the future of Yugoslavia. The republics of Serbia and Montenegro wanted to maintain a centralized federal state. These were the only two republics that held this view. Croatia, Slovenia, Bosnia and Herzegovina, and Macedonia all sought greater autonomy if not outright independence.

From the beginning, Bosnia and Herzegovina was in a particularly difficult position. Although the Muslims were the largest segment of the population, there were significant numbers of Serbs and Croats.[5] Furthermore, both the Serbs and the Croats had traditional claims on all or parts of Bosnian territory.

1.5.1 War in Croatia

In August 1990 Serbs in Croatia organized a referendum on political autonomy and in October declared the creation of the Autonomous Region of Krajina. The following February, the Serbs of Krajina expressed the desire to unite with Serbia and Montenegro.

Military clashes had taken place between the Croatian Government and the Serbs in late September 1990. The federal Yugoslav National Army (YNA) moved in to play a policing role but was viewed by the Croats with deep suspicion, since the federal forces were dominated by Serbs.

In June 1991 both Croatia and Slovenia declared independence. By mid-September, the YNA was openly fighting on the side of the Croat Serbs and battling Slovenian forces as well. During the summer, some one-fifth of Croatia fell to Serbian separatists.

---

[5] In 1991 the breakdown of the population in Bosnia and Herzegovina was as follows: Muslims, 43.7%; Serbs, 31.3%; Croats, 17.3%; 'Yugoslavs', 5.5%; others, 2.2%.

Map showing the new states of the former Yugoslavia

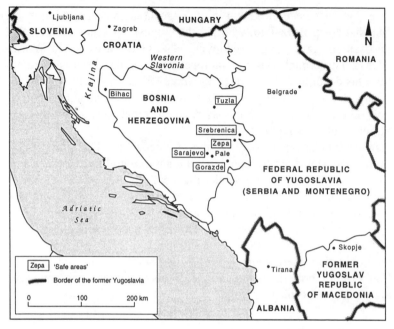

The conflict between Slovenia and the YNA ended in July when YNA forces withdrew. By January 1992 there had been 15 cease-fires mediated in Yugoslavia, either by the European Community (EC) or by the United Nations (UN). In that month the EC recognized the independence of Croatia and Slovenia.

1.5.2   The conflict spreads: Bosnia and Herzegovina

During discussions on the future of Yugoslavia, the Bosnian Serbs made it clear that they would not accept minority status in an independent Bosnia and Herzegovina or in a confederation with Croatia. They preferred to remain part of a federal Yugoslavia or in a Bosnia divided along ethnic lines.

On 29 February–1 March 1992 a referendum was held in Bosnia. It was boycotted by the Serb population and the result was 99 per cent in favour of independence. In April the EC and the USA recognized Bosnia's independence. Later in the month Serbia and Montenegro announced the formation of a new state, the Federal Republic of Yugoslavia. The Yugoslavia created by General Tito was no more.

Although the YNA withdrew from Bosnia and Herzegovina in May, Bosnian Serb officers and soldiers stayed behind and became part of the Bosnian Serb Army. Fighting which had been sporadic in the early spring became more intense and both the Croats and the Serbs sought to control regions where they were the dominant ethnic population.

1.5.3   The UN Protection Force in the former Yugoslavia

Diplomatic efforts to halt the bloodshed began with the EC and then became a joint EC–UN effort. To support an EC-led settlement of the crisis, the UN Security Council agreed to create a peacekeeping force, the UN Protection Force (UNPROFOR), in the former Yugoslavia. The force was first sent to Croatia in April 1992 where it served as a buffer between Croatia and territories within Croatia held by Serb forces.

The EC and the UN sponsored an International Conference on the Former Yugoslavia, which held its first meeting in August 1992. Cyrus Vance (a former US Secretary of State), representing the UN, and Lord Owen (a former British Foreign Minister), representing the EC, worked together to develop a peace plan for Bosnia. It is known as the Vance–Owen Plan.

The Vance–Owen Plan called for the division of Bosnia and Herzegovina into 10 autonomous provinces, with special status for Sarajevo. The agreement was accepted by all parties, only to be rejected by the Bosnian Serb Parliament in May 1993. Furthermore, after a foreign ministers' meeting later in May between France, Russia, Spain, the UK and the USA, it became clear that no one was willing to provide the troops necessary to enforce the provisions of the Vance–Owen Plan.

By this time, the UN had already directed UNPROFOR to provide humanitarian assistance in Bosnia, where the situation had become desperate. In addition, UNPROFOR was given the job of ensuring the security and functioning of the Sarajevo international airport.

In early 1993 the world became more familiar with the term 'ethnic cleansing'. It was the expression used to describe the Serb policy of driving other peoples (usually Muslim Bosnians) from territories Serb forces held or sought to hold.[6] A policy so blatantly directed against civilians of a particular group stirred international outrage. The UN Security Council responded by declaring six largely Muslim areas to be 'safe areas'. While the idea was to provide safe haven for Muslim civilians, UNPROFOR was not given the military capability needed to defend the safe areas.

Shortly after the safe areas were declared by the UN, the Security Council authorized UNPROFOR to reply to attacks on it as well as to any obstructions of its personnel or movements of humanitarian assistance. More importantly, it authorized member states of the UN to assist UNPROFOR by providing air support. The North Atlantic Treaty Organization (NATO) responded by offering to provide such assistance.[7]

1.5.4 Macedonia

In a preventive measure, in December 1992 the UN Security Council deployed UNPROFOR troops along the borders of the Former Yugoslav Republic of Macedonia (FYROM) with Serbia and Albania.[8] The UN hoped to prevent the spread of the wider Yugoslav conflict and was successful in this regard.

1.5.5 Diplomacy after the Vance–Owen Plan

The UN–EC diplomatic effort in Bosnia which was spearheaded by Cyrus Vance (and later Thorvald Stoltenberg) and Lord Owen gave way in early 1994 to the five-nation Contact Group. This group consisted of France, Germany, Russia, the UK and the USA.

The Contact Group oversaw a peace settlement between the Bosnian Croats and the Government of Bosnia and Herzegovina in March 1994. This agreement created a federation between the two. A second agreement followed which outlined a statement of principles linking Bosnia and Herzegovina to Croatia.

---

[6] Although 'ethnic cleansing' has most often been associated with the Serbs, Croats and Muslims have also been accused of atrocities against other ethnic groups residing in the territory they claim.

[7] NATO's role in the conflict actually began with the monitoring and enforcement of the 1991 international arms embargo against the republics of the former Yugoslavia. In Apr. 1993 it then began operations to enforce the no-fly zone over Bosnia and Herzegovina.

[8] In Mar. 1995 the Security Council established the UN Preventive Deployment Force (UNPREDEP) in Macedonia to succeed UNPROFOR. See also chapter 2, section 2.4.1.

The Contact Group then moved on to produce a peace plan which called for 51 per cent of the territory of Bosnia and Herzegovina to be allocated to the Bosnian Muslims and Croats, and the remainder to the Bosnian Serbs. The Contact Group held out various rewards and punishments in support of the plan. It also put great pressure on Serbia itself to pressure the Bosnian Serbs in turn to accept the agreement.

Once again, as it had done with the Vance–Owen Plan a year earlier, the Bosnian Serb Parliament rejected the Contact Group's plan. This time, Serbia responded by closing its border with Bosnia except for food, medicine and humanitarian aid, to force the Bosnian Serbs to agree to the peace plan. Bosnia's new peace between its Muslims and Croats, and Serbia's withdrawal of support for the Bosnian Serbs helped improve Bosnia's military situation.

In November 1994 a serious military/diplomatic crisis developed when the Bosnian Serbs put pressure on the safe area of Bihac. Using heavy weapons and aircraft, the Serbs attacked the city. After being authorized by the UN Security Council, NATO aircraft struck Serbian missile batteries and airfields. The Serbs responded by detaining UN peacekeepers near Bihac. Concern grew that peacekeepers were extremely vulnerable and that NATO strikes against the Serbs would simply translate into retaliation against UNPROFOR.

By the end of 1994 there were considerable divisions between the UN and NATO and within NATO and the Contact Group as to how to proceed.

1.5.6   The emergence of the Dayton Agreement

The year 1995 began with Croatia threatening not to renew the mandate of UNPROFOR in Croatia. It argued that UNPROFOR had merely preserved the status of the Serb territories that had been carved out of Croatia early in the war. As long as UNPROFOR stood as a buffer between the Croats and the breakaway Serbs, there was no incentive for the Serbs to negotiate. The UN Secretary-General essentially agreed with this view, saying that the Serbs had taken advantage of UNPROFOR's protection to establish their Republic of Krajina.

In May Croatia attacked Serbian territories in Western Slavonia. In August it attacked additional Serbian sectors, including Krajina. In both cases, the Federal Republic of Yugoslavia did not come to the aid of the Serbs. In November Croatia negotiated a settlement with the remaining Serb breakaway territories.

The success of Croatia's operations abruptly changed the complexion of the war. The Serbs no longer seemed invincible and the common front between Serbia and the Serbs in Croatia and Bosnia was crumbling.

In Bosnia, a cease-fire arranged by former US President Jimmy Carter collapsed in March and violence steadily increased. In late May Sarajevo suffered from fierce Serb shelling and the UN commander requested NATO air strikes, which were launched. Once again, the Bosnian Serbs hit back by taking UN soldiers hostage. On this occasion they held almost 400.

In July one of the most horrific events of the war took place. The Bosnian Serbs captured the 'safe area' of Srebrenica. Muslim women and children were sent by bus to Bosnian Government-held territory, while men of fighting age were transported to detention camps. Thousands of people went missing, many of whom became the victims of mass executions. Many believe it to have been the largest single mass killing in post-World War II Europe. For their role in this event and others, former Bosnian Serb leader Radovan Karadzic and Bosnian Serb General Ratko Mladic have been indicted for genocide by the UN International Criminal Tribunal for the Former Yugoslavia in The Hague.

In late August a single shell fell in central Sarajevo, killing 37 people. It fell very close to the marketplace where a shell in February 1994 had also killed many civilians, an event that received great publicity around the world. The UN announced that the shell had been fired from Bosnian Serb territory. On 30 August NATO launched the largest military operation in its history. NATO aircraft attacked targets throughout Bosnian Serb-held territory for two weeks, almost without pause.

In the midst of the NATO campaign, US Assistant Secretary of State Richard Holbrooke persuaded the foreign ministers of Bosnia and Herzegovina, Croatia and Yugoslavia (Serbia and Montenegro), which also represented the Bosnian Serbs, to agree on the basic principles of a peace settlement. On 5 October US President Clinton announced a 60-day cease-fire, during which the parties would conduct peace talks. The cease-fire took effect on 12 October 1995.

1.5.7 The uncertain peace in Bosnia and Herzegovina

In 1995, three weeks of talks took place at the Wright-Patterson Air Force Base in Dayton, Ohio, and resulted in November in what is commonly called the Dayton Agreement.[9] Its key element is a 51 : 49 per cent partition of Bosnia and Herzegovina between the Bosnian Croat Federation and the Republika Srpska (the Bosnian Serb territory), respectively.

To implement the agreement, a NATO Implementation Force (IFOR) of 60 000 troops from 33 countries at its peak was created to replace UNPROFOR. The OSCE was assigned the role of human rights and elections monitoring and discussions took place on funding for economic reconstruction.

The Dayton Agreement contains several key elements.

1. IFOR had a one-year mandate. Its commander was authorized to use force if necessary. In particular, force could be used against any party breaking the peace, failing to remove weapons from specified zones or failing to vacate areas to be transferred to others.

2. A new constitution was imposed on Bosnia that created the Muslim–Croat Federation of Bosnia and Herzegovina and the Bosnian Serb Republika Srpska—two entities within a single state, each entity maintaining separate armies.

3. The parties undertook to negotiate, under OSCE auspices, an agreement on balanced and stable defence force levels in and around the former Yugoslavia.[10]

4. No one charged with crimes by the International Criminal Tribunal in The Hague could hold appointive or elective or other public office.

5. Refugees have the right to go home or receive fair compensation for being displaced.

Following signature of the Dayton Agrement, IFOR was rapidly deployed and managed to successfully separate the warring parties, supervise the removal and storage of heavy weapons and end the

---

[9] The full title of the agreement is the General Framework Agreement for Peace in Bosnia and Herzegovina. The agreement has 11 annexes. It was first initialed in Dayton on 21 Nov. and then signed in Paris on 14 Dec. 1995.

[10] These negotiations were held in 1996 and led to the Agreement on Sub-Regional Arms Control—called the Florence Agreement—signed by Croatia, Bosnia and Herzegovina and its 2 entities, and Yugoslavia (Serbia and Montenegro). See also chapter 5, section 5.3.2.

fighting. A UN civilian police force helped supervise and monitor the activities of local police.

As called for in the Dayton Agreement, country-wide elections were held in September 1996. Before September, much concern was expressed that the elections would be so flawed that it was better that they be postponed. Although there was less violence than expected on election day, there was also little free movement of voters. This meant that in many cases neither Serb nor Muslim refugees were able to return to their former homes and territories to cast their ballots.

Alija Izetbegovic, the Muslim President of Bosnia, received the most votes and became the chairman of Bosnia's three-person presidency as well as Bosnian head of state.

Whether a durable peace can be established in Bosnia and Herzegovina remains to be seen. Economic reconstruction is proceeding slowly, as is the re-establishment of normal government functions. In late 1996 IFOR was replaced by the Stabilization Force (SFOR) of 32 000 troops, accompanied by an enlarged civilian police presence, to help ensure that fighting does not break out again in Bosnia.

2. Armed conflict prevention, management and resolution

2.1 Introduction

Conflict management, prevention and resolution are carried out by many actors in the international community—the United Nations, regional organizations, individual states or groups of states and even individuals. Non-governmental organizations (NGOs) and agencies also contribute to the peace process.

Often, success comes when several actors pursue an agreed approach to a conflict situation, drawing on their complementary skills and resources. If, however, the peacemaking parties are not careful to coordinate their efforts, a bad situation can be made worse.

The focus of this chapter is on multilateral efforts to deal with armed conflict. This is not to suggest that other approaches are not legitimate or important but simply to emphasize those cases where states have sought to pursue collective rather than individual action.

Some of the key concepts involved in looking at how the international community responds to conflict or potential conflict situations are defined below. These definitions are by no means absolute. In fact, these terms are subject to a great deal of debate. For example, even 'peacekeeping', which has been part of the international community's vocabulary for almost as long as 'United Nations', is a concept which continues to evolve.

Not only is it difficult to agree on these definitions, but it is also rare that measures taken by the international community can be so neatly categorized. Section 2.4 of this chapter presents several cases of conflict prevention, management and resolution in action. As these cases show, the international community draws on whatever instruments it needs, in whatever combination, to ensure or restore the peace.

2.1.1 Conflict prevention

Conflict prevention is intended to prevent disputes from escalating into armed conflicts, to prevent old conflicts from recommencing and to prevent existing conflicts from spreading. It includes measures

Types of diplomatic initiative and instrument

Arbitration • A process in which an outside party draws up a settlement for the parties to a dispute. In binding arbitration, the parties agree to be bound by the settlement devised by the arbitrator.

Conciliation • A process in which a third party tries to bring the parties to agreement by such things as improving communications, providing technical assistance and exploring potential solutions.

Fact-finding missions • These are carried out by third parties to determine, as far as possible, the objective facts at the heart of a dispute.

Good offices • A process in which a third party acceptable to all parties to the dispute offers his or her aid in opening up communication.

Inspections • Arms control and disarmament treaties often have provisions for inspections. Inspections are intended to build confidence and prevent misunderstanding between parties.

Judicial settlement • A decision rendered by a court or legal panel.

Preventive diplomacy • Action to try to head off a crisis or conflict.

Mediation • A process in which a third party assists the parties to a conflict to reach a negotiated settlement. 'Mediation' is sometimes used to cover the wide range of roles a third party can play.

Monitoring • An ongoing process of scanning the political environment to detect potential conflicts in advance.

Negotiation • The process of discussion and communication between two or more parties which is meant to lead to an agreement.

Warnings • In order to prevent the outbreak of a conflict, a state, group of states or international organization might issue warnings about possible consequences.

mentioned in Chapter VI of the UN Charter, including diplomatic initiatives—preventive diplomacy, negotiation, mediation, conciliation, arbitration and judicial settlement—and preventive deployment of troops. In the case of preventive deployments, civilians and/or military forces may be used. Conflict prevention also includes fact-finding missions, warnings, inspections and monitoring.

2.1.2 Peacekeeping

Peacekeeping is the use of neutral military personnel and/or civilians to help warring parties prevent, manage or resolve conflict between or within states. These forces are usually organized by an international organization and are therefore international in nature. Peacekeepers complement the political process of conflict resolution and the restoration and maintenance of peace. They are normally permitted to use force only in self-defence. They normally operate with the consent of the parties to the conflict.

Although peacekeeping is not specifically mentioned in the UN Charter, its roots are in Chapter VI, which concerns peaceful settlement of disputes.

2.1.3 Conflict resolution

Conflict resolution (or peacemaking) takes place after conflict has broken out. Its aim is to establish a peaceful settlement. As with conflict prevention, a range of diplomatic, judicial or conciliation initiatives may be used.

A last-resort method of conflict resolution is 'peace enforcement', which is action taken under Chapter VII of the UN Charter involving the use of political and economic sanctions and/or military force to restore peace. It is 'enforcement' in the sense that measures are taken against a state or party to convince it to act (or not act) in ways that it does not want to.

2.1.4 Peace-building

Peace-building takes place in the aftermath of a conflict. It is action to strengthen and solidify a political settlement, such as economic reconstruction and re-establishment of normal civilian life. Its purpose is to avoid a return to conflict. In some cases this may require ambitious 'nation-building' efforts.

2.2 The United Nations

The UN is the international community's principal mechanism for armed conflict prevention, management and resolution. Indeed, the

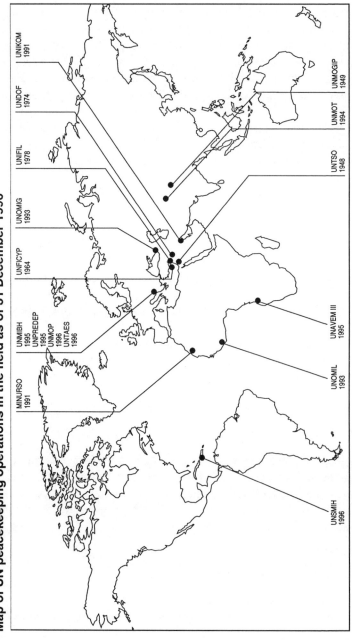

Map of UN peacekeeping operations in the field as of 31 December 1996

UNIKOM
1991

UNDOF
1974

UNIFIL
1978

UNOMIG
1993

UNFICYP
1964

UNMIBH
1995
UNPREDEP
1995
UNMOP
1996
UNTAES
1996

MINURSO
1991

UNMOGIP
1949

UNMOT
1994

UNTSO
1948

UNAVEM III
1995

UNOMIL
1993

UNSMIH
1996

Note: Dates refer to the start of operations. Acronyms are explained in the list of missions in the panel on pp. 42–50.

inspiration for much of our understanding of how to deal with international conflict is found in the UN Charter. In particular, two chapters are important—Chapter VI: Pacific Settlement of Disputes; and Chapter VII: Action with Respect to Threats to the Peace, Breaches of the Peace, and Acts of Aggression. The structure of the UN and its role in disarmament questions are discussed at greater length in chapter 6.

Within the UN system, the main responsibility for maintaining international peace and security rests with the Security Council. The Council has at its disposal a range of instruments up to and including the use of military force. In practice, however, force has rarely been used by the UN.[1] Instead, peacekeeping developed as the preferred method of dealing with international armed conflict.

The UN's experience with peacekeeping began in 1948, when it created the UN Truce Supervision Organization (UNTSO) in the wake of the Arab–Israeli War. The following year it established another observation force, this time in India/Pakistan, in response to the dispute over Kashmir. Like UNTSO, the UN Military Observer Group in India and Pakistan (UNMOGIP) is still in operation.

In 1956 the first large-scale peacekeeping force was created. The UN Emergency Force (UNEF I) was sent to supervise the cease-fire following the 1956 Suez Crisis. The contribution of peacekeeping to international peace and security was recognized in 1988 when the United Nations Peace-Keeping Forces (as opposed to an individual or organization) were awarded the Nobel Peace Prize.

When it comes to peacekeeping, the UN has many advantages over other international organizations. Almost every country in the world is a member and the UN gives its members many opportunities and ways to be heard. It is the only universal (or nearly universal) body to which states can turn for assistance in the case of a serious dispute which may lead to military conflict. When the UN focuses on a problem and acts, it carries with it the weight of international opinion in a way no other body can. Recent multilateral observer and peacekeeping missions are listed in the panel on pages 42–50, showing which

---

[1] The UN's authority to use force is set out in Chapter VII of the UN Charter. The Charter declares that the Security Council may take such action by 'air, sea, or land forces as may be necessary to maintain or restore international peace and security'. The Charter also sets out other measures to give effect to Security Council decisions which do not involve the use of armed force. These include the 'complete or partial interruption of economic relations and of rail, sea, air, postal, telegraphic, radio and other means of communication, and the severance of diplomatic relations'.

Multilateral observer and peacekeeping missions, 1994–96

Acronym/ (Legal instrument)	Name/type of mission (O: observer) (PK: peacekeeping)	Location	Start/ end date	Countries contributing[a]	Personnel strength[a]
UN PEACEKEEPING OPERATIONS					
UNTSO (SCR 50)	UN Truce Supervision Organization (O)	Egypt/ Israel/ Lebanon/ Syria	June 1948	Argentina, Australia, Austria, Belgium, Canada, Chile, China, Denmark, Finland, France, Ireland, Italy, Netherlands, New Zealand, Norway, Russia, Sweden, Switzerland, USA	163
UNMOGIP (SCR 91)	UN Military Observer Group in India and Pakistan (O)	India/ Pakistan (Kashmir)	Jan. 1949	Belgium, Chile, Denmark, Finland, Italy, South Korea, Sweden, Uruguay	45
UNFICYP (SCR 186)	UN Peace-keeping Force in Cyprus (PK)	Cyprus	Mar. 1964	Argentina, Australia, Austria, Canada, Finland, Hungary, Ireland, UK	1 197
UNDOF (SCR 350)	UN Disengagement Observer Force (O)	Syria (Golan Heights)	June 1974	Austria, Canada, Japan, Poland	1 046
UNIFIL (SCR 425, 426)	UN Interim Force in Lebanon (PK)	Lebanon (Southern)	Mar. 1978	Fiji, Finland, France, Ghana, Ireland, Italy, Nepal, Norway, Poland	4 505
UNIKOM (SCR 689)	UN Iraq–Kuwait Observation Mission (O)	Iraq/Kuwait (Khawr 'Abd Allah waterway and UN DMZ)	Apr. 1991	Argentina, Austria, Bangladesh, Canada, China, Denmark, Fiji, Finland, France, Germany, Ghana, Greece, Hungary, India, Indonesia, Ireland, Italy, Kenya, Malaysia, Nigeria, Pakistan, Poland, Romania, Russia, Senegal, Singapore, Sweden, Thailand, Turkey, UK, USA, Uruguay, Venezuela	1 102
UNAVEM II (SCR 696)	UN Angola Verification Mission (O)	Angola	June 1991/ Feb. 1995	Argentina, Brazil, Congo (Brazzaville), Guinea-Bissau, Hungary, India, Jordan, Malaysia, Morocco, Netherlands, New Zealand, Nigeria, Norway, Slovakia, Sweden, Zimbabwe	279

Mission (SCR)	Name	Location	Dates	Participating countries	No.
ONUSAL (SCR 693, 729)	UN Observer Mission in El Salvador (O)	El Salvador	July 1991/Apr. 1995	Brazil, Chile, Colombia, Guyana, Italy, Mexico, Spain, Venezuela	34
MINURSO (SCR 690)	UN Mission for the Referendum in Western Sahara (O)	Western Sahara	Sep. 1991	Argentina, Austria, Bangladesh, Belgium, China, Egypt, El Salvador, France, Germany, Ghana, Greece, Guinea, Honduras, Hungary, Ireland, Italy, Kenya, Malaysia, Nigeria, Norway, Pakistan, Poland, Portugal, Russia, South Korea, Togo, Tunisia, USA, Uruguay, Venezuela	231
UNPROFOR (SCR 743, 776, 795, 982)	UN Protection Force (PK)	Bosnia and Herzegovina	Mar. 1992/Dec. 1995	Argentina, Bangladesh, Belgium, Brazil, Canada, Colombia, Czech Rep., Denmark, Egypt, Estonia, Finland, France, Ghana, Indonesia, Ireland, Jordan, Kenya, Lithuania, Malaysia, Nepal, Netherlands, New Zealand, Nigeria, Norway, Pakistan, Poland, Portugal, Russia, Senegal, Slovakia, Spain, Sweden, Switzerland, Tunisia, Turkey, Ukraine, UK, USA	2 675
ONUMOZ (SCR 797, 898)	UN Operation in Mozambique (PK)	Mozambique	Dec. 1992/Jan. 1995	Argentina, Australia, Austria, Bangladesh, Botswana, Brazil, Canada, Cape Verde, China, Czech Rep., Egypt, Ghana, Guinea-Bissau, Guyana, Hungary, India, Indonesia, Italy, Japan, Jordan, Malaysia, Nepal, Netherlands, New Zealand, Nigeria, Pakistan, Portugal, Russia, Spain, Sri Lanka, Sweden, Togo, USA, Uruguay, Zambia	5 063
UNOSOM II (SCR 814)	UN Operation in Somalia (PK)	Somalia	May 1993/Mar. 1995	Australia, Bangladesh, Egypt, Ghana, India, Indonesia, Italy, Malaysia, Netherlands, Nigeria, Pakistan, Philippines, South Korea, Zambia, Zimbabwe	7 973
UNOMUR (SCR 846)	UN Observer Mission in Uganda–Rwanda (O)	Uganda/Rwanda	June 1993/Jan. 1994	Bangladesh, Botswana, Brazil, Hungary, Netherlands, Senegal, Slovakia, Zimbabwe	80
UNOMIG (SCR 849, 858)	UN Observer Mission in Georgia (O)	Georgia (Abkhazia)	Aug. 1993	Albania, Austria, Bangladesh, Cuba, Czech Rep., Denmark, Egypt, France, Germany, Greece, Hungary, Indonesia, Jordan, Pakistan, Poland, Russia, South Korea, Sweden, Switzerland, Turkey, UK, USA, Uruguay	124

Acronym/ (Legal instrument)	Name/type of mission (O: observer) (PK: peacekeeping)	Location	Start/ end date	Countries contributing[a]	Personnel strength[a]
UNOMIL (SCR 866)	UN Observer Mission in Liberia (O)	Liberia	Sep. 1993	Bangladesh, China, Czech Rep., Egypt, Guinea-Bissau, India, Jordan, Kenya, Malaysia, Nepal, Pakistan, Uruguay	78
UNMIH (SCR 867)	UN Mission in Haiti (PK)	Haiti	Sep. 1993 / June 1996	Algeria, Antigua & Barbuda, Argentina, Austria, Bahamas, Bangladesh, Barbados, Belize, Benin, Canada, Djibouti, France, Guatemala, Guinea-Bissau, Guyana, Honduras, India, Ireland, Jamaica, Jordan, Mali, Nepal, Netherlands, New Zealand, Pakistan, Philippines, Russia, St Kitts & Nevis, St Lucia, Suriname, Togo, Trinidad & Tobago, Tunisia, USA	2 245
UNAMIR (SCR 872)	UN Assistance Mission for Rwanda (PK)	Rwanda	Oct. 1993	Argentina, Australia, Austria, Bangladesh, Canada, Chad, Congo (Brazzaville), Djibouti, Ethiopia, Fiji, Germany, Ghana, Guinea, Guinea-Bissau, India, Jordan, Malawi, Mali, Niger, Nigeria, Pakistan, Poland, Russia, Senegal, Spain, Switzerland, Tunisia, UK, Uruguay, Zambia, Zimbabwe	688
UNASOG (SCR 915)	UN Aouzou Strip Observer Group (O)	Aouzou Strip (Libya/Chad)	May 1994 / June 1994	Bangladesh, Ghana, Honduras, Kenya, Malaysia, Nigeria	9
UNMOT (SCR 968)	UN Mission of Observers in Tajikistan (O)	Tajikistan	Dec. 1994	Austria, Bangladesh, Bulgaria, Denmark, Jordan, Poland, Switzerland, Ukraine, Uruguay	43
UNAVEM III (SCR 976)	UN Angola Verification Mission III (O)	Angola	Feb. 1995	Algeria, Bangladesh, Brazil, Bulgaria, Congo (Brazzaville), Egypt, Fiji, France, Guinea-Bissau, Hungary, India, Italy, Jordan, Kenya, Malaysia, Mali, Namibia, Netherlands, New Zealand, Nigeria, Norway, Pakistan, Poland, Portugal, Romania, Russia, Senegal, Slovakia, South Korea, Sweden, Tanzania, UK, Ukraine, Uruguay, Zambia, Zimbabwe	6 608

Mission	Location	Date	Contributing countries	Strength
UNCRO (SCR 981) UN Confidence Restoration Operation in Croatia (PK)	Croatia	Mar. 1995	Argentina, Bangladesh, Belgium, Brazil, Canada, Czech Rep., Denmark, Egypt, Estonia, Finland, France, Germany, Ghana, Indonesia, Jordan, Kenya, Lithuania, Malaysia, Nepal, Netherlands, New Zealand, Nigeria, Norway, Pakistan, Poland, Portugal, Russia, Senegal, Slovakia, Spain, Sweden, Switzerland, Tunisia, Turkey, UK, Ukraine, USA	3 752
UNPREDEP (SCR 983) UN Preventive Deployment Force (PK)	Macedonia	Mar. 1995	Argentina, Bangladesh, Belgium, Brazil, Canada, Czech Rep., Denmark, Egypt, Finland, France, Ghana, Indonesia, Ireland, Jordan, Kenya, Nepal, Netherlands, New Zealand, Nigeria, Norway, Pakistan, Poland, Portugal, Russia, Spain, Sweden, Switzerland, Turkey, UK, Ukraine, USA	1 101
UNMIBH (SCR 1035) UN Mission in Bosnia and Herzegovina (O)	Bosnia and Herzegovina	Dec. 1995	Argentina, Austria, Bangladesh, Bulgaria, Canada, Denmark, Egypt, Estonia, Finland, France, Germany, Ghana, Greece, Hungary, India, Indonesia, Ireland, Jordan, Kenya, Malaysia, Nepal, Netherlands, Nigeria, Norway, Pakistan, Poland, Portugal, Russia, Senegal, Spain, Sweden, Switzerland, Tunisia, Turkey, Ukraine, USA	1 709
UNTAES (SCR 1037) UN Transitional Administration for Eastern Slavonia, Baranja and Western Sirmium (PK)	Croatia	Jan. 1996	Argentina, Austria, Bangladesh, Belgium, Brazil, Czech Rep., Denmark, Egypt, Fiji, Finland, France, Ghana, Greece, Indonesia, Ireland, Jordan, Kenya, Lithuania, Nepal, Netherlands, New Zealand, Nigeria, Norway, Pakistan, Poland, Portugal, Russia, Senegal, Slovakia, Sweden, Switzerland, Tunisia, Turkey, UK, Ukraine, USA	5 344
UNMOP (SCR 1038) UN Mission of Observers in Prevlaka (O)	Croatia	Jan. 1996	Argentina, Bangladesh, Belgium, Brazil, Canada, Czech Rep., Denmark, Egypt, Finland, France, Ghana, Indonesia, Ireland, Jordan, Kenya, Nepal, New Zealand, Nigeria, Norway, Pakistan, Poland, Portugal, Russia, Sweden, Switzerland, UK, Ukraine	28
UNSMIH (SCR 1063) UN Support Mission in Haiti (PK)	Haiti	July 1996	Algeria, Bangladesh, Canada, Djibouti, France, India, Mali, Pakistan, Russia, Togo, Trinidad & Tobago, USA	1 549

OTHER UN OPERATIONS

Acronym/ (Legal instrument)	Name/type of mission (O: observer) (PK: peacekeeping)	Location	Start/ end date	Countries contributing[a]	Personnel strength[a]
OSGAP (SG)	Office of the Secretary-General in Afghanistan and Pakistan (O)	Afghanistan/ Pakistan	Mar. 1990/ Dec. 1994	Austria, Canada, Denmark, Fiji, Finland, Ghana, Ireland, Nepal, Poland, Sweden	10
CIAV/OAS	International Commission for Support and Verification (O)	Nicaragua	May 1990	..	..
MICIVIH (GAR 47/20B)	International Civilian Mission to Haiti (O)	Haiti	Feb. 1993	..	..
UNSMA (GAR 48/208)	UN Special Mission to Afghanistan (O)	Afghanistan/ Pakistan	Mar. 1994	Ghana, Ireland	2
MINUGUA (GAR 48/267)	UN Mission for the Verification of Human Rights and of Compliance with the Commitments of the Comprehensive Agreement on Human Rights in Guatemala (O)	Guatemala	Oct. 1994	Argentina, Brazil, Canada, Colombia, Italy, Spain, Sweden, Uruguay, Venezuela	66
OSGA (SG Jan. 1995)	Office of the Secretary-General in Afghanistan (O)	Afghanistan/ Pakistan	Jan. 1995/ June 1996	Ghana, Ireland	2
MINUSAL (SG Feb. 1995)	Mission of the UN in El Salvador (O)	El Salvador	May 1995/ Apr. 1996	..	..

ONUV (GAR 50/226)	UN Office of Verification	(O)	El Salvador	May 1996/ Dec. 1996	..	3

ORGANIZATION FOR SECURITY AND CO-OPERATION IN EUROPE (OSCE)

– (CSO 18 Sep. 1992)	SCE Spillover Mission to Skopje	(O)	Former Yugoslav Rep. of Macedonia	Sep. 1992	..	4
– (CSO 6 Nov. 1992)	OSCE Mission to Georgia	(O)	Georgia (S. Ossetia; Abkhazia)	Dec. 1992	..	17
– (CSO 13 Dec. 1992)	OSCE Mission to Estonia	(O)	Estonia	Feb. 1993	..	6
– (CSO 4 Feb. 1993)	OSCE Mission to Moldova	(O)	Moldova	Apr. 1993	..	8
– (CSO 23 Sep. 1993)	OSCE Mission to Latvia	(O)	Latvia	Nov. 1993	..	7
– (1 Dec. 1993)	OSCE Mission to Tajikistan	(O)	Tajikistan	Feb. 1994	..	8
– (2 June 1994)	OSCE Mission in Sarajevo	(O)	Bosnia and Herzegovina	Oct. 1994	..	6
– (CSO 15 June 1994)	OSCE Mission to Ukraine	(O)	Ukraine	Nov. 1994	..	6
– (11 Apr. 1995)	OSCE Assistance Group to Chechnya	(O)	Chechnya	Apr. 1995	..	8

Acronym/ (Legal instrument)	Name/type of mission (O: observer) (PK: peacekeeping)	Location	Start/ end date	Countries contributing[a]	Personnel strength[a]
– (8 Dec. 1995)	OSCE Mission to Bosnia and Herzegovina (O)	Bosnia and Herzegovina	Dec. 1995	..	8
– (18 Apr. 1996)	OSCE Mission to Croatia (O)	Croatia	July 1996	..	..
CIS/RUSSIA					
– (Bilateral agreement)	'South Ossetia Joint Force' (PK)	Georgia (S. Ossetia)	July 1992	Georgia, Russia, North and South Ossetia	..
– (Bilateral agreement)	'Moldova Joint Force' (PK)	Moldova (Trans-Dniester)	July 1992	Moldova, Russia, 'Trans-Dniester Rep.'	..
– (CIS 24 Sep. 1993)	CIS 'Tajikistan Buffer Force' (PK)	Tajikistan (Afghan border)	Aug. 1993	Kazakhstan, Kyrgyzstan, Russia, Uzbekistan	..
– (CIS 15 Apr. 1994)	CIS 'Peacekeeping Forces in Georgia' (PK)	Georgian–Abkhazian border	June 1994	Russia	..
OTHER					
NNSC (Armistice Agreement)	Neutral Nations Supervisory Commission (O)	North Korea/ South Korea	July 1953	Sweden, Switzerland	10
MFO (Protocol to treaty)	Multinational Force and Observers in the Sinai (O)	Egypt (Sinai)	Apr. 1982	Australia, Canada, Colombia, Fiji, France, Hungary, Italy, New Zealand, Norway, Uruguay, USA	1 896

Operation (authorization)	Name	Type	Location	Dates	Participating countries	No.
ECOMOG (ESMC 7 Aug. 1990)	ECOWAS Monitoring Group	(PK)	Liberia	Aug. 1990	Gambia, Ghana, Guinea, Mali, Nigeria, Niger, Sierra Leone, Uganda	7 500
ECMM (Brioni Agreement)	EC Monitoring Mission	(O)	Former Yugoslavia	July 1991	Austria, Belgium, Czech Rep., Denmark, Finland, France, Germany, Greece, Ireland, Italy, Netherlands, Norway, Poland, Portugal, Slovakia, Spain, Sweden, UK	211
UNMLT (SCR 880)	UN Military Liaison Team	(O)	Cambodia	Nov. 1993/ May 1994	Austria, Bangladesh, Belgium, China, France, India, Indonesia, Malaysia, New Zealand, Pakistan, Poland, Russia, Thailand, Uruguay	20
OMIB (OAU 1993)	OAU Mission in Burundi	(O)	Burundi	Dec. 1993	Burkina Faso, Guinea, Mali, Niger, Tunisia	1
TIPH (Mar. 1994 Agreement)	Temporary International Presence in the City of Hebron	(O)	West Bank	May 1994/ Aug. 1994	Denmark, Italy, Norway	117
– (SCR 929)	Opération Turquoise	(PK)	Rwanda	June 1994/ Aug. 1994	Chad, Congo (Brazzaville), Egypt, France, Guinea-Bissau, Mauritania, Niger, Senegal	3 060
WEUPF (Washington Agreement 16 Mar. 1994)	Western European Union Police Force	(O)	Bosnia and Herzegovina (Mostar)	July 1994	Austria, Belgium, Finland, France, Germany, Greece, India, Luxembourg, Netherlands, Portugal, Spain, Sweden, UK	180
MNF (SCR 940)	Operation Uphold Democracy	(PK)	Haiti	Sep. 1994/ Mar. 1995	Antigua & Barbuda, Argentina, Australia, Bahamas, Bangladesh, Barbados, Belgium, Belize, Benin, Bolivia, Costa Rica, Denmark, Dominica, Grenada, Guatemala, Guyana, Israel, Jamaica, Jordan, Netherlands, Philippines, Poland, St Kitts & Nevis, St Lucia, St Vincent and Grenadines, Trinidad and Tobago, UK, USA	7 797
– (Agreement Sep. 1994; SCR 943)	Mission of the International Conference on the Former Yugoslavia	(O)	Serbia/Bosnia and Herzegovina border area	Sep. 1994	Belgium, Canada, Czech Rep., Denmark, Finland, France, Germany, Greece, Ireland, Italy, Netherlands, Norway, Portugal, Russia, Spain, Sweden, UK, USA	..

Acronym/ (Legal instrument)	Name/type of mission (O: observer) (PK: peacekeeping)	Location	Start/ end date	Countries contributing[a]	Personnel strength[a]
SPPKF (Agreement 1994)	South Pacific Peacekeeping Force (PK)	Bougainville, Papua New Guinea	10–14 Oct. 1994	Fiji, Tonga. Vanuatu	400
MOMEP (Decl. of Itamaraty)	Mission of Military Observers Ecuador/ Peru (O)	Ecuador/ Peru	Mar. 1995	Argentina, Brazil, Chile, Ecuador, Peru, USA	35
IFOR (SCR 1031)	Implementation Force (PK)	Bosnia and Herzegovina	Dec. 1995	Albania, Austria, Belgium, Bulgaria, Canada, Czech Rep., Denmark, Egypt, Estonia, Finland, France, Germany, Greece, Hungary, Italy, Jordan, Latvia, Lithuania, Luxembourg, Malaysia, Morocco, Nether- lands, Norway, Poland, Portugal, Romania, Russia, Slovakia, Spain, Sweden, Turkey, UK, Ukraine, USA	40 000
SFOR (SCR 1088)	Stabilization Force (PK)	Bosnia and Herzegovina	Dec. 1996	Albania, Austria, Belgium, Bulgaria, Canada, Czech Rep., Denmark, Egypt, Estonia, Finland, France, Germany, Greece, Hungary, Italy, Jordan, Latvia, Lithuania, Luxembourg, Malaysia, Morocco, Nether- lands, Norway, Poland, Portugal, Romania, Russia, Spain, Sweden, Turkey, UK, Ukraine, USA	32 000

[a] The information given refers to 1996 or the last year of operation.

Notes: SCR = Security Council Resolution; SG = UN Secretary-General; DMZ = demilitarized zone; OAS = Organization of American States; GAR = General Assembly Resolution; CSO = OSCE Committee of Senior Officials; CIS = Commonwealth of Independent States; ESMC = ECOWAS Standing Mediation Committee; EC = European Community; OAU = Organization of African Unity.
'.' = not available or nor applicable. Missions are in order of starting date. Figures on the number of personnel are as of 31 Dec. 1996 and include both military and civilian staff.

Sources: SIPRI *Yearbooks 1995–1997. The Yearbooks* should be consulted for a more complete presentation of this information.

countries have contributed troops, military observers and civilian police.

Because the UN has a permanent Secretariat, headed by the Secretary-General, it also has the advantage of a pool of expertise and experience upon which to draw. Whether the Secretary-General is conducting a fact-finding mission, or the Security Council has approved a peacekeeping operation, experience in these matters can make the difference between success and failure.

There is also the fundamental issue of resources. While mediation, fact-finding and negotiation are within the reach of regional organizations, large-scale peacekeeping usually is not. Only by drawing upon the resources—financial and other—of many countries, can peacekeeping missions be put together.

2.3   Regional organizations

As noted above, regional organizations are another type of actor involved in armed conflict prevention, management and resolution. They have less experience in this field than the UN and only a modest record of success.[2]

Sometimes the UN will cooperate with a regional organization in addressing a particular dispute. This cooperation may take the form of the regional organization assuming the diplomatic lead to resolve a conflict with the UN following up with peacekeeping.

An important issue is how to make sure that UN and regional efforts are properly coordinated. In 1995 the UN Secretary-General suggested that, in relations with the Organization of African Unity (OAU), a more formal and ongoing mechanism would be helpful. He proposed that a UN liaison officer be posted to OAU headquarters to ensure effective coordination and communications.

Because funding is often an issue for regional organizations, the UN can help draw attention to a regional conflict and secure funds. In October 1995, the UN convened a funding conference on the conflict in Liberia. One of the aims of the conference was to fund the peacekeeping efforts of the Economic Community of West African States (ECOWAS) in Liberia.

---

[2] See chapter 9, section 9.3, for membership of the main regional organizations.

2.3.1   The Organization of African Unity

The Organization of African Unity (OAU) has been involved in a number of observer missions, many of which have concerned election monitoring, but it has not attempted major peacekeeping operations. In some cases, the OAU has assisted with peace negotiations. This is what happened in 1993 when it acted as broker between the Rwanda Patriotic Front and the Government of Rwanda.

To develop a more systematic role in conflict prevention in Africa, the OAU established a Conflict Prevention, Management and Resolution Mechanism in 1993. The mechanism meets at the level of ambassador and is supported by a secretariat. In 1995 the mechanism received funding assistance from Canada, France, Japan, the UK, the USA and the UN. In June 1996 OAU generals reached agreement on earmarking numbers of national troops for peacekeeping, and under OAU auspices leaders of states in the Great Lakes region imposed economic sanctions on Burundi.

Despite these initiatives, the OAU has not been able to take on a more ambitious role in conflict prevention, largely because of its financial difficulties and its lack of a permanent decision-making body. The UN and Western states are trying to help the OAU to overcome these deficiencies.

2.3.2   The Organization for Security and Co-operation in Europe

The Organization for Security and Co-operation in Europe (OSCE) began as the Conference on Security and Co-operation in Europe (CSCE). It first met in 1973 in Helsinki, Finland. Its founding members included most of the states of Europe as well as Canada and the United States. The membership has since grown as new states have emerged in Europe. In January 1995, the CSCE became the OSCE.

The CSCE was originally a broad forum to discuss issues relating to cooperation and security in Europe. During the 1970s and the 1980s it was generally viewed as a lesser player in European security matters, taking a back seat to the North Atlantic Treaty Organization (NATO) and the Warsaw Treaty Organization (the WTO, or Warsaw Pact). In the early 1990s, however, with the collapse of the Soviet Union, the organization took on new significance as the one pan-European institution which could serve as a vehicle for cooperation and security in post-cold war Europe.[3]

The CSCE quickly found itself busy launching fact-finding and good-offices missions to the states which were former Soviet republics and members of the WTO. The purpose of these missions was generally to identify and possibly defuse potential sources of conflict. Some missions have had a specific mandate to promote negotiations between the parties in conflict. In other missions, the mandates were less concrete. For example, the OSCE Mission to Tajikistan was mandated to maintain contact and facilitate dialogue between the parties. It was also to encourage confidence building and promote respect for human rights.

Since early 1995 the OSCE has been prepared for its first peace-keeping mission, to Nagorno-Karabakh, but has been unable to deploy because the warring parties have not given their consent to the mission. Its overseeing of the elections in Bosnia and Herzegovina in September 1996 was not entirely successful. Unforeseen assistance from the NATO Implementation Force (IFOR, see pages 54–55) was necessary, and the elections were widely criticized as being unfair.

The OSCE has also acted through its High Commissioner for National Minorities (HCNM). The Commissioner's work has focused on preventing the outbreak or escalation of conflict involving national minority groups. This has included providing advice to some countries on how to deal with specific minority situations.

2.3.3   The Commonwealth of Independent States

In 1992 the members of the Commonwealth of Independent States (CIS)[4] agreed to cooperate in peacekeeping as needed within their territories. In the autumn of 1993, members further decided that CIS peacekeeping forces would be made up of national units with joint supply and logistical support.

Joint CIS peacekeeping operations have been conducted in Tajikistan and Abkhazia (in Georgia). Peacekeeping forces involving CIS states, but not under a CIS mandate, have also been sent to South Ossetia (Georgia) and eastern Moldova. In all cases, these forces are

---

[3] See also chapter 7, section 7.2.5.
[4] The CIS was created in 1991, after the breakup of the Soviet Union. It is an organization of 12 former Soviet republics for political and economic cooperation. For the CIS member states, see chapter 9, section 9.3.

dominated by Russia. They have operated under different rules from those of the UN. This is particularly the case in connection with the minimum use of force, impartiality and operating with the consent of the parties to the dispute.

The CIS and Russia have sought international recognition of their peacekeeping operations. The UN Security Council has chosen not to endorse them because of concern about their lack of conformity with UN peacekeeping norms and standards.

2.3.4 The North Atlantic Treaty Organization

Until recently, a discussion on armed conflict prevention, management and resolution probably would not have included NATO. NATO is an alliance that was established in 1949 to provide for the collective defence of its members. Through the strength of its members and their commitment to each other's defence, NATO is meant to deter acts of aggression against its member states. If deterrence fails, the alliance has the forces and command structure in place to respond. With the collapse of the Soviet Union and the Warsaw Pact, the search began for a modified role for NATO.

The most visible change is the role it has played in the conflict in the former Yugoslavia. This conflict provided NATO with an opportunity to do something that would have been quite impossible during the cold war. NATO lent its military muscle to the UN's peacekeeping operation.[5] Not only was this the first time NATO forces had engaged in combat, but it was also the first time NATO had operated beyond its members' territory and in support of broader security interests.

NATO became involved in the former Yugoslavia in several ways. It helped enforce the no-fly zone over Bosnia and Herzegovina imposed by the UN Security Council. It also provided fighter aircraft, reconnaissance and airborne early-warning aircraft, and naval vessels in support of the UN arms embargo against all the states of the former Yugoslavia. Troops of the UN Protection Force (UNPROFOR) in the former Yugoslavia also operated under the protective air power of NATO. However, the command procedures for the use of air power became a sore point between the two organizations. NATO air power was eventually used to coerce the Bosnian Serbs into suing for peace.

---

[5] The conflict in the former Yugoslavia is also discussed in chapter 1, section 1.5.

With the signing of the Dayton Agreement, NATO became further involved in Bosnia and Herzegovina by providing the troops for IFOR. IFOR was the largest peacekeeping force in 1996. It was authorized under Chapter VII of the UN Charter and had more 'robust' rules of engagement, authorizing the use of force beyond self-defence. It did not, however, use significant military force. Nor has its successor, the Stabilization Force (SFOR).

With the successful IFOR mission as an example, in June 1996 NATO leaders agreed on the basic principles for Combined Joint Task Forces—international task forces tailored for specific missions which could be controlled by the Western European Union (WEU) and use NATO military assets and US logistical and tactical support.

While NATO's assistance to UNPROFOR and role in IFOR and SFOR have been its most well-known attempts to reshape its mandate in the post-cold war world, the alliance has taken some other initiatives. Through the North Atlantic Cooperation Council (NACC),[6] which includes the NATO member states, former Warsaw Pact states and former Soviet republics, NATO has tried to develop a common approach to peacekeeping and humanitarian assistance. Another initiative is the Partnership for Peace (PFP) programme, which allows for cooperation with NACC and other OSCE states in such areas as military planning, budgeting and training. Since 1994 NATO forces have held an expanding series of exercises focusing on peacekeeping techniques.

2.3.5   The Economic Community of West African States

In 1990 ECOWAS established the ECOWAS Cease-fire Monitoring Group (ECOMOG) in Liberia to oversee a cease-fire agreed by Liberia's warring factions. In October 1991 ECOMOG became a self-described 'peacekeeping/peace enforcement' operation, whose biggest contributor was Nigeria.

In July 1993 talks jointly sponsored by the UN, the OAU and ECOWAS led to the Cotonou Peace Agreement, which set out a process that began with a cease-fire and was to end with an election in 1994. ECOMOG would monitor this process, assisted by the newly created UN Observer Mission in Liberia (UNOMIL). UNOMIL

---

[6] As of May 1997, the activities of NACC and the PFP were merged in the Euro-Atlantic Partnership Council. See chapter 7, section 7.2.2.

became the first UN peacekeeping mission undertaken in cooperation with an existing mission run by another organization.

ECOMOG has had serious difficulties in stabilizing the situation in Liberia. In April 1996 most of UNOMIL withdrew when ECOMOG lost control of the situation and renewed fighting devastated Monrovia. At times ECOMOG has become involved in the conflict itself. It is dominated by Nigeria, does not have enough resources and has strayed from the principles of good peacekeeping behaviour. By the end of 1996, however, it appeared that the peace process in Liberia was beginning to take root and the efforts of ECOMOG and UNOMIL were receiving increasing support and recognition.

2.4 Examples of conflict prevention, management and resolution

2.4.1 Conflict prevention

UN Preventive Deployment Force in Macedonia

Although best known for its operations in Bosnia and Herzegovina and Croatia, UNPROFOR established a small mission in the Former Yugoslav Republic of Macedonia (FYROM) in 1992. It later became known as the UN Preventive Deployment Force (UNPREDEP). UNPREDEP was invited by the Macedonian Government to help prevent a spillover of the Yugoslav conflict into Macedonia. The force had about 1000 troops at its disposal and monitored borders shared between Macedonia, Yugoslavia (Serbia and Montenegro) and Albania. This preventive deployment was the first operation of its kind in UN history.

2.4.2 Conflict resolution

Special Mission to Afghanistan

In 1994 the UN Secretary-General sent the Special Mission to Afghanistan (UNSMA) to explore the future role of the UN in fostering national dialogue and reconstruction in Afghanistan. Discussions were held with Afghan refugees, Iran, Russia, Saudi Arabia, Turkey, Uzbekistan and the former King of Afghanistan. Options considered included a substantial UN presence in Afghanistan, a cease-fire and the holding of free and fair elections. To date, these talks have been continually sidelined by rapidly changing events on the ground.

2.4.3 Peacekeeping

UN Peace-keeping Force in Cyprus

Until 1960 Cyprus was a colony of the United Kingdom. When it became independent, power was to be shared between the Greek Cypriot majority and the Turkish Cypriot minority. In late 1963 fighting broke out between the two communities on Cyprus and the UN responded by creating the UN Peace-keeping Force in Cyprus (UNFICYP).

The situation became more complicated in 1974 when the President of Cyprus was overthrown by Greek Cypriots, supported by the military regime in Greece. Those who led the coup wanted union with Greece. Turkey feared the coup would lead to an invasion of Cyprus by Greek troops and responded by occupying the northern 40 per cent of the island. In response, UNIFICYP was redeployed along a buffer zone between the two communities. In 1983 Turkish Cypriot authorities declared independence for their sector and renamed it the Turkish Republic of Northern Cyprus. The declaration of independence was rejected by the UN Security Council and has been recognized by no other country except Turkey.

Despite numerous plans and initiatives by the UN, the USA, the UK and others, Cyprus is still divided. UNFICYP remains, although its strength has been reduced by half in recent years. In 1996 there was concern at the inceasing militarization of the island and fighting flared up along the 'Green Line' which divides it, leading to civilian deaths. Critics of UNFICYP claim that the continued presence of peacekeepers has made it possible for the two sides to avoid settling the dispute, and there exists a long-standing proposal to replace it with a NATO-led multinational force including Greek and Turkish components. Supporters claim that UNFICYP's withdrawal would lead to renewed fighting.

UN Transitional Authority in Cambodia

The UN Transitional Authority in Cambodia (UNTAC) marked a new phase in the international community's experience with peacekeeping.

Although it included traditional peacekeeping elements, such as cease-fire monitoring, UNTAC's mandate was more ambitious. Essentially, it was charged with overseeing the political reconstruction of Cambodia over a short period of time. Peace-building was an important aspect of UNTAC's work.

In 1991 the Paris Peace Accords were signed to end the civil war in Cambodia. The accords were signed by the four contending Cambodian factions, the five permanent members of the Security Council and 12 other interested regional states.

Elements of the accords included:

• a cease-fire and withdrawal of foreign forces;
• an end to external military assistance;
• the demobilization of military forces and their eventual incorporation into a new, national army;
• release of all prisoners of war and civilian political prisoners; and
• elections for a Constituent Assembly which would write a new constitution before becoming Cambodia's National Assembly.

One of UNTAC's roles was to oversee those government activities that could most influence the outcome of Cambodia's elections. These activities included foreign affairs, defence, finance, public security and information. Never before had the UN exercised such power over the affairs of a sovereign member state.

UNTAC was also successful in returning to Cambodia 350 000 Cambodian refugees from the Thailand/Cambodia border and getting over 90 per cent of eligible voters on the voting list.

In May 1993 elections were held and were proclaimed free and fair by the UN, which had organized, supervised and observed them. The resulting Constituent Assembly drew up a constitution and, at the end of September, became the National Assembly. A new Royal Cambodian Government was established under King Sihanouk comprising a coalition of two of the former warring parties.

The success of the May elections has been identified as a key factor in the implementation of the Paris Peace Accords and UNTAC's operations. Cambodians voted in such overwhelming numbers and under such difficult circumstances that they created a powerful wave of momentum in support of reconstruction and reconciliation. Although UNTAC was not without its flaws, it did establish a foundation for Cambodia's future as a democratic, open and prosperous society.

Recent events, in which one faction deposed the other from the coalition, have unfortunately demonstrated that Cambodia's political leadership lacks the ability to build on this foundation.

UN Aouzou Strip Observer Group

In 1994 the International Court of Justice handed down a decision on the territorial dispute between Chad and Libya over the Aouzou Strip. It ruled in favour of Chad, and Libya withdrew from the territory, something it had agreed to do before the Court reached its decision.

The UN Aouzou Strip Observer Group (UNASOG) was given the mandate of monitoring Libyan withdrawal from the contested strip of land. The operation consisted of nine military observers and six civilian staff, lasted 40 days and had the shortest mandate in UN peacekeeping history.

2.4.4   Peace enforcement

United Nations Operation in Somalia II

When it agreed on the mandate for the UN Operation in Somalia II (UNOSOM II), the United Nations Security Council authorized the use of force beyond self-defence as part of a peacekeeping operation for the first time in over 30 years. UNOSOM II taught the international community some hard lessons about this relatively rare approach to dealing with conflict.

The story of UNOSOM II began in December 1992, when the Security Council authorized a multilateral—although not UN—mission to deliver humanitarian aid to Somalia. The government had collapsed in Somalia and, in addition to civil war, the people were suffering from famine and drought. The Unified Task Force (UNITAF), led by the USA, arrived to replace the existing small and ineffective UN Operation in Somalia (UNOSOM I). UNOSOM I had been unable to provide sufficient security to safely deliver relief to the people.

UNITAF made important strides in relieving the effects of the famine, but the USA did not wish to maintain a long-term presence in Somalia. In May 1993, UNOSOM II was created by the UN to replace UNITAF. It had a very ambitious mandate. Among other things, UNOSOM II was to:

- restore peace, stability, law and order;
- provide security and assistance in bringing home refugees and resettling displaced persons;
- monitor the arms embargo against the various Somali factions and facilitate disarmament; and
- assist in the provision of relief and in the economic development of Somalia.

Under UNITAF, there had been only modest efforts to disarm the Somali factions which battled in the capital, Mogadishu. When UNOSOM II tried to disarm General Mohammad Farah Aidid's faction, the UN suffered its worst death toll in peacekeeping history in such a short period of time: 23 killed and 54 wounded. Somali civilian casualties were even higher. When US forces not under UN command stepped up actions against Aidid, they and UNOSOM II suffered further losses. The reaction of Western troop-contributing countries to the fighting and loss of lives was fatal to the mission's future. The USA announced that it would withdraw by March 1994 and other contributors set timetables as well.

The Security Council responded by setting March 1995 as the cut-off point for the Somalia operation. UNOSOM II gave up its attempts to force disarmament and withdrew to secure positions in Mogadishu. Although conditions in the countryside generally improved, life in the capital grew worse. UNOSOM II left Somalia on schedule, assisted by a seven-nation combined task force, 'United Shield'.

In the end, about 800 urban guerrilla fighters managed to severely disrupt a UN force of 28 000. From this experience, a number of conclusions have been drawn.

Peace enforcement cannot be conducted by a peacekeeping force. Even when force is used by a properly mandated peace enforcement operation, political negotiations rather than peace enforcement will alone provide the ultimate solution to civil conflict. Where UN troops and national forces of a UN member are operating in the same theatre, command of the two forces should be united or tightly coordinated. All contingents operating under UN command should be prepared to abide by the decisions of UN commanders. Peace-enforcement operations demand a strategic plan and a credible military force. Nation-building exercises, as in Somalia and Cambodia, require a broad approach, substantial resources, an integrated plan and the determination to stay the course.

2.4.5 Peace-building

Peace-building involves all the elements normally associated with healthy, well-managed, open and stable societies. Such elements include social and economic development, a vigorous civil society and efficient, effective and humane governance.

Electoral operations

Increasingly, the international community is using international oversight and observation of democratic elections as a way of building the peace. For countries which have no tradition of free and fair elections, the international community can make a significant contribution. Peace agreements and elections may fail if the parties are unable to carry them out properly. The UN has played a leading role in this regard. The panel on pages 62–63 lists a selection of the UN-assisted electoral observer missions that operated in 1994 and 1995.

This development only became possible with the end of the cold war. Before that, the UN could not promote democracy as a universal value since many of its members—essentially the Soviet Union, its allies and many developing states—would have viewed this approach as interference in the internal affairs of states.

Beginning with just a few requests in 1989, and peaking at over 30 in 1992, the UN has provided electoral assistance to countries under various circumstances. In 1989, in a major operation, the UN supervised the electoral process which marked the transition of Namibia from the control of South Africa to independence, while in Cambodia it actually organized an entire electoral process in a member state for the first time. Normally, however, its role is restricted to observation, verification and provision of technical assistance.

Drawing up electoral laws, educating the population in democratic concepts and showing how to create and maintain voting lists are among the services that the UN, working with other organizations and governments, has provided in recent years.

Select substantial UN-assisted electoral observer missions, 1994–95

Acronym/ (Legal instrument)	Name of observer coordinating unit	Location	Start date	Elections conducted in 1994–95 with UN assistance	Date of elections	Electoral observers
– (Request Nov. 1993)	Supreme Electoral Council	Nicaragua	Jan. 1994	Elections for regional councils on the Atlantic coast	27 Feb.	29
ONUSAL (SCR 693, 832)	UN Observer Mission in El Salvador, Electoral Division	El Salvador	Sep. 1993	Elections for President, the National Assembly, municipal legislatures and the Central American Parliament	20 Mar.	c. 850
				President elections, second round	24 Apr.	900
– (Request July 1993)	Joint International Observer Group	Uganda	..	Elections to Constituent Assembly	28 Mar.	110
UNOMSA (SCR 772, 894)	UN Observer Mission in South Africa	South Africa	Sep. 1992	Elections for the National Assembly and the 9 provincial parliaments	26–29 Apr.	2 120
EUNELSA	EU Election Unit in South Africa	South Africa	..	Elections for the National Assembly and the 9 provincial parliaments	26–29 Apr.	322
–	OAU Observer Mission	South Africa	..	Elections for the National Assembly and the 9 provincial parliaments	26–29 Apr.	102
COGSA	Commonwealth Observer Group in South Africa	South Africa	Feb. 1994	Elections for the National Assembly and the 9 provincial parliaments	26–29 Apr.	118
– (Request Oct. 1993)	UN Electoral Assistance Secretariat	Malawi	Jan. 1994	Presidential and parliamentary elections	17 May	250
– (Request Dec. 1992)	International Observer Group	Guinea-Bissau	..	Presidential and legislative elections	3 July	100
				Presidential elections, second round	7 Aug.	100

ETONU-MEX (Request May 1994)	UN Technical Assistance team in Mexico	Mexico	June 1994	Presidential and congressional elections	21 Aug.	c. 30 000
ONUMOZ (SCR797)	UN Operation in Mozambique, Electoral Division	Mozambique	Mar. 1993	Presidential and parliamentary elections	27–29 Oct.	c. 2 300
– (Request July 1994)	Namibian Directorate of Elections	Namibia	..	Presidential and legislative elections	7–8 Dec.	150
UNMIH (SCR 940 Request Sep. 1994)	UN Mission in Haiti	Haiti	Nov. 1994	Legislative, municipal and local elections Complimentary legislative and municipal elections Second round of legislative elections and additional re-runs Presidential elections	25 June 13 Aug. 17 Sep. 17 Dec.	293
– (Request Jan. 1995)	OSCE/UN Joint Operation for the Election Monitoring in Armenia	Armenia	June 1995	Parliamentary elections Parliamentary elections, second round	5 July 19 July	90
– (Request June 1995)		Tanzania	Aug. 1995	Presidential elections in Zanzibar Presidential and parliamentary elections in Tanzania	22 Oct. 29 Oct.	405
– (Request June 1995)	OSCE/UN Joint Electoral Observation Mission in Azerbaijan	Azerbaijan	Sep. 1995	Parliamentary elections Parliamentary elections, second round	12 Nov. 26 Nov.	122

Sources: SIPRI Yearbooks 1995–1996.

3. Military expenditure, arms production and the arms trade

3.1 Introduction

One of the great challenges for people who study military expenditure, arms production and the arms trade is coming up with reliable data. Fortunately, there is a considerable 'open literature' on these subjects, that is, publicly available sources of information. This literature includes the following: newspapers; periodicals and journals; books, monographs and annual reference works; official national documents; company annual reports; and documents issued by international and intergovernmental organizations.

SIPRI also uses questionnaires to add to the information it can gather from the open literature. Even so, gaps and incomplete data mean that we can never know the true and complete picture of the military sector of some countries. In these cases, the specialist will often have to make certain assumptions and estimates based on expert knowledge of the subject.

The message, then, is that the data must be treated with some degree of caution. None the less, this chapter shows that enough is known about military expenditure, arms production and the arms trade to make informed judgements about their role in international security.

3.2 Military expenditure

Total world military spending has been dropping since it reached a peak in 1987. However, there are indications that the decline was levelling off in 1996.[1] Most of the decline has been because of reductions by the United States and Russia due to the end of the cold war. US spending was cut by one-third during its period of decline, 1986–96. The cuts in Russia's military budget started in 1991 but have been much sharper, although there are no precise estimates of

[1] *SIPRI Yearbook 1997*, p. 163.

the cuts in real terms. Military spending by other member states of the former cold war blocs have also decreased, although these cuts have not been so great. The European members of the North Atlantic Treaty Organization (NATO) have cut their military expenditures by 15 per cent since their peak in 1990, and the Central and East European (CEE) countries have cut their defence budgets significantly (precise data are not available) since the dissolution of the Warsaw Treaty Organization (WTO) in 1991.

The global figures, however, obscure increased spending in certain countries and regions. Spending in the Middle East, South Asia and South-East Asia, for example, has not followed the consistent decline seen in global expenditure. Some countries in these regions continue to boost their military spending.

Many developing countries pursue a level of military strength that limits their opportunities to address social and economic problems. In turn, internal social and economic difficulties can quickly become the source of violent instability and conflict.

3.2.1   Definitions and methods: understanding figures on military spending

Comparing the military spending of various countries around the world is no simple matter. For one thing, there is no internationally standardized definition of military expenditure. Because of this, military spending that one might expect to be accounted for in a defence budget might be located elsewhere in the national budget. For example, although Russia's 1995 budget allocated 2.9 trillion roubles ($644 million) for Border Troops, this expense is found not as a defence item in the state budget but as a civilian item under the heading 'Law Enforcement and State Security'.[2]

Where possible, the following items arc included in the military expenditure figures in the above table: all current and capital expenditure on the armed forces and the running of defence departments and other government agencies engaged in defence projects and space activities; the cost of paramilitary forces, border guards and police when judged to be trained and equipped for military operations; military research and development, testing and evaluation costs; and costs of retirement pensions of service personnel and civilian employees.

[2] *SIPRI Yearbook 1996,* p. 333.

World military expenditure in constant price figures, 1992–96[a]

Figures are in US $m. at 1990 prices (CPI-deflated) and exchange rates unless otherwise indicated.

State		1992	1993	1994	1995	1996
NATO						
North America						
Canada		10 482	10 433	10 191	9 549	8 817
USA		284 116	269 111	254 038	238 176	226 369
Europe						
Belgium		3 760	3 571	3 551	3 479	3 443
Denmark		2 648	2 653	2 587	2 561	2 544
France		41 502	41 052	41 260	39 234	38 432
Germany		37 697	34 002	31 621	31 478	30 507
Greece		3 808	3 716	3 780	3 849	4 072
Italy		23 024	23 147	22 575	20 612	23 059
Luxembourg		111	102	112	109	107
Netherlands		7 174	6 590	6 358	6 175	6 180
Norway		3 569	3 326	3 495	3 156	3 380
Portugal		1 977	1 908	1 861	2 000	2 156
Spain		8 113	8 823	7 940	8 230	8 094
Turkey		5 747	6 355	6 213	6 200	6 306
UK		37 141	36 312	35 116	31 961	31 475
NATO Europe		*176 273*	*171 556*	*166 469*	*159 046*	*159 756*
NATO Total		*470 872*	*451 100*	*430 698*	*406 771*	*394 943*
Other Europe						
Albania		46	28	30	31	28
Austria		1 507	1 528	1 514	1 522	1 586
Bulgaria		244	209	223	256	234
Croatia	1993 prices/ER	[845]	[851]	[956]	[1 023]	. .
Cyprus		373	I 168	176	293	286
Czech Rep.[b]	1993 prices/ER		828	857	762	793
Czechoslovakia		1 520	. .	. .	. .	. .
Estonia	1993 prices/ER	10	13	17	17	[15]
Finland		2 277	2 211	2 176	1 959	2 133
Hungary		404	944	349	(254)	(216)
Ireland		505	510	525	630	653
Latvia	1993 prices/ER	. .	16	19	(17)	(18)
Lithuania	1993 prices/ER	3	20	11	(12)	(13)
Malta		26	27	29	. .	. .
Poland		1 075	1 192	1 150	1 158	1 220
Romania		1 023	617	(735)	(722)	748
Slovakia[b]	1993 prices/ER		280	298	337	347
Slovenia	1993 prices/ER	212	184	181	208	177

State		1992	1993	1994	1995	1996
Sweden		5 325	5 243	5 295	5 477	5 619
Switzerland		4 086	3 639	3 725	3 669	3 493
Middle East						
Bahrain		250	244	246	245	..
Egypt		1 475	1 462	[1 787]	..	..
Iran		14 784	19 162	(17 902)	(17 629)	(18 231)
Israel		6 879	6 137	8 751	8 633	6 619
Jordan		296	359	351	372	327
Kuwait	1989 prices/ER	8 417	5 575	4 119	2 852	..
Oman		2 164	1 672	1 597	1 559	..
Saudi Arabia		113 759	15 541	(15 619)	(15 697)	(15 776)
Syria		2 460	1 947	1 971	(2 116)	..
UAE		1 945	[2 007]	1 994	1 944	[3 889]
Yemen		76	62	..	..	..
South Asia						
Bangladesh		362	416	432	427	420
India		7 421	7 747	8 416	8 345	8 333
Pakistan		3 071	3 101	2 978	(2 938)	(3 003)
Sri Lanka		257	276	320	(490)	(630)
Far East						
China		7 184	7 063	7 505	7 487	8 162
Indonesia		(2 206)	(2 495)	(2 844)	(2 706)	(2 674)
Japan		29 644	29 982	30 135	30 428	31 028
Korea, South		10 779	10 654	11 531	(12 133)	(12 765)
Malaysia		1 522	1 617	1 690	1 821	[2 101]
Myanmar		812	..	..	..	..
Philippines		555	595	631	697	698
Singapore		1 921	1 961	2 035	2 540	2 718
Taiwan		8 154	8 444	8 172	(8 134)	(8 101)
Thailand		2 293	2 712	2 793	2 563	3 150
Viet Nam		408	301	393	..	..
Oceania						
Australia		7 174	7 390	7 237	6 735	5 423
Fiji		28	28	23	23	..
New Zealand		632	632	625	710	718
Papua New Guinea		54	61	(61)	..	..
Africa						
Algeria		[1 355]	1 666	2 027	(1 963)	(2 187)
Angola		(1 709)	(2 147)	..	(1 221)	..
Botswana		(156)	..	..	..	..
Burkina Faso		69	62	50	..	..

State	1992	1993	1994	1995	1996
Burundi	..	..	..	35	..
Cameroon	182	193	191	..	..
Cape Verde	..	2.5	..	..	..
Central African Rep.	23 I	21	(19)	(17)	..
Côte d'Ivoire	145	143	126	..	..
Eritrea[c]		55	..	..	..
Ethiopia	215 I	219	205	191	..
Gambia	3	2	2	3	4
Ghana	55	75	..	..	..
Kenya	121	100	98	112	..
Lesotho	[18]	[19]	20	21	..
Madagascar	37	35	30	25	..
Malawi	18	15	25	25	..
Mauritania	(37)	(36)	(34)	(33)	..
Mauritius	11	10	11	11	..
Morocco	1 114	1 176	1 207	1 109	..
Mozambique	127	144	(108)	(86)	..
Namibia	104	62	49	(50)	(68)
Rwanda	110	..	..	..	..
Senegal	109	..	..	..	..
Seychelles	19	12	6	10	..
Sierra Leone	20	..	..	..	..
South Africa	2 831	2 631	2 714	2 455	(2 330)
Sudan	628	669	..	..	..
Swaziland	19	20	21	21	..
Togo	47	52	38	..	..
Tunisia	317	332	332	280	(281)
Uganda	73	71	..	(191)	(202)
Zambia	101	48	31	38	..
Zimbabwe	418	368	273	238	..
Central America					
Belize	5	6	(8)	..	..
Costa Rica	112	147	..	..	..
El Salvador	95	73	62	60	..
Guatemala	121	111	126	(126)	..
Honduras	(96)	(90)	(98)	(86)	..
Mexico	1 137	1 245	1 615	1 245	1 197
Panama	84	91	94	91	..
South America					
Argentina	2 583	2 323	2 471	2 377	2 330
Bolivia	109	115	(115)	(114)	(60)
Brazil	1 162	..	..	..	..
Chile	707	728	733	(738)	(991)

State	1992	1993	1994	1995	1996
Colombia	444	537	625	(423)	..
Ecuador	301	329	301	..	..
Guyana	11	13	15	14	13
Paraguay	90	87	(81)	(84)	(85)
Peru	603	[563]	(582)	..	..
Uruguay	204	159	234	(174)	..
Venezuela	(1 339)	[971]	(751)	(723)	(588)

Conventions

..	Data not available or not applicable	I	Series break when data not comparable
( )	Uncertain data	CPI	Consumer price index
[ ]	SIPRI estimate	ER	Exchange rate

Notes:

[a] Only those states for which data were available for at least one year in the period 1992–96 are included in this table. For the purpose of making comparisons over time and between countries, data in this table have been converted to constant US dollars, using national CPIs and the annual average exchange rates as published by the International Monetary Fund.

[b] The Czech Republic and Slovakia became independent in Jan. 1993.

[c] Eritrea became independent in May 1993.

Source: *SIPRI Yearbook 1997*, pp. 195–200. The *Yearbook* should be consulted for a more complete presentation of the data and the sources and methods.

Once all the military-related items in a budget have been identified, another challenge is how to compare them. If the exchange rate and national rate of inflation are known, figures can be converted (for example, to US dollars). Unfortunately, economic conditions in some countries can be so unstable or poorly documented that meaningful comparisons are impossible.

As noted above, there is also the question of getting solid data in the first place. Some countries have no interest in the rest of the world knowing exactly what they spend on defence. Others are quite open and figures are easily obtained. Figures in the panel on pages 66–69 are drawn from such sources as the United Nations, the International Monetary Fund (IMF), NATO, national ministries of defence and finance, statistical offices, central banks, and specialized journals and newspapers.

Priorities in resource use

The sums of money devoted to world military expenditure are over-whelming by any measure. They are especially great when compared to the continuing poverty and needs of many people throughout the world. The following facts are striking.

- In spite of a recent decline, in 1995 world military expenditures still amounted to more than $1.4 million per minute.

- The US military budget exceeds the total military expenditures of the 13 biggest spenders ranking below it.

- Although there were 4.6 million fewer soldiers in 1995 than in 1989, 22.4 million men and women remained under arms, 65% of whom in the developing countries.

- There are as many land-mines planted in Cambodia as there are people. One person out of every 236 is an amputee.

- The World Bank estimated in 1990 that an increase of one year in average years of education may lead to a 3% rise in the world's gross domestic product (GDP).

- In 1994 the life expectancy of people in the industrial countries was 77 years; in the transition countries it was 69 years and in the developing countries 63 years.

- In 1990 the world spent 5% of the gross national product (GNP) on education, 4.6% on health and 3.8% on the military.

- In the major armed conflicts fought in the 1990s, the large majority of deaths were civilian.

- The end of the cold war left many countries with large holdings of 'surplus' weapons, many of which have been given away.

The information in this panel is drawn from: Sivard, R. L., *World Military and Social Expenditures 1996*, 16th edition (World Priorities: Washington, DC, 1996). As used in this panel, the term 'industrial countries' includes 24 countries in North America, most of Europe and Oceania, and Israel and Japan. The 27 'transition countries' are some of those in Central and Eastern Europe and the former Soviet Union. The term 'developing countries' refers to 109 countries in Latin America, Africa, Asia (excluding Israel and Japan); Malta and Turkey in Europe; and Fiji and Papua New Guinea in Oceania.

3.3 Arms production

The downward trend in world military spending has resulted in a drop in arms production in most parts of the world. Arms production fell by around one-third between 1990 and 1995. This has had a considerable effect on the world's arms industry. However, recent evidence suggests that the decline in arms sales may now be levelling out.[3]

3.3.1 Characteristics of the arms industry

Arms production is not a specific industrial sector, but cuts across several industries, particularly aerospace, electronics, shipbuilding and the manufacture of other transport equipment. In addition, most companies which produce military equipment also produce goods for civilian markets. Few firms sell only military goods. 'The arms industry', then, cannot be precisely defined. The term is used to denote the sum of companies involved in the production of military equipment, although these companies often produce significant output for the civilian market as well.

Military production has particular characteristics. For example, governments often protect it through state ownership, by barring foreign competition or by providing financial support. Foreign sales of military equipment are regulated in most countries. As a result, the export control policies of home governments are very important, not to mention domestic arms sales. Finally, weapon systems involve high research and development costs, making long production runs and/or subsidies crucial.

These factors make it difficult for arms manufacturers to react to changes in demand for their products. There is also political resistance from many governments to seeing their defence industrial capacity drop below a certain level.

Even so, the world arms industry has not been able to avoid the impact of the end of the cold war and the globalization of the economy.

---

[3] *SIPRI Yearbook 1997*, pp. 239–40.

3.3.2 Recent trends in arms production

By the mid-1990s, several trends were clear. With reduced domestic demand, there was increased pressure to sell arms abroad. Competition in most markets has become more fierce and arms production is being concentrated in fewer and larger companies. Finally, as in the global economy at large, there is growing internationalization through take-overs, joint ventures and cooperative arrangements.

These trends have been driven mostly by decreased demand for arms and the rapidly increasing research and development costs for military equipment. In contrast, an important trend—although it is not related to cuts in arms purchases—is the changing relationship between civil and military technology. It used to be the case that military industry was the technology leader in many fields. Today, civil technology is just as likely to be on the cutting edge of the latest technological developments.

The combined arms sales of the top 100 companies in member states of the Organisation for Economic Co-operation and Development (OECD) and the developing countries (except China) declined in value by 2 per cent in 1994 and 6 per cent in 1993,[4] but rose by nearly 5 per cent in 1995.[5]

This is not to say that the arms industry does not continue to be profitable. In fact, in the USA, the military aerospace industry has had record profits. Nevertheless, the arms industry continues to make major adjustments to cope with the lower global demand for its products.

Military industries in the United States have dealt with reduced demand by rationalization, merging and becoming more concentrated. As a result, from 1990 to 1995, employment in the military aircraft, missiles and space sectors fell from 627 000 to 326 000.

In Western Europe there has been both an increased national concentration of the arms industry (although the opportunities for concentration may soon be exhausted) and more European joint ventures focused on specific weapon projects or categories. While most governments and industrialists repeatedly state the need to form a

---

[4] The members of the OECD are listed in chapter 9, section 9.3. Only 4 countries in the developing world (apart from China) had companies among the top 100 in those years: India, Israel, South Korea and South Africa.

[5] The actual volume increase was smaller because of the effects of inflation and fluctuations in exchange rates.

Europe-wide defence industrial base, this has proved difficult to achieve.

France was until 1995 something of an exception to these developments in Europe. The French arms industry has had a very close relationship with the French Government. This has meant that the French industry has been cushioned against the more dramatic effects of a reduction in the demand for arms. This policy has resulted in cost increases for weapon systems which finally became unacceptable to the French Government. Several measures were therefore proposed during 1996 to change this system. The change of government in the summer of 1997 will delay the implementation of some of these measures, but the change in direction is expected to remain.

The Western European Armaments Group (WEAG) was established in 1993 within the Western European Union (WEU) with a primary task to form a European Armaments Agency with supranational authority for common European arms procurement. Little progress has been made because of strong differences between the participating countries.[6] In 1996, therefore, a more pragmatic approach was taken with the creation of a looser structure for armaments cooperation outside the WEU framework—the Joint Armaments Cooperation Organization (JACO),[7] with participation of France, Germany, Italy and the UK and open to any other European country. The final aim is to harmonize national weapon requirements and establish a Europe-wide defence market according to the belief that a large European home market would create better conditions for European competitiveness with the USA.

The decline in the Russian arms industry has been swift and steep. According to official Russian statistics, by the end of 1996 military production had declined to one-eighth of its 1991 level.[8] The effect of this fall is significant when one considers that the Russian defence complex was the core of Russian industry as a whole and was certainly the most technologically advanced part of it. Military enterprises have suffered not only because of defence budget cutbacks but also because once Russian defence budgets have been set the funds have been made available only very slowly. This lag in distributing

---

[6] For the list of countries participating in WEAG, see chapter 9, section 9.3.
[7] It is also often referred to by its French acronym, OCCAR.
[8] *SIPRI Yearbook 1997*, pp. 254–55.

The 100 largest arms-producing companies in the OECD and developing countries, 1995

Figures in columns 6, 7 and 8 are in US $ million.

1	2	3	4	5	6	7	8	9
Rank					Arms sales		Total sales	Col. 6 as
1995	1994	Company	Country	Sector	1995	1994	1995	% of col. 8
1	1	Lockheed Martin	USA	Ac El Mi	13 800	14 400	22 853	60
2	2	McDonnell Douglas	USA	Ac El Mi	9 620	9 230	14 332	67
3	3	British Aerospace	UK	A Ac El Mi SA/O	6 720	7 030	9 062	74
4	6	Loral	USA	El Mi	6 500	5 100	6 700	97
5	4	General Motors, GM	USA	El Eng Mi	6 250	5 900	168 800	4
S	S	Hughes Electronics (GM)	USA	El Mi	5 950	5 590	14 772	40
6	5	Northrop Grumman	USA	Ac El Mi SA/O	5 700	5 670	6 818	84
7	7	Thomson	France	El	4 630	4 270	14 388	32
S	S	Thomson–CSF (Thomson)	France	El	4 620	4 260	7 111	65
8	8	Boeing	USA	Ac El Mi	4 200	4 050	19 515	22
9	12	GEC	UK	El Sh	4 100	3 190	17 348	24
10	10	Raytheon	USA	El Mi	3 960	3 550	11 716	34
11	9	United Technologies, UTC	USA	El Eng	3 650	3 800	22 624	16
12	11	Daimler Benz, DB	FRG	Ac El Eng MV Mi	3 350	3 510	72 255	5
13	15	DCN	France	Sh	3 280	2 730	3 352	98
S	S	Daimler–Benz Aerospace (DB)	FRG	Ac El Eng Mi	3 250	3 430	10 493	31
14	13	Litton	USA	El Sh	3 030	3 160	3 320	91
15	14	General Dynamics, GD	USA	MV Sh	2 930	2 860	3 067	96
16	18	TRW	USA	Oth	2 800	2 480	10 172	28

17	21	IRI	Italy	Ac El Eng Mi Sh	2 620	2 070	41 904	6
18	20	Westinghouse Electric	USA	El	2 600	2 450	9 605	27
19	19	Aérospatiale Groupe	France	Ac Mi	2 550	2 450	9 862	26
20	16	Mitsubishi Heavy Industries	Japan	Ac MV Mi Sh	2 430	2 730	32 067	8
21	17	Rockwell International	USA	El Mi	2 430	2 550	12 981	19
S	S	Finmeccanica (IRI)	Italy	Ac El Eng Mi	2 380	1 860	6 326	38
22	32	Rolls Royce	UK	Eng	2 050	1 360	5 678	36
23	24	Alcatel Alsthom	France	El	2 000	1 800	32 138	6
S	S	Pratt & Whitney (UTC)	USA	Eng	1 840	. .	6 170	30
24	29	CEA	France	Oth	1 740	1 540	3 854	45
25	27	Texas Instruments	USA	El	1 740	1 710	13 128	13
26	25	General Electric	USA	Eng	1 700	1 800	70 028	2
27	30	Kawasaki Heavy Industries	Japan	Ac Eng Mi Sh	1 670	1 450	11 548	14
28	26	Tenneco	USA	Sh	1 670	1 750	8 899	19
S	S	Newport News (Tenneco)	USA	Sh	1 670	1 750	1 670	100
29	28	Textron	USA	Ac El Eng MV	1 600	1 600	9 973	16
30	39	GIAT Industries	France	A MV SA/O	1 280	1 030	1 671	77
31	33	Dassault Aviation Groupe	France	Ac	1 270	1 340	2 323	55
32	34	Allied Signal	USA	Ac El	1 220	1 300	14 346	9
33	50	Alliant Tech Systems	USA	SA/O	1 190	760	1 190	100
34	63	GKN	UK	Ac MV	1 180	550	5 217	23
35	42	Mitsubishi Electric	Japan	El Mi	1 150	940	37 331	3
36	35	Celsius	Sweden	A El SA/O Sh	1 150	1 190	2 079	55
37	38	SNECMA Groupe	France	Eng	1 080	1 060	3 605	30
38	36	Israel Aircraft Industries	Israel	Ac El Mi	1 050	1 150	1 400	75
39	41	ITT Industries	USA	El	1 000	1 000	8 884	11
40	46	Lagardère Groupe	France	Mi	980	820	10 534	9
41	37	FMC	USA	A MV	970	1 100	4 567	21

1	2	3	4	5	6	7	8	9
Rank					Arms sales		Total sales	Col. 6 as
1995	1994	Company	Country	Sector	1995	1994	1995	% of col. 8
42	43	Siemens	FRG	EI	910	870	61 938	1
43	48	AT&T	USA	EI	900	790	79 609	1
44	53	Diehl	FRG	SA/O	870	740	2 191	40
45	57	Thyssen	FRG	MV Sh	780	640	28 032	3
46	67	NEC	Japan	EI	780	520	46 749	2
S	S	Matra Défense (Lagardère)	France	Mi	750	680	765	97
47	51	Oerlikon–Bührle	Switzerl.	A Ac EI Mi SA/O	730	750	3 225	23
48	44	GTE	USA	EI	730	850	19 957	4
49	45	Harris	USA	EI	720	840	3 444	21
50	62	Tracor	USA	Comp (Ac EI Mi)	720	560	887	81
51	52	Bremer Vulkan, BV	FRG	EI Sh	690	740	4 187	16
52	40	Teneo	Spain	A Ac EI MV Sh	670	1 020	17 884	4
53	54	Hunting	UK	Comp (EI Mi)	670	690	1 780	38
54	64	SAGEM Groupe	France	EI	650	540	3 020	21
55	59	Denel	S. Africa	A Ac EI MV Mi SA/O	650	600	938	69
56	58	FIAT	Italy	Eng MV	640	620	42 845	1
S	S	SNECMA (SNECMA Groupe)	France	Eng	630	650	1 735	36
S	S	STN Atlas Elektronik (BV)	FRG	EI	620	680	1 012	61
57	68	Dassault Electronique	France	EI	610	490	852	72
58	55	Eidgenössische Rüstungsbetriebe	Switzerl.	A Ac Eng SA/O	610	660	666	91
59	66	Ishikawajima–Harima	Japan	Eng Sh	600	520	11 537	5
60	65	Ordnance Factories	India	A SA/O	590	520	719	82
S	49	Bath Iron Works (GD)	USA	Sh	590	770	640	92

		Company	Country	Sector				
61	–	Vickers	UK	Eng MV SA/O	560	260	1 806	*31*
62	70	Rheinmetall	FRG	A EI MV SA/O	550	480	2 384	*23*
63	84	Toshiba	Japan	EI Mi	540	400	54 434	*1*
64	74	Racal Electronics	UK	EI	540	450	1 661	*33*
65	72	Dyncorp	USA	Comp (Ac)	540	470	909	*60*
66	73	Ceridian	USA	EI	510	460	1 333	*38*
S	56	VSEL (GEC)	UK	Sh	510	650	..	*:*
67	88	Rafael	Israel	SA/O Oth	490	360	500	*98*
68	60	Gencorp	USA	EI Eng	490	580	1 772	*28*
S	S	CASA (Teneo)	Spain	Ac	490	440	866	*56*
S	S	Aerojet (Gencorp)	USA	EI Eng	490	580	520	*94*
69	S	BDM International	USA	EI Oth	480	430	890	*54*
70	89	Saab	Sweden	Ac EI Mi	470	350	1 111	*42*
71	69	Lucas Industries	UK	Comp (Ac)	460	490	4 629	*10*
72	75	Honeywell	USA	EI Mi	460	450	6 731	*7*
73	86	Avondale Industries	USA	Sh	450	380	576	*78*
74	76	Motorola	USA	EI	450	450	27 040	*2*
75	96	Olin	USA	SA/O	440	320	3 150	*14*
S	S	SAGEM (SAGEM Groupe)	France	EI	430	360	1 659	*26*
76	77	Mitre	USA	Oth	420	430	576	*73*
77	90	Koor Industries	Israel	A EI	410	340	3 390	*12*
78	71	Smiths Industries	UK	Comp (Ac)	410	470	1 420	*29*
79	93	Logicon	USA	EI Oth	410	340	476	*85*
80	80	Hindustan Aeronautics	India	Ac Mi	400	410	433	*92*
S	S	Hollandse Signaalapparaten (Thomson-CSF, France)	Netherl.	EI	400	360	410	*99*
S	S	Agusta (Finmeccanica)	Italy	Ac	390	450	499	*77*
81	91	MKEK[f]	Turkey	SA/O	380	340	640	*59*

| Rank | | | | | Arms sales | | Total sales | Col. 6 as |
| 1 | 2 | 3 | 4 | 5 | 6 | 7 | 8 | 9 |
1995	1994	Company	Country	Sector	1995	1994	1995	% of col. 8
S	S	Tadiran (Koor Industries)	Israel	EI	370	310	1 049	35
82	–	Wegmann Group	FRG	MV	350	280	424	82
83	–	The Japan Steel Works	Japan	SA/O	350	190	1 253	28
84	85	Esco Electronics	USA	EI	350	390	441	78
85	95	Devonport Management	UK	Sh	340	330	354	97
S	S	Sextant Avionique (Thomson-CSF)	France	EI	340	330	978	35
86	98	Bombardier	Canada	EI Mi	330	310	5 190	6
87	92	Vosper Thornycroft	UK	Sh	330	340	376	87
S	S	FIAT Aviazione (FIAT)	Italy	Eng	330	350	946	35
S	S	Allison (Rolls Royce, UK)	USA	Eng	330	..	750	44
88	79	Preussag	FRG	Sh	320	410	18 389	2
S	S	HDW (Preussag)	FRG	Sh	320	410	732	44
89	–	Nissan Motor	Japan	A MV	310	290	64 216	..
S	S	Oto Melara (Finmeccanica)	Italy	A MV Mi	310	270	310	100
90	100	SNPE Groupe	France	A SA/O	300	290	877	35
91	–	Elbit	Israel	EI	300	290	968	31
92	–	Fuji Heavy Industries	Japan	Ac	300	240	11 453	3
93	–	Babcock International Group	UK	Sh	290	280	..	..
S	–	Thomson Sintra (Thomson-CSF)	France	EI	290	..	307	96
94	–	UNC	USA	Comp (Ac)	280	210	536	52
S	S	Saab Military Aircraft (Saab)	Sweden	Ac	280	180	357	78
95	83	TAAS	Israel	A MV SA/O	270	400	405	66
96	–	Ericsson	Sweden	EI	270	270	13 848	2

		Company	Country					
S	S	Ericsson Microwave (Ericsson)	Sweden	El	270	270	516	52
97	87	Thiokol	USA	Eng SA/O	260	370	957	27
98	78	Oshkosh Truck	USA	MV	260	430	438	60
99	31	Unisys	USA	El	260	1 400	6 202	4
100	-	Komatsu	Japan	MV SA/O	260	230	10 624	2

Notes: Companies are ranked by their arms sales in 1995. Rankings and sales data from 1994 are provided for comparison. Where a company is a subsidiary of a parent firm, this is marked by an 'S' in cols 1 and 2 and the company is ranked as if it were independent. Names in brackets under 'Company' are the parent firms.

Data on total sales in col. 8 are for the entire company, not for the arms-producing sector alone. Data are reported on the fiscal-year basis reported by the company in its annual report.

Data in local currencies have been converted to US dollars to allow for comparisons. The period-average of market exchange rates of the International Monetary Fund, in *International Financial Statistics*, is used for conversion to US dollars.

Data on Japanese firms are based on military contracts with the Japan Defense Agency, rather than on military sales.

Abbreviations: A = artillery, Ac = aircraft, El = electronics, Eng = engines, Mi = missiles, MV = military vehicles, SA/O = small arms/ordnance, Sh = ships; Oth = other. 'Comp ( )' = components of the product within the parentheses. This is used only for companies which do not produce any final systems.

Conventions
'. .' = not applicable or not available.
'(-) = company did not have any arms sales in 1994, or did not exist as it was structured in 1995, or was not among the 100 largest companies in 1994.

Source: SIPRI Yearbook 1997, pp. 261-66. For a more complete presentation of data on the top 100 arms-producing companies, consult the *Yearbook*.

funds has meant that the Russian armed services have built up a considerable debt to their suppliers.

However, 1996 saw major changes in Russia's defence industrial policy on ownership and management of the Russian arms enterprises. Increased competition, new corporate structures and increased state intervention to support the process of change, including exports, are expected.

China's arms industry is in the early stage of cutbacks. This contraction is due to two factors. China has enjoyed a favourable security situation since the early 1980s and responded by cutting its armed forces by 25 per cent. No longer would it prepare to fight a mass 'People's War'; instead, China chose to focus on limited wars using sophisticated weapon systems. In addition to needing fewer weapons from its arms industry, China's military has resisted buying domestic weapons which do not meet the high-technology specifications it wishes to set.

The precise size of the Chinese military industry is unknown. Estimates range from 1000 production facilities and 3 million workers to 50 000 production facilities and 25 million workers.[9] Coordinating arms development and production has never been easy under the Chinese system. It is likely to become less easy as the industry shrinks, becomes decentralized and faces the free market conditions that have already been introduced to other sectors of the Chinese economy.

3.3.3 Definitions and methods: understanding figures on arms production

The panel on pages 74–79 presents information on the 100 largest arms-producing companies in the OECD and the developing countries (except China). Data were gathered from questionnaires sent to over 400 companies, annual reports, newspapers, military journals, company archives and marketing reports, and government publications. Estimates were made for companies which did do not respond or report their arms sales separately from their other business activities.

---

[9] *SIPRI Yearbook 1996*, p. 438. The real number is likely to be in the lower end of this range. *SIPRI Yearbook 1995*, p. 374; and Arnett, E. (ed.), SIPRI, *Military Capacity and the Risk of War: China, India, Pakistan and Iran* (Oxford University Press: Oxford, 1997), pp. 243–76.

3.4   Arms transfers

From the end of the cold war in 1991 until 1996, the trade in major conventional weapons, that is, major weapons that are not weapons of mass destruction (nuclear, chemical or biological), remained fairly steady as compared to the period 1986–90.[10] In this earlier period there was a sharp decline in arms transfers after they reached a peak in 1987.

According to the SIPRI evaluation system, the value of world transfers of major conventional weapons in 1996 was $22.98 billion (in 1990 US dollars). For an explanation of the SIPRI evaluation system in calculating the arms trade, see section 3.4.4.

3.4.1   Suppliers

The dominant sources of major conventional weapons are six suppliers: the United States, Russia, Germany, the United Kingdom, France and China. In 1996 they accounted for 80 per cent of total deliveries. Indeed, these countries ranked as the leading six suppliers for the entire period 1992–96.

In the period 1991–95, the USA became the world's dominant arms supplier, a position held in 1986–90 by the Soviet Union. With the collapse of the Soviet Union there was a steep decline in Russian arms sales, bottoming out at 3.5 per cent of world sales in 1994. Russian sales did pick up in 1995 to a level closer to those of 1991–93 and in 1996 surpassed that level.

3.4.2   Recipients

Countries in Asia have boosted their receipts of arms deliveries from 26 per cent of total deliveries in 1986 to 48 per cent in 1996.

Looking more closely at Asia, the subregion of North-East Asia recorded some sharp increases in imports. While imports to Japan have fallen over the past five years, deliveries to China, South Korea and Taiwan have increased and even accelerated when compared to

---

[10] The term 'major conventional weapons' in this chapter refers to those included in 5 categories of weapons or systems: aircraft, armour and artillery, guidance and radar systems, missiles, and warships. See also chapter 6, section 6.4.2, for a discussion of the United Nations Register of Conventional Arms.

The trade in major conventional weapons, 1992–96*

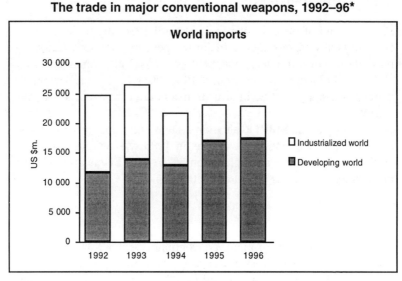

The industrialized world: Albania, Armenia, Australia, Austria, Azerbaijan, Belarus, Belgium, Bosnia and Herzegovina, Bulgaria, Canada, Croatia, Czechoslovakia (until 1992), Czech Republic (since 1993), Denmark, Estonia, Finland, France, Georgia, Germany, Greece, Hungary, Iceland, Ireland, Italy, Japan, Kazakhstan, Kyrgyzstan, Latvia, Liechtenstein, Lithuania, Luxembourg, Macedonia, Malta, Moldova, Monaco, Netherlands, New Zealand, Norway, Poland, Portugal, Romania, Russia, Slovakia (since 1993), Slovenia, Spain, Sweden, Switzerland, Tajikistan, Turkey, Turkmenistan, UK, Ukraine, USA, Uzbekistan and Yugoslavia (Serbia and Montenegro). The developing world comprises all other nations of the world.

* Transfers are measured using the SIPRI evaluation system, in US $ million at 1990 prices.

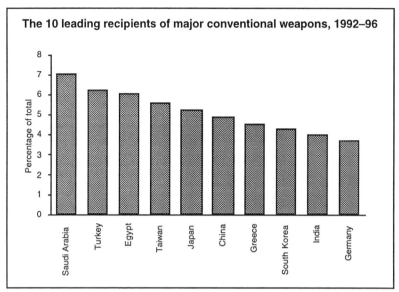

The 10 leading recipients of major conventional weapons, 1992–96

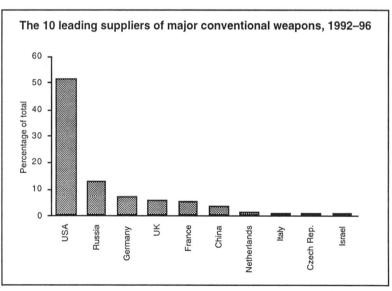

The 10 leading suppliers of major conventional weapons, 1992–96

the period 1986–90. These three countries now account for 30 per cent of total deliveries.

In the Middle East, the share of arms deliveries going to the Persian Gulf subregion has dropped. In 1986 Iran, Iraq and Saudi Arabia accounted for 57 per cent of deliveries to the Middle East. In 1995 this figure fell to 27 per cent. However, it must be kept in mind that Iraq is subject to a United Nations arms embargo.

The arms market in the Central and East European countries may grow as these countries undertake major investment in equipment compatible with that of NATO, either in preparation for hoped-for membership or for exercises with NATO countries under the Partnership for Peace (PFP) framework. Some programmes are already being implemented.

3.4.3 General observations

The trade in major conventional weapons in the period 1992–96 tends to reinforce the traditional understanding of the arms trade.

• The trade is concentrated among a small number of suppliers and relatively small number of recipients.
• The suppliers closely match the group of major world powers as identified by such factors as size of economies and permanent membership of the UN Security Council.
• The pattern of arms transfers is heavily influenced by the security arrangements between supplier and recipient.
• The bilateral relationships between suppliers and recipients tend to become durable over time.

3.4.4 Definitions and methods: understanding figures on the arms trade

The figures in section 3.4 of this chapter are generated by the SIPRI arms transfers database. The system of evaluation used is intended to capture the trend in the total flow of major weapons and its geographic pattern.

First, it is important to note that the data cover five categories of weapons or systems: aircraft, armour and artillery, guidance and radar systems, missiles and warships. Small arms, artillery under 100-mm calibre, ammunition, support items, services and components or component technology (except for specific items) are not included in the statistics.

To be considered a major weapon or system, the weapon transferred must have a clear military application and be destined for the armed forces, paramilitary forces, intelligence agencies or police forces of another country.

Data include transfers of final systems and licensed production of final systems.

Second, the SIPRI evaluation system expresses arms transfers in 1990 US dollars and produces values based on actual deliveries during the year(s) in question. These values are not the actual prices paid for weapons in a particular deal but are trend-indicator values constructed by SIPRI.

It is understandable to ask why data on revenues from sales are not used to measure the arms trade. One reason is that sales data for arms transfers are only available for a small number of countries. Even then, the data are often not broken down in detail.

Sales-revenue data can also be misleading. For example, the transfer of a radar system to one country may include military aid and grants to reduce the price of the system. Another country receiving this radar system might not get aid and grants. Although receiving essentially the same thing, these two countries would end up paying very different prices. The SIPRI evaluation system takes into account these and other factors, so that similar weapon systems are given similar values—a qualitative measurement of the weapons transferred, not the economic cost for the buyer.

The panel on pages 82–83 gives a snapshot of the imports, exports, recipients and suppliers of major conventional weapons on a global basis.

4. Weapons of mass destruction

4.1 Introduction

'Weapons of mass destruction' is the term commonly applied to nuclear, biological and chemical weapons, also called NBC weapons. It captures effectively the shared characteristic of these weapons—their ability to kill on a large scale and in an indiscriminate way.

The task before the international community is twofold—to reduce and eventually eliminate weapons of mass destruction and to prevent their spread or proliferation. The issues connected with this task are presented in detail in chapter 5.

This chapter reviews the known and assumed stockpiles of nuclear, chemical and biological weapons and describes several of the international arms control agreements and other efforts to prevent the proliferation of weapons of mass destruction. It concludes with a look at the activities of the United Nations Special Commission on Iraq (UNSCOM), the unique case of the international community acting to rid itself of the threat posed by one country's programme for weapons of mass destruction.

4.2 Nuclear weapons

Most states in the world fall into two categories: nuclear weapon states and non-nuclear weapon states. Indeed, this is an important distinction that is fundamental to one of the world's major multilateral arms control agreements—the 1968 Treaty on the Non-proliferation of Nuclear Weapons, or Non-Proliferation Treaty (NPT). States can also be categorized by whether or not they have declared that they possess nuclear weapons. There are states which have not declared that they possess nuclear weapons but are known to have or are strongly suspected of having them none the less.

The following section presents the five nuclear weapon programmes which are declared and relatively well known.

4.2.1   Declared nuclear weapon states

Five states are declared nuclear weapon states: China, France, Russia, the United Kingdom and the United States.[1] At the beginning of 1997, the number of nuclear weapons in their operational inventories totalled at least 20 000.

The panel on pages 88–89 summarizes the nuclear forces of China, France and the United Kingdom and the strategic nuclear weapons of the USA and Russia but not their tactical nuclear weapons. These figures are best estimates based on public information. There are some uncertainties, especially in the case of China. The breakdown of weapons among these five countries is as follows:

- The USA: about 7150 strategic and 1150 tactical warheads;
- Russia: about 7250 strategic and over 3000 tactical warheads;
- The UK: about 300 warheads;
- France: just under 500 warheads; and
- China: about 275 strategic and perhaps 120 tactical warheads.[2]

4.2.2   Undeclared nuclear weapon states

A state which could relatively quickly build an inventory of nuclear weapons, has indicated that it might do so if it chose to, and is not a party to the 1968 Non-Proliferation Treaty (NPT) is known as a 'threshold state'. India and Pakistan are threshold states by this definition. Israel—a state which is assumed to possess nuclear weapons—is generally also categorized as a threshold state. Suspicions arise from several factors which are common to these countries. These include statements from officials, the capability to produce or acquire the fissile materials needed to produce nuclear weapons and the necessary technical capabilities.

It is notable that the number of states suspected of possessing nuclear weapons, or seeking to develop such a capability, has declined in recent years. In fact, 30 years ago some experts feared there would be as many as 20 nuclear weapon states in the world by the 1980s.[3]

---

[1] The NPT defines a nuclear weapon state as 'one which has manufactured and exploded a nuclear weapon or other nuclear explosive device prior to 1 January 1967'.

[2] A strategic nuclear weapon has a range usually of over 5500 km (intercontinental range) and is intended to strike the home territory of the opposing power. A tactical nuclear weapon has a short range and is intended for battlefield use.

[3] *SIPRI Yearbook 1994*, p. 608.

The nuclear forces of the five declared nuclear weapon states, as of January 1997

Type/designation	No. deployed[a]	No. warheads in stockpile
US strategic nuclear forces		
Bombers		
B-52H Stratofortress	71/44	400
B-1B Lancer	95/48	400
B-2 Spirit	13/10	1 000
Total	**179/102**	**1 800**
ICBMs		
Minuteman III		
Mk-12	200	600
Mk-12A	325	975
MX/Peacekeeper	50	500
Total	**575**	**2 075**
SLBMs		
Trident I C4	192	1 536
Trident II D5	216	1 728
Mk-4	..	1 344
Mk-5	..	384
Total	**408**	**3 264**
Russian strategic nuclear forces[b]		
Bombers		
Tu-95M Bear-H6 32	192	
Tu-95M Bear-H16	56	896
Tu-160 Blackjack	25	300
Total	**113**	**1 388**
ICBMs		
SS-18	180	1 800
SS-19	160	960
SS-24 M1/M2	36/10	460
SS-25	369	389
Total	**755**	**3 589**
SLBMs		
SS-N-18 M1	208	624
SS-N-20	120	1 200
SS-N-23	112	448
Total	**440**	**2 272**

Type/designation	No. deployed[a]	No. warheads in stockpile
British nuclear forces		
Aircraft		
GR.1/1A Tornado	96	100
SLBMs		
Trident II D5	32	160
French nuclear forces		
Land-based aircraft		
Mirage 2000N/ASMP	45	45
Carrier-based aircraft		
Super Étendard	24	20
SLBMs		
M4A/B	48	288
M45	16	96
Chinese nuclear forces		
Aircraft		
H-6	120	120
Q-5	30	30
Land-based missiles		
DF-3A	50	50
DF-4	20	20
DF-5A	7	7
DF-21A	36	36
SLBMs		
Julang-1	12	12
Tactical weapons		
Artillery/ADMs, Short-range missiles		120

Acronyms: ADM = atomic demolition munition; ALCM = air-launched cruise missile; ASMP = air-sol moyen portée; ICBM = intercontinental ballistic missile; SLBM = submarine-launched ballistic missile; SRAM = short-range attack missile; SSBN = nuclear-powered, ballistic-missile submarine.

[a] For US bombers, number deployed, the second figure is the operational number available for both nuclear and conventional missions. The 2 figures for the number of Russian SS-24 ICBMs deployed are for the rail-based M1/silo-based M2, respectively.

[b] For Russian forces, the designation refers to the NATO designation.

Source: SIPRI Yearbook 1997, pp. 394–401. The *Yearbook* should be consulted for additional data and detailed explanations of how the figures were derived.

The legality of nuclear weapons

• On 8 July 1996 the International Court of Justice (ICJ) delivered its opinion on the legality of using nuclear weapons. It made its decision after being asked by the UN General Assembly in December 1994 whether the threat or use of nuclear weapons was 'consistent with international law'.

• The Court's decision was complex but it concluded that, overall, there was no 'comprehensive and universal prohibition of the threat or use of nuclear weapons'. The Court ruled that 'the threat or use of nuclear weapons would generally be contrary to the rules of international law applicable in armed conflict, and in particular the principles and rules of international human-itarian law', with the possible exception in an extreme circumstance of self-defence.

This may seem a setback for those who hoped the ICJ would rule firmly against nuclear weapons. It is important to note, however, that the judges also recalled that there exists an obligation in international law to pursue in good faith and bring to a conclusion negotiations leading to nuclear disar-mament in all its aspects under strict and effective international control.

In South Asia it is the long-standing rivalry between India and Pak-istan that is the source of nuclear proliferation concerns.

The Indian programme is the most advanced of the two. In 1974 India tested a 12-kiloton 'peaceful nuclear device', and it has been suspected of working to improve its nuclear weapon capabilities ever since. Besides the concerns raised by the 1974 nuclear explosion, India has production facilities capable of producing weapon-usable fissile materials that are not subject to international safeguards.

India insists that a global disarmament treaty is a superior approach to the NPT. It is believed to have enough weapon-grade material for between 45 and 75 nuclear warheads.[4]

Pakistan has the capability to produce highly enriched uranium suit-able for weapons and is reported to have the components to assemble nuclear weapons. Pakistani officials have made such claims. However, there is continuing uncertainty over whether it possesses nuclear weapons. While Pakistan has not signed the NPT, it has

---

[4] *SIPRI Yearbook 1996*, p. 626. The number of warheads is an estimate based on plutonium on hand.

declared a willingness to enter into non-proliferation commitments when India does the same. Pakistan is estimated potentially to have between 5 and 10 nuclear weapons.[5]

Long-standing tensions in the Middle East have contributed to suspicions that some countries in the region possess nuclear weapons. Until recently, Iraq was a prime candidate in this regard. It is now known without doubt that Iraq—a party to the Non-Proliferation Treaty—did have a considerable nuclear weapon programme (see section 4.5).

Israel is assumed to have a substantial nuclear arsenal, consisting of up to 100 warheads which could be delivered by aircraft and missiles. Israel has not signed the NPT, nor has it declared that it possesses nuclear weapons. It has stated that it might sign the treaty provided a secure and stable peace is achieved in the Middle East.

South Africa became a party to the NPT in 1991 as a non-nuclear weapon state. Despite this development, it was still suspected of possessing nuclear weapons. This was confirmed by then South African President F. W. de Klerk in March 1993. He admitted that South Africa had possessed nuclear weapons but said that they had been destroyed and South Africa's nuclear weapon-making programme dismantled. After inspections, International Atomic Energy Agency (IAEA) officials were satisfied that this was the case.

4.2.3   The NPT and the NPT Review Conferences

The Non-Proliferation Treaty was opened for signature in 1968. As of 1 January 1997, 186 states had ratified, acceded or suceeded to the treaty.

Almost from the moment the first atomic bomb was dropped, the international community has tried to both stop the spread of nuclear weapons and at the same time encourage disarmament. The United Nations was the focus of many debates on how this could be achieved. The NPT was negotiated in the Eighteen-Nation Committee on Disarmament (ENDC) in 1965–68. It struck a balance between the interests of the states which did and did not possess nuclear weapons. This balance is found in the combined effect of Articles I–VI of the treaty:

[5] *SIPRI Yearbook 1995*, p. 657.

• Nuclear weapon states agreed not to transfer nuclear weapons to other states or to assist them to acquire nuclear weapons. Non-nuclear weapon states undertook not to receive nuclear weapons and not to manufacture them.

• Non-nuclear weapon states agreed to accept safeguards administered by the International Atomic Energy Agency (IAEA) to ensure that nuclear materials were not diverted from peaceful uses to nuclear weapon development. In return, non-nuclear weapon states could participate fully in the peaceful application of nuclear technology.

• All the NPT parties agreed to pursue negotiations in good faith on ending the nuclear arms race and on a treaty on general and complete disarmament.

The NPT contains a provision which has ensured that non-proliferation issues will remain at the top of the international community's arms control agenda: after an initial and mandatory review conference five years after the treaty came into force (1970), additional review conferences could be held every five years thereafter. In addition, after 25 years, the parties to the treaty would have to decide its future. In 1995, after four review conferences (in 1975, 1980, 1985 and 1990), the NPT Review and Extension Conference took place in April–May. The was decided to extend the treaty indefinitely, change the process by which the treaty's implementation is reviewed and set detailed 'yardsticks' for evaluating implementation.

In the future, review conferences will not be limited to looking back and examining the implementation of the treaty over the previous five years. The conferences will also look ahead at what can be done to strengthen the treaty and convince all states to sign it.

Making the NPT permanent was an important achievement for the international community. It ensures that nuclear non-proliferation will remain a priority indefinitely. Another result is that the elaborate safeguards measures that are the responsibility of the International Atomic Energy Agency stay in place. Future disarmament initiatives would be threatened without the confidence provided by IAEA safeguards.

Now that the NPT machinery will continue indefinitely, attention is likely to focus on the few parties to the NPT that have been alleged to be seeking nuclear weapons. In addition, making the treaty universal and dealing with the commitment to work towards general and complete disarmament will also figure prominently in future review conferences.

4.3   Chemical weapons

Chemical weapons (CW) are chemical substances—gas, liquid or solid—when used or intended for use as weapons because of their toxic effect on humans, animals or plants.

Chemical weapons are the only class of non-conventional weapons to have been systematically used in war and incorporated into military doctrine. First used on a large scale during World War I, they were also employed in the Russian Civil War (1919–21), in Spanish Morocco (1922–27), during Italy's invasion of Ethiopia (1935–36), in Japan's war in China (1937–45), by Egypt in the Yemeni Civil War (1963–67), in the Viet Nam War (1962–75) and in the Iraq–Iran War (1980–88). During the 1991 Persian Gulf War, it was feared that Iraq might use its chemical weapons against the international coalition formed to liberate Kuwait.

These events have both helped and complicated efforts by the international community to ban chemical weapons. Europe's experience with CW during World War I led to the 1925 Protocol for the Prohibition of the Use in War of Asphyxiating, Poisonous or Other Gases, and of Bacteriological Methods of Warfare (Geneva Protocol). While the Protocol bans the use of CW, it does not ban their production or possession. About 30 of the states which signed and ratified the Protocol reserved for themselves the right of retaliation should they be attacked with chemical or biological weapons. Several of these states have withdrawn their reservations.

In 1993, after over 20 years of negotiations, the Convention on the Prohibition of the Development, Production, Stockpiling and Use of Chemical Weapons and on their Destruction—the Chemical Weapons Convention (CWC)—was opened for signature. It entered into force on 29 April 1997.

4.3.1   Possessors of chemical weapons and allegations of CW use

As of August 1997 only India, Russia and the USA have formally declared that they possess a CW arsenal. UN fact-finding missions conducted in 1984–88 and UNSCOM's activities, however, confirmed that Iraq also possessed chemical weapons (see section 4.5).

It is very difficult to determine which other states have CW programmes, although there continue to be allegations that India, Russia and the USA are not alone. In 1994, for example, the US Congressional Research Service reported that Afghanistan, China, Egypt, Ethiopia, Iran, Israel, Kazakhstan, North Korea, Myanmar (formerly Burma), Syria, Taiwan, Ukraine and Viet Nam had been identified as possible possessors of chemical weapons and that Chile, Cuba, France, South Korea, Libya, Pakistan, Somalia, South Africa and Thailand were suspected of having CW programmes.[6]

There have been numerous allegations of chemical weapon use in recent years. Often, these allegations have been made by one or more parties to an internal conflict. In such cases, it is very difficult for independent experts to determine the truth of the situation. Sometimes the sites of alleged CW use are so remote that it may be difficult for outsiders even to gain access. Added to this is the fact that allegations can be used to generate international support or sympathy.

4.3.2   Chemical weapon destruction

All the parties to the multilateral CWC are required to destroy their CW stockpiles within 10 years of the convention entering into force. An extension period of no more than 5 years may be granted in exceptional cases. As the states which possess the most extensive stockpiles of chemical weapons, the USA and Russia have the largest and most expensive destruction programmes to undertake. The USA has ratified the CWC but as of August 1997 Russia had not.

In 1990 the USA and the USSR had signed an agreement known as the Bilateral Destruction Agreement.[7] This agreement was never ratified by either country and thus did not enter into force. US assistance is provided under the Cooperative Threat Reduction programme, discussed in chapter 5, section 5.2.3.

Some of the key issues surrounding the CW stockpiles are the cost of destruction, the safety of current destruction technologies, and the design and implementation of technologies which take into account citizens' concerns. At the moment, the USA is using the incineration method at the Johnston Atoll in the Pacific Ocean and at Tooele, Utah, although other methods continue to be studied.

---

[6] *SIPRI Yearbook 1995*, p. 340; and *SIPRI Yearbook 1996* p. 665. See the panel on pages 125–35 in chapter 5 for the list of states which have signed or ratified the CWC.

[7] The full title of the bilateral US–Russian agreement is the Agreement on Destruction and Non-Production of Chemical Weapons and on the Measures to Facilitate the Multilateral Convention on Banning Chemical Weapons.

In the USA a destruction schedule is being implemented: the target date for the complete elimination of CW stockpiles is 31 December 2004. Russia, which has a larger CW stockpile to destroy than the USA, has not begun destruction operations and has had difficulties finding the necessary funding. Germany, the Netherlands, Sweden and the USA are providing assistance, and Finland and Italy are considering doing so.

Under the Chemical Weapons Convention, states parties are required to declare their CW stockpiles. At the time of writing, the identity of other possessors in addition to India, Russia and the USA as well as the size of their arsenals were still unknown. Iraq, which is still not a signatory to the CWC, must destroy its chemical weapons under the supervision of UNSCOM. It is not yet certain whether Iraq has declared its entire chemical arsenal.

4.3.3   Old CW munitions[8]

Belgium and France have for decades been retrieving sizeable quantities of chemical munitions from the World War I front-line areas. Until the late 1970s, most were dumped into the deep sea, but as a consequence of international environmental laws alternative disposal methods had to be sought. Many of the recovered shells had failed to detonate, which poses an additional hazard to dealing with them. Others have deteriorated to such an extent that their destruction is complicated by the contamination of the explosive charge and the chemical agent by reactions in the soil. A major difficulty is determining whether or not a shell that is to be retrieved is filled with chemicals. Germany faces similar problems at former production and storage sites.

There have been other reports of dumping of old chemical weapons in the sea. For example, in 1992 it was reported that the German Democratic Republic dumped World War II chemical munitions in the Baltic Sea as recently as 1965. There have also been reports that the former Soviet Union dumped chemical bombs in 1946–48 off the coast of Latvia and that large amounts of CW were dumped in the

[8] See Stock, T. and Lohs, Kh., *The Challenge of Old Chemical Munitions and Toxic Armament Wastes,* SIPRI Chemical & Biological Warfare Studies no. 16 (Oxford University Press: Oxford, 1997).

North Sea in the 1950s and 1960s and 'small amounts' in the Black Sea.

Old chemical weapons were also dumped off the coasts of Denmark, Norway, Sweden and the UK after World War II. Responding to a parliamentary inquiry, the British Ministry of Defence admitted that approximately 120 000 tonnes of CW were dumped by the UK after the war and an additional 25 000 tonnes between 1955 and 1957.

For the first time, in the spring of 1995 Japan officially confirmed Chinese claims that it had abandoned old chemical weapons in China during World War II. Two Japanese teams removed chemical weapons from sites in China and negotiations began between the two governments on the cost of recovery and destruction of abandoned CW in China.

4.4   Biological and toxin weapons

Biological weapons (BW) contain living organisms or infective material derived from them. They are intended to cause disease or death in humans, animals or plants, and their effectiveness depends both on the organism's ability to multiply and on the means by which they are delivered to the target. As with chemical weapons, the international community views biological and toxin weapons as particularly repulsive and inhumane. Accordingly, they are the subject of two international agreements: the 1925 Geneva Protocol and the 1972 Convention on the Prohibition of the Development, Production and Stockpiling of Bacteriological (Biological) and Toxin Weapons and on their Destruction, or the BTWC. However, the threat posed by biological weapons has not been removed.

4.4.1   Possessors of biological and toxin weapons

Several factors make it very difficult positively to identify states which possess BW. First, the technology and know-how involved in the production of BW can also be used for peaceful purposes—the basic know-how of BW is similar in both cases. In fact, the BTWC allows for the development of pathogens or toxins for peaceful, prophylactic or protective purposes. It is therefore not possible to be certain that a state's BW-related activities necessarily indicate an intention to produce weapons.

Second, because BW are viewed so negatively by the international community and their production is outlawed by the BTWC, states pursuing a BW programme must do so in secret. As a result, firm evidence is difficult to come by. The source of information on possessors of BW is usually an 'intelligence' report that cannot be independently verified.

In 1995, in his annual Report to Congress on Adherence to and Compliance with Arms Control Agreements, US President Bill Clinton expressed concerns about the compliance with the BTWC of eight countries: China, Egypt, Iran, Iraq, Libya, Russia, Syria and Taiwan.[9]

4.4.2 Violations of the BTWC

Alleged violations of the BTWC have been few and are generally unconfirmed by independent sources. However, in 1993 additional information came to light about the outbreak of anthrax in Sverdlovsk (today Yekaterinburg), Russia, in 1979. Anthrax is an infectious disease caused by a bacterium. Humans can contract the disease via cuts in the skin by being exposed to infected animals, by consuming animal products or from anthrax aerosols. At the time of the outbreak, Soviet officials claimed that it was due to tainted meat. This explanation was always questioned since Sverdlovsk is home to a biological facility on a military complex. A team of Russian and US experts concluded, however, that those who died had inhaled aerosols containing the anthrax bacterium. This finding followed Russian President Boris Yeltsin's admission in June 1992 that the epidemic was indeed the consequence of military research to make biological weapons. However, the results of a subsequent joint investigation by Russian and US experts also indicated that the amount of spores released could have been consistent with research activities permitted under the BTWC, namely, for medical or protection purposes. The incident illustrates the difficulties in confirming alleged violations of the BTWC.

4.4.3 The BTWC Review Conferences

Four review conferences of the BTWC have been held since the convention was signed in 1972; the fourth was held in 1996.

---

[9] Egypt and Syria have not ratified the BTWC; see the panel on pages 125–35 in chapter 5.

At the Second Review Conference, held in 1986, the parties to the convention decided to exchange information annually on research facilities, biological products and outbreaks of rare diseases. This information exchange was designed to build confidence in the BTWC and between the parties. By 1995 there had been nine rounds of information exchange, but this process has not lived up to expectations. For example, less than half the parties to the BTWC participated in the exercise in 1995. Very few states have participated in all nine rounds.

The Third Review Conference, held in 1991, moved the issue of verification measures to the top of the agenda by creating an Ad Hoc Group of Governmental Experts to Identify and Examine Potential Verification Measures from a Scientific and Technical Standpoint (VEREX). The mandate of the group was to identify measures which could determine whether a state party to the BTWC was engaged in prohibited activities. These activities could be with regard to biological agents, weapons or means of delivery.

A Special Conference in 1994 considered the VEREX Report and created an Ad Hoc Group of Experts, to investigate the options for legally binding measures to strengthen the BTWC. The Fourth Review Conference considered a report by the Ad Hoc Group and instructed it to intensify its activities with the aim of completing its work before the Fifth Review Conference, to be held not later than the year 2001.

Verifying the BTWC is especially challenging. The problem is that the activities that could lead to the development of biological weapons are virtually the same as legitimate activities for peaceful purposes. In addition, any state with a modestly developed pharmaceutical industry could develop biological weapons if it wanted to do so.

Measures to strengthen and verify the BTWC must be balanced with the desire of developing states to have access to the high technologies and benefits of biological industries. In fact, the BTWC explicitly states in its Article X that the convention should encourage cooperation and not hamper the scientific and technological development of states 'in the field of peaceful bacteriological (biological) activities'.

The Fourth Review Conference emphasized the increasing importance of Article X in the light of recent scientific and technological developments and suggested measures to promote the fullest possible exchange of materials and knowledge for peaceful purposes and international cooperation. Some parties to the BTWC have stated that agreement on a verification regime will be possible only if there is progress towards implementing Article X.

4.5 The United Nations Special Commission on Iraq

On 3 April 1991 the UN Security Council passed Resolution 687. It set the terms for the cease-fire between Iraq and the multinational coalition which was created in response to Iraq's invasion of Kuwait.

Part C of the resolution addresses Iraq's weapons of mass destruction. It calls for all of them to be declared, identified, located and destroyed. In addition, a monitoring system is to be established to ensure that new weapons are not reintroduced by Iraq. The prohibited weapons are ballistic missiles with a range greater than 150 km and nuclear, biological and chemical weapons.

The Security Council took additional action in October 1991, when it passed Resolution 715. This resolution approved two plans, one each for nuclear and non-nuclear items, respectively. They deal with monitoring Iraq's obligations under the cease-fire not to use, develop, construct or acquire any of the prohibited weapons.

To put Part C of Resolution 687 into effect, the Security Council created the United Nations Special Commission on Iraq as a subsidiary body of the Council. Its mandate is to supervise and execute the elimination and to conduct on-site inspection of Iraq's biological, chemical and missile capabilities. In dealing with Iraq's nuclear weapon programme, UNSCOM cooperates with the International Atomic Energy Agency, which has the lead role.

UNSCOM consists of 21 experts from around the world, appointed by the Secretary-General. It is organized in four groups—nuclear, chemical/biological, ballistic missiles and future compliance monitoring. Individual inspectors who carry out inspections in Iraq are drawn from various countries.

4.5.1 UNSCOM's tools

To do its work, UNSCOM has various tools, both legal and operational. For example, in order to carry out their inspections, the Security Council empowered UNSCOM and the IAEA with the right to unconditional and unrestricted access to any and all areas, facilities, equipment and records in Iraq.

This right has not gone unchallenged by Iraq. There are numerous incidents in which the Iraqi authorities attempted to impose limits on UNSCOM and otherwise make its work difficult.

A very serious moment came in January 1993, when Iraqi officials advised UNSCOM that it could no longer land its aircraft in Iraq. Instead, it would have to use Iraqi aircraft or land in Jordan and travel overland. This was a breach of Iraq's obligations under Security Council resolutions. Iraq did not back down from its position until after US and British air forces attacked Iraqi military targets.

In addition to its legal mechanism, UNSCOM has operational tools at its disposal. Information is gathered by overflights of US U-2 reconnaissance aircraft. Inspection teams are transported within Iraq by UNSCOM helicopters, and transport aircraft move such things as analysis instruments, detection devices and medical equipment. Remote-controlled camera systems have even been installed to monitor activities at sites that are associated with chemical and biological weapons.

4.5.2 UNSCOM's findings[10]

Chemical weapons

Iraq had a substantial chemical weapon programme. It had chemical warfare agents, such as mustard and nerve agents, and numerous means of delivery. These included aerial bombs, mortar bombs, artillery shells and rockets, rocket-propelled grenades and chemical warheads for its Scud missiles. Iraq also admitted having missile warheads armed with biological weapons.

Chemicals were destroyed or neutralized by various means, while production equipment and munitions were destroyed mechanically. On 16 June 1994, UNSCOM's Chemical Destruction Group was able to disband, after successfully completing its work. The focus is now on the ongoing monitoring and verification of Iraq's dual-purpose chemical industry, that is, those sectors of the industry whose products can be used for peaceful or military purposes.

---

[10] For SIPRI's most recent account of UNSCOM findings, see *SIPRI Yearbook 1997*, pp. 457–65.

Biological weapons

Iraq initially did not declare any biological warfare programme. It later admitted that it had conducted some early, basic research for defensive purposes. In June 1995 Iraq acknowledged that it had been involved in more than just research and had an offensive biological weapon programme which included the production of BW agents. Then came the admission that the programme included preparing biological agents to be delivered as weapons, or 'weaponizing' the agents. By the end of 1996, UNSCOM was still seeking to determine the extent of the Iraqi programme.

Nuclear weapons

When it made its initial declaration under Resolution 687 in May 1991, Iraq claimed that it had no nuclear weapons or nuclear weapon programme of any sort. Inspections by UNSCOM and the IAEA Action Team later determined that Iraq had an ambitious programme that fell just short of the manufacture of nuclear weapons. It was revealed that Iraq's secret enrichment programme had been intended to produce large amounts of highly enriched uranium by the mid-1990s. In addition, in 1995 Iraq admitted that it had a radiological weapon programme. The principal effect of these weapons is to spread massive quantities of radiation. This contrasts with nuclear weapons, whose principal effects are heat, blast and radiation.

Efforts continue to ensure that the prohibition under Resolution 687 on the possession of separated plutonium and HEU by Iraq is upheld.

Ballistic missiles

Iraq's initial claim about the size of its missile inventory was not accurate. UNSCOM proved that Iraq held a greater quantity than it admitted. The missiles have been destroyed by Iraq either on its own initiative, without international control, or under UNSCOM's supervision. UNSCOM has since conducted numerous inspections and set up monitoring systems to determine the capabilities of Iraqi industry to build prohibited missile systems.

5. Arms control

5.1 Introduction

For many years, arms control and disarmament initiatives were largely in the hands of the superpowers of the day—the United States and the Soviet Union. As the states with the largest military establishments—and with particular advantages in nuclear, biological and chemical weapons—their priorities and relationship with each other dominated the arms control agenda. They also had a leadership role within their respective alliances—the North Atlantic Treaty Organization (NATO) and the Warsaw Treaty Organization (WTO, or Warsaw Pact)—which gave them another channel for influencing the course of events.

Today, the USA and Russia are still highly influential players on the arms control scene, but they are not the only states with sophisticated weapons.

Arms control and disarmament talks take place in two types of forum, bilateral and multilateral. For the purposes of this chapter, bilateral talks are those between the USA and Russia. Multilateral talks are carried out on a regional basis or an international basis between several parties.

This chapter examines some of the agreements and negotiating bodies through which arms control talks take place. It then provides summaries of international arms control treaties in force.

5.2 Bilateral agreements

5.2.1 START I and START II

Two treaties signed in the 1990s form the basis of the bilateral arms control regime governing US and Russian (former Soviet) strategic nuclear weapons. These are the 1991 START I and 1993 START II treaties.[1]

---

[1] START is the acronym for Strategic Arms Reductions Treaty. Before the START treaties were signed, the United States and the Soviet Union first agreed to limit their strategic nuclear weapons in 2 treaties, SALT I and SALT II—Strategic Arms Limitation Talks/ Treaty. SALT II, while signed by the US President, was never ratified by the US Senate.

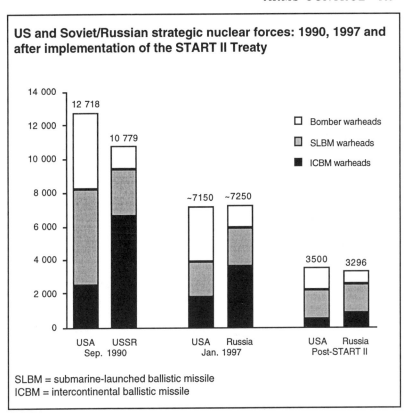

US and Soviet/Russian strategic nuclear forces: 1990, 1997 and after implementation of the START II Treaty

SLBM = submarine-launched ballistic missile
ICBM = intercontinental ballistic missile

After almost 10 years of negotiations, US President George Bush and Soviet President Mikhail Gorbachev signed the START I Treaty in 1991. The treaty entered into force in 1994. The terms of the treaty require Russia (which, as the legal successor to the USSR, agreed to abide by all treaties previously binding on the USSR) and the USA to make phased reductions in their strategic nuclear forces over a seven-year period. In 1992 Belarus, Kazakhstan and Ukraine—former Soviet republics then with nuclear weapons on their territories—signed the Lisbon Protocol, pledging to join the 1968 Non-Proliferation Treaty (NPT) as non-nuclear weapon states and thereby becoming parties to the START I Treaty.[2]

[2] Belarus became a party to the NPT in 1993, and Kazakhstan and Ukraine became parties in 1994. START I thus became a multilateral treaty.

In January 1993, less than 18 months after the signing of START I, President Bush and Russian President Boris Yeltsin signed the follow-on START II Treaty. It calls for further phased reductions in strategic forces as well as a ban on all land-based strategic ballistic missiles with multiple independently targetable re-entry vehicles (MIRVs). A missile with MIRVs can deliver warheads to multiple targets.

START II was submitted to the US Senate for ratification the same month. Although there was little opposition in the Senate, it was not approved by that body until three years later.

The fate of the treaty in Russia is uncertain. Ratification in the Russian Parliament has been held up by internal domestic crises and concerns about the technical and economic aspects of some treaty provisions. There has also been frustration with the US position on the 1972 Anti-Ballistic Missile (ABM) Treaty and opposition to the enlargement of NATO membership to include states in Central and Eastern Europe.

Presidents Yeltsin and Clinton have announced their desire to move beyond START II and enter a new phase of talks on deeper strategic arms reductions. Despite this commitment to keep the bilateral process moving, there will probably not be further progress until START II has been ratified by Russia.

5.2.2   The Anti-Ballistic Missile Treaty

In 1972 the United States and the Soviet Union signed the ABM Treaty. It prohibits the two parties from building a nationwide defence system against ballistic missile attack. It also limits the development and deployment of missile defence systems. The 1974 Protocol to the treaty allows each side to build no more than one ballistic missile defence site.

The idea behind the ABM Treaty was that it was better that both the USSR and the USA remain vulnerable to nuclear attack. With each side being vulnerable, there would be no incentive to launch a first strike.

A first strike would be futile because each side had enough weapons to survive an attack and hit back with devastating results. This is the essential idea behind the theory of mutual assured destruction (MAD). However, if one side could defend itself with an ABM system, it might be tempted to launch a first strike after all. The side with such a defence might calculate that it could inflict massive destruction on its opponent and survive a retaliatory strike.

The ABM Treaty established the Standing Consultative Committee (SCC) as the body to address questions about the treaty's implementation. Russia strongly insists that the ABM Treaty cannot be reinterpreted by one party alone and that all issues relating to treaty compliance must be negotiated.

The issue of ballistic missile defences and the ABM Treaty resurfaced in 1993 when the USA brought theatre ballistic missile defence (TMD) systems to the negotiating table in the SCC. The USA argues that TMD systems are needed to protect its troops operating overseas and its allies from future conflicts with adversaries who might possess ballistic missiles. Theatre ballistic missiles are not defined in the ABM Treaty, and this has led to the difficulties between the USA and Russia. TMD systems have raised a difficult question—that is, how to define or recognize a system whose missile defence capabilities are limited to a theatre of conflict, as opposed to a system which may have the potential to defend against strategic forces as well. This has been a very complex technical and political issue between the USA and Russia. However, in August 1997 they reached agreement in the SCC on the delimitation of strategic and non-strategic ABM systems.

In the USA, the Congress has made the matter more complicated by pushing legislation that would require the US Department of Defense (DOD) to develop a multi-site, nationwide ballistic missile defence system. Although the Clinton Administration has continued to resist efforts to pass such legislation, it is clear that the issue is not over and the debate between the USA and Russia will remain a lively one.

5.2.3 The Cooperative Threat Reduction programme

In 1991 the Soviet Union entered a period of instability which ended in its collapse. The growing uncertainty led to fears about the fate of the thousands of nuclear warheads on Soviet territory. In September 1991 US President George Bush called for the USA and the USSR to work together to find a safe way to store, transport, dismantle and destroy nuclear warheads. The Soviet Union was agreeable to the idea. In November, the US Congress passed legislation allowing for up to $400 million of Pentagon funds to be used to assist with safely storing and dismantling nuclear weapons.

Congress provided further funding in 1992, by which time the Soviet Union had split up. Accordingly, this funding provided bilateral assistance to Belarus, Kazakhstan, Russia and Ukraine for their denuclearization activities. These were the states holding Soviet nuclear weapons when the Soviet Union dissolved.

These initiatives led to a cooperative arms control forum, known as the Safe and Secure Dismantlement (SSD) Talks, where bilateral US assistance to Belarus, Kazakhstan, Russia and Ukraine could be discussed. The overall programme became known as the Cooperative Threat Reduction (CTR) programme. (It is also often called the Nunn–Lugar programme, after the two US senators who sponsored the original authorizing legislation.) It expanded to include converting the former Soviet Union's nuclear weapon industry to non-military pursuits where possible.

Most of the assistance agreed to under the CTR programme has been to help the former Soviet republics safely dismantle the nuclear weapons on their territories. For example, the USA has provided mobile cranes and bulldozers to eliminate missiles, special railway cars to transport liquid fuel from retired missiles and incinerators to burn the fuel. Assistance to Russia has also included help with control and accounting, nuclear material security and export regulations. The USA and Russia will share the costs of a new storage facility at Mayak, in Russia. In addition, CTR programme assistance has been used to help safely dismantle chemical weapons.

The USA has negotiated separate umbrella agreements with each of these four former Soviet republics—Belarus, Kazakhstan, Russia and Ukraine. Under these umbrella agreements, more specific arrangements have been made. By the end of 1996, the USA had committed nearly $1.5 billion to the CTR programme, 52 per cent of it for Russia.

5.2.4   Other bilateral initiatives

The US–Russia Highly Enriched Uranium Agreement

In 1993 the USA signed an agreement with Russia to purchase, over a 20-year period, up to 500 tonnes of highly enriched uranium (HEU). The source of the HEU is dismantled nuclear warheads. The HEU is to be blended down by Russia into fuel (low-enriched uranium, or LEU) which can be used by civilian nuclear power plants.

The programme is meant to reduce the likelihood that HEU left over from dismantled warheads will fall into the wrong hands and become a security threat. The funds paid to Russia are to be used for environmental clean-up, improved safety at nuclear power plants and other such purposes.

Progress was made on implementing the agreement during 1996. Certain differences over price and compensation were settled and agreement was reached in principle on verification measures to ensure that the LEU is indeed derived from dismantled Russian nuclear warheads.

Fissile material stockpile agreements

US–Russian bilateral talks have been under way on measures which seek to build confidence and increase the transparency of each side's fissile material stockpiles.[3] Both sides want as clear and accurate a picture as possible of how much nuclear weapon-grade material the other has and want to monitor how much is used. However, despite the support of Presidents Clinton and Yeltsin, the negotiations to work out the necessary data exchange agreements have made little progress.

5.3 Multilateral forums

5.3.1 The Conference on Disarmament

The Conference on Disarmament (CD) is based in Geneva, Switzerland, and has existed under its present name since 1984. It is the successor to the Ten-Nation Committee on Disarmament (1959–60), the Eighteen-Nation Committee on Disarmament (1962–69), the Conference of the Committee on Disarmament (1969–78) and the Committee on Disarmament (1979–83).

Since 1996 the CD has had 60 members,[4] drawn from all the regions of the world. States which are not members may send their representatives to the plenary sessions of the CD and are sometimes invited to other meetings as well. Although not part of the United

---

[3] See Albright, D., Berkhout, F. and Walker, W., SIPRI, *Plutonium and Highly Enriched Uranium 1996: World Inventories, Capabilities and Policies* (Oxford University Press: Oxford, 1997).

[4] Formally, the CD has 61 member states, but Yugoslavia (Serbia and Montenegro) has been suspended since 1992.

Nations organization, it is closely linked to the UN. Its budget is part of the UN budget, it is served by UN personnel, the Secretary-General of the CD is appointed by the Secretary-General of the UN and the CD itself reports to the UN General Assembly. When an arms control agreement is drawn up in the CD, it is transmitted to the General Assembly to be recommended for signature and ratification by UN member states.

The CD adopts a specific agenda for each session. To carry out its work, the Conference creates subsidiary bodies such as ad hoc committees, working groups, technical groups or groups of governmental experts. The CD works on the basis of consensus, not majority voting (the new members which joined in 1996 have waived their right to block consensus for two years).

The CD has over the years (as the ENDC and the CCD) negotiated arms control treaties such as the 1968 Non-Proliferation Treaty, the 1971 Seabed Treaty, the 1972 Biological Weapons Convention, the 1977 Enmod Convention, the 1993 Chemical Weapons Convention and the 1996 Comprehensive Nuclear Test-Ban Treaty. The last two of these negotiations are described in the section below.

Negotiations on the CWC and the CTBT

For some two decades, one of the most important tasks of the CD was to negotiate a treaty on chemical weapons. Although the 1925 Geneva Protocol prohibits the use of chemical and bacteriological weapons in conflict, it does not ban their possession. In 1992 the CD completed the Convention on the Prohibition of the Development, Production, Stockpiling and Use of Chemical Weapons and on their Destruction (CWC), which closed this loophole.

In January 1993 the CWC was opened for signature. Important elements of the convention include: a total ban on chemical weapons and a timetable for their destruction; the establishment of the Organization for the Prohibition of Chemical Weapons (OPCW) to verify the provisions of the treaty; and a commitment by the parties to ensure that persons and organizations under their jurisdiction do not undertake activities in violation of the CWC.

After two and a half years of negotiation, the CD concluded the text of the Comprehensive Nuclear Test-Ban Treaty (CTBT) in 1996. It was transmitted to the UN, and the General Assembly voted on 10 September to open it for signature.

Talks on a CTBT took place, in one form or another, almost continuously from 1958 until 1996. They began with negotiations chiefly between the Soviet Union on the one side and the USA and the UK on the other, in Geneva.

Initially, the force behind the call for a CTBT was the danger posed by radioactive fallout. Until the Partial Test Ban Treaty (PTBT) of 1963, there were no restrictions against testing in the atmosphere, under water or in outer space. Large nuclear explosions in the atmosphere raised public concern about the threat posed by the resulting radiation.

The PTBT went a long way in easing fears about the environment, but because it placed no restrictions on underground tests it did little to slow nuclear weapon programmes. In fact, the USA, the UK and the USSR stepped up their testing after the PTBT was signed.

Although there were various proposals for a CTBT, negotiations did not resume until the CD agreed on a mandate in 1994. The negotiations were difficult throughout 1995.

When the CD ended its second session of 1996, it had a complete draft text of the treaty. India, however, among other things, was concerned that the CTBT did not commit the five nuclear weapon states to a fixed timetable for complete nuclear disarmament. Furthermore, in its view, the CTBT would not prevent nuclear weapon states from improving their nuclear weapons in the laboratory. If India continues to object to the CTBT, it will not enter into force. This is because it is one of the 44 states whose ratification is needed before the CTBT can enter into force.[5]

Ban on production of fissile material for nuclear explosives

In 1995 the CD agreed on a mandate to pursue a ban on the production of fissile material for nuclear explosives. Such a ban would end the production of plutonium and uranium that can be used for nuclear weapons and explosives. An Ad Hoc Committee was established to negotiate a treaty, but as of 1 September 1997 the negotiations had not started.

[5] For the list of 44 states, see section 5.7.25 in this chapter. After 3 years, however, the states that have signed it can apply it on a provisional basis. According to Article XIV, paragraph 2, if it has not entered into force 3 years after the anniversary of its opening for signature a conference of the states that have already deposited their instruments of ratification will decide what measures consistent with international law may be undertaken to accelerate the ratification process in order to facilitate early entry into force.

5.3.2 The Organization for Security and Co-operation in Europe

The Organization for Security and Co-operation in Europe (OSCE) began its life as the Conference on Security and Co-operation in Europe (CSCE). The CSCE first met in 1973 in Helsinki, Finland. Its founding members included all the states of Europe except for Albania, as well as Canada and the USA. Membership has since grown as new states have emerged in Europe.

The CFE Treaty

The OSCE provided the framework for negotiating the 1990 Treaty on Conventional Armed Forces in Europe (CFE Treaty). The treaty was concluded in the last days of the cold war by NATO and the Warsaw Treaty Organization (WTO). It covered five categories of heavy weapons (battle tanks, armoured combat vehicles, artillery, combat aircraft and attack helicopters) and its area of application extends from the Atlantic to the Urals (the so-called ATTU zone), excluding the three Baltic states. The territory of each of the two alliances was divided into a system of zones with regional limitations designed to avoid excessive force concentrations on the line of confrontation between the blocs. In 1992–95 the states parties scrapped or converted over 50 000 items of weapons. Furthermore, Russia pledged to destroy 14 500 items beyond the Ural Mountains.

Begun in January 1997, the CFE adaptation talks aim at adjusting the treaty to the post-cold war realities, including the forthcoming enlargement of NATO, and replacing the outdated bloc structure with national/territorial levels for weapon holdings. It will result in further reductions and enhancement of conventional stability throughout the ATTU area. These negotiations are planned to come to a close in 1998.

The Open Skies Treaty

The 1992 Treaty on Open Skies was negotiated within the framework of the OSCE but may, after it has entered into force, be acceded to by any state which is 'able and willing' to contribute to its objectives. It calls upon all signatories to submit their territories to short-notice unarmed aerial surveillance and it initiated a new phase in the process of increasing transparency among states.

The Forum for Security Co-operation and the Florence Agreement

The OSCE has a forum for all its participating states to negotiate conventional arms control issues, called the Forum for Security Co-operation (FSC). At the OSCE Lisbon Summit of December 1996, it was decided that the FSC should revise its priorities and focus on a new agenda. This agenda includes implementation of arms control agreements and arrangements, regional measures, and confidence- and security-building measures (CSBMs) for preventive diplomacy, crisis management and post-conflict rehabilitation.

The OSCE, in the FSC, assisted in negotiation of the 1996 Florence Agreement on Sub-Regional Arms Control in the former Yugoslavia. Modelled on CFE solutions, it aims at reducing some 6000 heavy weapon items of the former combatants in the former Yugoslavia (Bosnia and Herzegovina and its two entities—the Federation of Bosnia and Herzegovina and the Republika Srpska—plus Croatia and Serbia and Montenegro) by November 1997. After conclusion of the reduction process, negotiations on a regional balance 'in and around the former Yugoslavia' are to start.

5.3.3 The United Nations

A number of UN bodies and committees are the scene of arms control debates and discussions, but not treaty negotiations. These organs are the Security Council, the General Assembly (including UN Special Sessions on Disarmament and the First Committee) and the Disarmament Commission. For information on their role in furthering arms control and disarmament, see chapter 6.

5.4 Nuclear weapon-free zones

The idea of establishing nuclear weapon-free zones (NWFZs) in populated parts of the globe (as distinct from uninhabited areas, such as the Antarctic) was conceived primarily with a view to preventing the emergence of new nuclear weapon states.

So far, five agreements intended to ensure the absence of nuclear weapons in the respective territories have been concluded. Of these, the 1967 Tlatelolco Treaty, for Latin America; the 1985 Treaty of Rarotonga, for the South Pacific; and the 1992 Joint Declaration on the Denuclearization of the Korean Peninsula have entered into force. One new treaty entered into force in 1997—the 1995 Treaty of Bangkok, for South-East Asia—and one has been opened for signature but not yet entered into force—the 1996 Pelindaba Treaty, for Africa.

Certain uninhabited areas have also been formally denuclearized: Antarctica, under the 1959 Antarctic Treaty; outer space, the moon and other celestial bodies, under the 1967 Outer Space Treaty and the 1979 Moon Agreement; and the seabed, the ocean floor and the subsoil thereof, under the 1971 Seabed Treaty.

5.5   Ban on anti-personnel land-mines

Anti-personnel land-mines, which pose a great danger not only to military forces but also to civilians—a danger which persists long after hostilities have ended—have been a matter of growing concern among individuals, non-governmental organizations (NGOs), governments and international organizations for many years.[6] The humanitarian impact of anti-personnel land-mines on civilians is far in excess of their military utility.

In 1995 the Review Conference of the Convention on Prohibitions or Restrictions on the Use of Certain Conventional Weapons Which May be Deemed to Be Excessively Injurious or to Have Indiscriminate Effects (the CCW Convention, often called the Inhumane Weapons Convention) was held. It adopted an amended Protocol II on prohibitions or restrictions on the use of mines, booby-traps and other devices, including further restrictions on the use, production and transfer of anti-personnel land-mines. This Protocol will enter into force six months after 20 states have ratified it. In 1996 the UN passed a resolution, supported by 156 states, on a ban on the use, stockpiling, production and transfer of anti-personnel land-mines and calling on all states to accede to the CCW Convention and its amended Protocol II.

In 1996 the so-called Ottawa Group began to meet to negotiate a global ban on anti-personnel land-mines. In October they issued the Ottawa Declaration 'Towards a Global Ban on Anti-Personnel Mines', which was signed by 50 states. A follow-on conference in June 1997 produced the Brussels Declaration, signed by 97 states. At

[6] See, e.g., *SIPRI Yearbook 1996*, pp. 753–60; and *SIPRI Yearbook 1997*, pp. 495–500.

the meeting of the Ottawa Group held in Oslo in September, 89 states adopted the text of the Convention on the Prohibition of the Use, Stockpiling, Production and Transfer of Anti-personnel Mines and on their Destruction. It was opened to all states for signature in Ottawa on 3–4 December and at United Nations Headquarters in New York on 5 December 1997.[7]

In October it was announced that the International Campaign to Ban Landmines had been awarded the Nobel Peace Prize.

5.6   Multilateral export controls

During the cold war the international discussion of export controls was subordinate to the East–West conflict. For example, the objective of the main instrument for multilateral export control—the Coordinating Committee for Multilateral Export Control (COCOM)—was to maintain an embargo on transfers of technologies that could raise the military capacity of state socialist countries.

With the end of the cold war and the dismantling of the bloc system in Europe, there is a recognition that enhanced trade and industrial cooperation—including that in military and dual-use goods—is desirable. At the same time, there is a need to prevent the misuse or diversion of military and dual-use technology.

The relevant regimes are, in order of their formation:

• the Zangger Committee and the Nuclear Suppliers Group, which address transfers of nuclear dual-use technologies;
• the Australia Group, which addresses chemical and biological weapon precursors and technologies with civilian applications which can be used in the development and/or production of chemical and biological weapons;
• the Missile Technology Control Regime, which addresses cruise and ballistic missile systems capable of delivering a chemical, biological or nuclear weapon along with technologies related to the development and production of such missiles;
• the Wassenaar Arrangement on Export Controls for Conventional Arms and Dual-Use Goods and Technologies, which addresses con-

---

[7] The USA and some other countries have sought negotiations on a global ban in the CD, involving all the major land-mine producers and exporters. The CD managed only to appoint a Special Coordinator in June 1997 'to conduct consultations on a possible mandate on the question of anti-personnel landmines'.

Membership of multilateral military-related export control regimes, as of 1 January 1997

State	Zangger Committee 1974	NSG[a] 1978	Australia Group[b] 1985	MTCR[c] 1987	EU regulation 1995	Wassenaar Arrangement 1996
Argentina	x	x	x	x	n.a.	x
Australia	x	x	x	x	n.a.	x
Austria	x	x	x	x	x	x
Belgium	x	x	x[d]	x	x	x
Brazil		x		x	n.a.	
Bulgaria	x	x			n.a.	x
Canada	x	x	x	x	n.a.	x
Czech Republic	x	x	x		n.a.	x
Denmark	x	x	x	x	x	x
Finland	x	x	x	x	x	x
France	x	x	x	x	x	x
Germany	x	x	x	x	x	x
Greece	x	x	x	x	x	x
Hungary	x	x	x	x	n.a.	x
Iceland			x[d]	x	n.a.	
Ireland	x	x	x	x	x	x
Italy	x	x	x	x	x	x
Japan	x	x	x	x	n.a.	x
Korea, South[e]		x	x[d]		n.a.	x
Luxembourg	x	x	x[d]	x	x	x
Netherlands	x	x	x	x	x	x
New Zealand		x	x	x	n.a.	x
Norway	x	x	x	x	n.a.	x
Poland	x	x	x		n.a.	x
Portugal	x	x	x	x	x	x
Romania	x	x	x		n.a.	x
Russia	x	x		x	n.a.	x
Slovakia	x	x	x		n.a.	x
South Africa	x	x		x	n.a.	
Spain	x	x	x	x	x	x
Sweden	x	x	x	x	x	x
Switzerland	x	x	x	x	n.a.	x
Turkey					n.a.	x
UK	x	x	x	x	x	x
Ukraine		x			n.a.	x
USA	x	x	x[d]	x	n.a.	x

Note: The years in the column headings indicate when the export control regime was formally established, although the groups may have met on an informal basis before then.

[a] The Nuclear Suppliers Group.

[b] The European Commission is represented in the Australia Group as an observer.

[c] The Missile Technology Control Regime.

[d] A member of the Australia Group which had not ratified the Chemical Weapons Convention as of 1 Jan. 1997.

[e] South Korea is an observer to the Zangger Committee.

ventional arms as well as certain civilian high technologies with potential military applications.

In addition, the members of the European Union (EU) are developing export controls in which both the member states and the European Commission play a part in the framework of a common export control system. The EU dual-use export control system is different in kind from the other regimes because of its different legal status. Whereas the other regimes are informal arrangements between sovereign states, the EU is a treaty-governed international organization within which members have given the organization itself considerable powers, in particular in the area of international trade policy.[8]

Two events have raised the profile and accelerated the development of all the regimes described here; namely, the end of the cold war and revelations regarding the extent of Iraq's weapon programmes.[9]

A central focus of most of the regimes has been the gradual integration of former members of COCOM with countries that were neutral and non-aligned during the cold war as well as with former members of the Warsaw Treaty Organization (WTO). As shown in the panel on page 114, by 1997 much of this integration had been accomplished.

The *Zangger Committee* established guidelines for exports of nuclear-related goods and technologies to countries that were not members of the NPT. The detonation of a nuclear explosive device by India in 1974 stimulated discussions among nuclear suppliers that led to the establishment of the *Nuclear Suppliers Group* (NSG), also known as the London Club. Although these groups existed earlier, the end of the cold war assisted the reinvigoration of nuclear export-control arrangements in response to the revelations regarding Iraq's nuclear programme in 1990–91. In 1992 the NSG agreed on Guidelines for Transfers of Nuclear-Related Dual-Use Equipment, Material and Related Technology (the so-called 'Warsaw Guidelines'). The members of the NSG agreed a common policy requiring application of full-scope IAEA safeguards to all nuclear activities as a condition of nuclear exports to non-nuclear weapon states. In 1994 discussions were held on rules for transfers of nuclear materials and equipment to

---

[8] For additional information on the EU dual-use export control system, see *SIPRI Yearbook 1997*, pp. 359–63.

[9] See chapter 4, section 4.5.

countries which participated fully in IAEA safeguards but which were nevertheless considered to be causes of proliferation concern.[10]

The *Australia Group* is a forum in which countries that supply or trade in chemicals, biological agents and/or production equipment that could be used in weapon programmes harmonize their national export controls.

The *Missile Technology Control Regime* (MTCR) was initially intended to reduce the risk that missiles which could act as delivery systems for nuclear weapons would spread widely. This was reflected in the initial Guidelines for Sensitive Missile-Relevant Transfers and its accompanying Equipment and Technology Annex in 1987. Subsequently, again after the revelation that Iraq had developed both chemical and biological weapons that could be delivered using missiles, the scope of the regime was expanded to include all missiles capable of delivering nuclear, chemical or biological warheads.

The discussions that led to the creation of the *Wassenaar Arrangement* on Export Controls for Conventional Arms and Dual-Use Goods and Technologies were a response to the recognition that under certain circumstances conventional arms could represent a threat to international peace and stability. Whereas there are strong international norms against the possession and use of nuclear, chemical and biological weapons, the same is not true for conventional weapons—which are seen as important instruments of defence policy by all states. However, after the invasion of Kuwait by Iraq in August 1990 many European governments acknowledged that in order to preserve peace and stability it is necessary for states to avoid excessive and destabilizing accumulations of conventional arms.

According to the initial elements of the Wassenaar Arrangement, the obligations on participating states are to exchange information and conduct discussions that will lead to greater awareness within the group about arms transfers and transfers of sensitive dual-use goods and technologies. This process of discussion is expected to assist in developing common understandings of the risks associated with given transfers. However, for these goods and technologies no specific conditions under which transfers should be denied have been elaborated, and decisions are to be taken on a national basis.

---

[10] For additional information see *SIPRI Yearbook 1995*, pp. 601–607.

5.7 Summaries of arms control treaties

Once international arms treaties are agreed upon, they are opened for signature by states. Some treaties are open to only certain states, as stipulated in the treaty. For example, the Treaty of Rarotonga is open to members of the South Pacific Forum. Other treaties are open to all states. Multilateral treaties may require the signature and ratification of a specific number of states or specific states before they enter into force, that is, become fully binding in international law.

Before a treaty can enter into force for a state, the state must ratify it according to its national laws. For example, in the USA, while the president may sign a treaty, the Senate must ratify, or approve, it before it becomes binding upon the USA. States with parliamentary systems usually require parliament's approval of treaties. Once ratification has taken place, each state must deposit a copy of the legal instrument which effects or confirms the ratification. This instrument is deposited with the treaty's depositary, for example, a government or an international organization. Some treaties have more than one depositary. The depositary, in turn, has an obligation to register the international agreement with the UN Secretariat. This requirement is set out in Article 102 of the UN Charter.

If states do not sign a treaty when it is first agreed upon they are not prevented from joining at a later date. When a treaty has entered into force, states can still accede to it and become a party when they are prepared to do so and meet the necessary requirements, and new states (such as those which emerged after decolonialization or from the breakup of Czechoslovakia or Yugoslavia) can succeed to it by making a declaration of continuity of the arms control obligations undertaken by the predecessor state.

The arms control and disarmament treaties below are listed in order of the date on which they were opened for signature. There is a brief summary of the nature of each treaty, followed by the date and place of signature. The information is valid as of 1 January 1997 unless otherwise indicated. These are complex legal agreements. For a complete presentation, consult the *SIPRI Yearbook 1997,* pages 527–46.

5.7.1 Protocol for the prohibition of the use in war of asphyxiating, poisonous or other gases, and of bacteriological methods of warfare (Geneva Protocol)

Prohibits the use of these methods of warfare and declares that this prohibition should be universally accepted as part of international law.

Opened for signature at Geneva on 17 June 1925; entered into force on 8 February 1928; 132 parties to the protocol.

5.7.2 Antarctic Treaty

Declares the Antarctic to be exclusively for peaceful purposes and prohibits any military measures in this area.

Opened for signature at Washington, DC, on 1 December 1959; entered into force on 23 June 1961; 43 parties to the treaty.

5.7.3 Treaty banning nuclear weapon tests in the atmosphere, in outer space and under water (Partial Test Ban Treaty, PTBT)

Prohibits nuclear explosions: (*a*) in the atmosphere, beyond its limits, including outer space, or under water, including territorial waters or the high seas; and (*b*) in any other environment if such explosion causes radioactive debris to be present outside the territorial limits of the state under whose jurisdiction or control the explosion is conducted.

Opened for signature at Moscow on 5 August 1963; entered into force on 10 October 1963; 124 parties to the treaty.

5.7.4 Treaty on principles governing the activities of states in the exploration and use of outer space, including the moon and other celestial bodies (Outer Space Treaty)

Prohibits the placing into orbit around the earth of any objects carrying nuclear weapons or any other kinds of weapons of mass destruction, the installation of such weapons on celestial bodies, or the stationing of them in outer space. The establishment of military bases, installations and fortifications, the testing of any type of weapons and the conduct of military manoeuvres on celestial bodies is also forbidden.

Opened for signature at London, Moscow and Washington, DC, on 27 January 1967; entered into force on 10 October 1967; 95 parties to the treaty.

5.7.5 Treaty for the prohibition of nuclear weapons in Latin America and the Caribbean (Treaty of Tlatelolco)

Provides for the military denuclearization of Latin America and the Caribbean. The treaty prohibits the testing, use, manufacture, production or acquisition by any means, as well as the receipt, storage, installation, deployment and any form of possession of any nuclear weapons by Latin American and Caribbean countries.

The parties to the treaty agree to apply IAEA safeguards to their peaceful nuclear activities. The five nuclear states and states with territories within the zone for which they are internationally responsible agree to respect the military denuclearization of the zone and not to use or threaten to use nuclear weapons against the parties to the treaty.

Opened for signature at Mexico City on 14 February 1967; entered into force on 22 April 1968. The treaty was amended in 1990, 1991 and 1992; 31 parties to the original treaty.

5.7.6 Treaty on the non-proliferation of nuclear weapons (Non-Proliferation Treaty, NPT)

Prohibits the transfer by nuclear weapon states, to any recipient, of nuclear weapons or other nuclear explosives or of control over them. The Treaty prohibits nuclear weapon states from encouraging or assisting any non-nuclear weapon state to acquire or manufacture such weapons or devices.

Non-nuclear weapon states are prohibited from acquiring nuclear weapons or nuclear explosive devices by any means. Non-nuclear weapon states agree to apply IAEA safeguards to their peaceful nuclear activities.

The parties will cooperate to encourage the peaceful use of nuclear energy. They will undertake negotiations on effective measures relating to stopping the nuclear arms race at an early date and to nuclear disarmament, and on a treaty on general and complete disarmament.

At a review conference in 1995, it was decided that the treaty should remain in force indefinitely.

Opened for signature at London, Moscow and Washington, DC, on 1 July 1968; entered into force on 5 March 1970; 186 parties to the treaty.

5.7.7 Treaty on the prohibition of the emplacement of nuclear weapons and other weapons of mass destruction on the seabed and the ocean floor and in the subsoil thereof (Seabed Treaty)

Nuclear weapons and other types of weapons of mass destruction, as well as their associated facilities, are banned from being placed on the seabed, ocean floor and their subsoil beyond the 12-mile seabed zone.

Opened for signature at London, Moscow and Washington, DC, on 11 February 1971; entered into force on 18 May 1972; 93 parties to the treaty.

5.7.8 Convention on the prohibition of the development, production and stockpiling of bacteriological (biological) and toxin weapons and on their destruction (Biological and Toxin Weapons Convention, BTWC)

Prohibits the development, production, stockpiling, retention or acquisition by other means of biological agents or toxins which have no peaceful purposes. The means to deliver and use these agents for hostile purposes is also banned. The destruction of the agents, toxins, weapons, equipment and means of delivery in the possession of the parties to the Convention, or their diversion to peaceful purposes should take place not later than nine months after the Convention enters into force.

Opened for signature at London, Moscow and Washington, DC, on 10 April 1972; entered into force on 26 March 1975; 140 parties to the convention.

5.7.9 Treaty on the limitation of anti-ballistic missile systems (ABM Treaty)

Prohibits the parties from building a nationwide defence system against strategic ballistic missile attack and limits the development and deployment of permitted defence systems.

Signed by the USA and the USSR at Moscow on 26 May 1972; entered into force on 3 October 1972.

Note: In 1997 Belarus, Kazakhstan, Russia and Ukraine signed a memorandum according to which they assume the obligations of the USSR regarding the treaty.

5.7.10 Treaty on the limitation of underground nuclear weapon tests (Threshold Test Ban Treaty, TTBT)

The parties agree not to carry out any underground nuclear weapon test having a yield exceeding 150 kilotons.

Signed by the USA and the USSR at Moscow on 3 July 1974; entered into force on 11 December 1990.

5.7.11 Treaty on underground nuclear explosions for peaceful purposes (Peaceful Nuclear Explosions Treaty, PNET)

The parties agree not to carry out any underground nuclear explosion for peaceful purposes having a yield exceeding 150 kilotons.

Signed by the USA and the USSR at Moscow and Washington, DC, on 28 May 1976; entered into force on 11 December 1990.

5.7.12 Convention on the prohibition of military or any other hostile use of environmental modification techniques (Enmod Convention)

Prohibits military or any other hostile use of environmental modification techniques having widespread, long-lasting or severe effects as the means of destruction, damage or injury to the states party to the Convention.

Opened for signature at Geneva on 18 May 1977; entered into force on 5 October 1978; 64 parties to the convention.

5.7.13   Convention on prohibitions or restrictions on the use of certain conventional weapons which may be deemed to be excessively injurious or to have indiscriminate effects (CCW Convention, or Inhumane Weapons Convention)

An umbrella treaty, under which specific agreements can be concluded in the form of protocols. Protocol I prohibits the use of weapons intended to injure by fragments which cannot be detected in the human body by X-rays. Protocol II prohibits or restricts the use of mines, booby-traps and similar devices. (Amendments adopted in 1996, but the amended Protocol II was not in force on 1 January 1997.) Protocol III restricts the use of incendiary weapons. Protocol IV, agreed in 1995, prohibits the use of laser weapons specifically designed to cause permanent blindness to unenhanced (unprotected) vision. Protocol IV requires 20 states to notify their consent to be bound by it before it enters into force. It was not in force on 1 January 1997.

Opened for signature at New York on 10 April 1981; entered into force on 2 December 1983; 63 parties to the convention.

5.7.14   South Pacific nuclear free zone treaty (Treaty of Rarotonga)

Prohibits the manufacture or acquisition by other means of any nuclear explosive device, as well as possession or control over such device by parties anywhere inside or outside the zone area. There are three additional protocols which describe various undertakings of the five nuclear weapon states and of states with territories within the zone for which they are internationally responsible.

Opened for signature at Rarotonga, Cook Islands, on 6 August 1985; entered into force on 11 December 1986; 12 parties to the treaty.

5.7.15   Treaty on the elimination of intermediate-range and shorter-range missiles (INF Treaty)

Obliges the parties to destroy all land-based missiles with a range of 500–5500 km and their launchers by 1 June 1991.

Signed by the USA and the USSR at Washington, DC, on 8 December 1987; entered into force on 1 June 1988.

5.7.16   Treaty on conventional armed forces in Europe (CFE Treaty)

Sets ceilings on five categories of military equipment in an area stretching from the Atlantic Ocean to the Ural Mountains in Russia (the ATTU zone). In January 1997 negotiations were started to adapt the treaty to the new security environment in Europe.

Opened for signature at Vienna on 19 November 1990; entered into force on 9 November 1992; 30 parties to the treaty.

5.7.17   Treaty on Open Skies

Obliges the parties to submit their territories to short-notice unarmed surveillance flights. The area of application stretches from Vancouver, Canada,
eastwards to Vladivostok, Russia. The treaty will enter into force when 20
states have ratified it, including all parties with more than eight 'passive
quotas' (Belarus, Canada, France, Germany, Italy, Russia, Turkey, the UK,
Ukraine and the USA).

Opened for signature at Helsinki on 24 March 1992 Not in force as of
1 January 1997.

Total ratified: 22; signed but not ratified: 5 (including Belarus, Russia and
Ukraine).

5.7.18   Treaty on the reduction and limitation of strategic offensive arms (START I Treaty)

Reduces US and Russian (at the time of signing the Soviet) offensive
strategic nuclear weapons to roughly equal aggregate levels over a seven-
year period. In 1992 Belarus, Kazakhstan and Ukraine assumed the obligations of the former USSR and pledged to eliminate all former Soviet strategic weapons on their territories.

Signed by the USA and the USSR at Moscow on 31 July 1991; entered
into force on 5 December 1994.

5.7.19   The Concluding Act of the negotiation on personnel strength of conventional armed forces in Europe (CFE-1A Agreement)

Limits the personnel of the conventional land-based armed forces within the
ATTU zone.

Opened for signature by the parties to the CFE Treaty at Helsinki on
10 July 1992; entered into force simultaneously with the CFE Treaty on
9 November 1992; 30 parties to the agreement.

5.7.20   Treaty on further reduction and limitation of strategic offensive arms (START II Treaty)

Requires the USA and Russia to eliminate their ICBMs with MIRVs and
reduce their deployed strategic nuclear warheads to no more than
3000–3500 by 1 January 2003.

Signed by the USA and the USSR at Moscow on 3 January 1993; not in
force as of 1 January 1997.

5.7.21   Convention on the prohibition of the development, production, stockpiling and use of chemical weapons and on their destruction (Chemical Weapons Convention, CWC)

Prohibits not only the use of chemical weapons but also the development,
production, acquisition, transfer and stockpiling of chemical weapons. Each
party undertakes to destroy its chemical weapons and production facilities.

Opened for signature at Paris on 13 January 1993; entered into force on 29 April 1997; 67 parties to the convention.

5.7.22 Southeast Asia nuclear-weapon-free zone treaty (Treaty of Bangkok)

Prohibits the development, manufacture, acquisition or testing of nuclear weapons inside or outside the zone area as well as the stationing and transport of nuclear weapons. The parties should conclude agreements to apply IAEA safeguards to their peaceful nuclear activities.

The treaty is open for signature by all states in South-East Asia: Brunei, Cambodia, Indonesia, Laos, Malaysia, Myanmar (Burma), the Philippines, Singapore, Thailand and Viet Nam.

Under a Protocol to the treaty the five nuclear weapon states are to undertake not to use or threaten to use nuclear weapons against any state party to the treaty or within the Southeast Asia nuclear-weapon-free zone.

Opened for signature at Bangkok on 15 December 1995. The treaty will enter into force upon the seventh ratification.

Total ratified: 5; signed but not ratified: 5.

Note: By early 1997, 8 states had ratified the treaty. It entered into force in March 1997.

5.7.23 African nuclear-weapon-free zone treaty (Treaty of Pelindaba)

Declares the continent of Africa, the island states that are members of the Organization of African Unity (OAU) and all islands considered by the OAU to be part of Africa to be a nuclear weapon-free zone. The treaty prohibits parties from developing, manufacturing, stockpiling, possessing or otherwise acquiring any kind of nuclear device. The parties agree to apply IAEA safeguards to their peaceful nuclear activities.

There are three Protocols which describe various undertakings of the five nuclear weapon states and of states with territories within the zone for which they are internationally responsible.

Opened for signature at Cairo on 11 April 1996. The treaty will enter into force upon the 28th ratification.

Total ratified: 2; signed but not ratified: 46.

5.7.24 Agreement on sub-regional arms control (Florence Agreement)

Sets numerical limits on five categories of armaments—battle tanks, armoured combat vehicles, artillery pieces, combat aircraft and attack helicopters—of the former combatants in a ratio of 5:2:2 for Yugoslavia (Serbia and Montenegro), Bosnia and Herzegovina, and Croatia, respectively; and a ratio of 2:1 for Bosnia's two entities. The arms reductions are to be completed by 1 November 1997.

Signed by Bosnia and Herzegovina and its two entities (the Muslim–Croat Federation of Bosnia and Herzegovina and the Bosnian Serb Republika

Srpska), Croatia, and Yugoslavia (Serbia and Montenegro) at Florence on 14 June 1996. The treaty entered into force upon signature.

5.7.25 Comprehensive nuclear test-ban treaty (CTBT)

All states parties are prohibited from conducting any nuclear weapon test explosion or any other nuclear explosion. The Comprehensive Nuclear Test-Ban Treaty Organization (CTBTO) will ensure treaty implementation.

Opened for signature at New York on 24 September 1996.

The treaty will enter into force 180 days after the date of the deposit of the instrument of ratification of the 44 states listed in an annexe to the treaty, but in no case earlier than two years after its opening for signature. All the 44 states possess nuclear power reactors and/or nuclear research reactors.

Total ratified: 1; signed but not ratified: 137.

Note: The 44 states whose ratification is required for entry into force: Algeria, Argentina, Australia, Austria, Bangladesh, Belgium, Brazil, Bulgaria, Canada, Chile, China, Colombia, Congo, Democratic Republic of (formerly Zaire), Egypt, Finland, France, Germany, Hungary, India, Indonesia, Iran, Israel, Italy, Japan, Korea (North), Korea (South), Mexico, Netherlands, Norway, Pakistan, Peru, Poland, Romania, Russia, Slovakia, South Africa, Spain, Sweden, Switzerland, Turkey, UK, Ukraine, USA, Viet Nam

5.8 Parties to multilateral arms control agreements

The panel on pages 125–35 lists the parties to the major multilateral arms control or disarmament agreements.

Some states have made important reservations or declarations in connection with the signing or ratification of or the accession or succession to some treaties. Consult the *SIPRI Yearbook 1997*, pages 527–46, for further information, including notes on the most important of these reservations and declarations.

The following symbols and abbreviations are used in the panel:

•	Ratification, accession or succession
s	Signed but not ratified
SA	Nuclear safeguards agreement in force with the International Atomic Energy Agency (IAEA) as required by the treaty or concluded by a nuclear weapon state on a voluntary basis
PI, PII	Additional Protocols to the Treaty of Tlatelolco
P1, P2, P3	Protocols to the Rarotonga Treaty
PI, PII, PIII	Protocols to the Pelindaba Treaty

Status of implementation of the major multilateral arms control and disarmament agreements, as of 1 January 1997

State	Geneva Protocol 1925	Antarctic Treaty 1959	PTBT 1963	Treaty of Tlatelolco 1967	NPT 1968	Seabed Treaty 1971	BTWC 1972	CCW Convention 1981	Rarotonga Treaty 1985	CWC 1993	Bangkok Treaty 1995	Pelindaba Treaty 1996	CTBT 1996
Afghanistan	•	•	•		•SA	•	•	s		s			
Albania	•		•		•		•			•			s
Algeria	•		s		•	•				•		s	s
Andorra					•								s
Angola	•											s	s
Antigua & Barbuda	•		•	•SA	•SA	•	•						
Argentina	•	•	•	•	•	•	•	•		•		s	s
Armenia	•		•		•SA		•			•			s
Australia	•	•	•		•SA	•	•	•	•	•			s
Austria	•	•	•		•SA	•	•	•		•			s
Azerbaijan					•					s			
Bahamas	•		•		•	•	•			s			
Bahrain	•				•	•	•			s			s
Bangladesh	•		•		•SA		•			s			s
Barbados	•			•SA	•SA		•						
Belarus	•		•		•SA		•	•		•			s

State	Geneva Protocol 1925	Antarctic Treaty 1959	PTBT 1963	Treaty of Tlatelolco 1967	NPT 1968	Seabed Treaty 1971	BTWC 1972	CCW Convention 1981	Rarotonga Treaty 1985	CWC 1993	Bangkok Treaty 1995	Pelindaba Treaty 1996	CTBT 1996
Belgium	•	•	•		•SA	•	•	•		s			s
Belize				•			•						
Benin	•	•	•		•	•	•	•		s		s	s
Bhutan	•		•		•SA	•	•						
Bolivia	•	•	•	•	•SA	•	•			s			s
Bosnia and Herzegovina					•	s	•	•					s
Botswana			•		•	•	•			•			
Brazil	•	•	•	•	•	•	•	•		s			s
Brunei					•SA	•	•	•		s	•	s	s
Bulgaria	•	•	•		•SA	•	•	•		•		s	s
Burkina Faso	•		s		•	•				s		s	s
Burundi		s	s		•	s	s			s		s	s
Cambodia	•				•	s	•			s	s		s
Cameroon	•	s			•	s	•			•		s	
Canada	•	•	•		•SA	•	•	•		•			s
Cape Verde	•		•		•	•	•			s		s	s
Central African Rep.	•		•		•	•	s			s		s	s
Chad	•		•		•					s		s	s

Country										
Chile	•	•	•SA	•	•	•	•	•		s
China	•	•	•PII	•	•	•	s	s	P2, 3	s PI, II	s
Colombia	•	•	•SA	•	s	•	•	s	s	s
Comoros			•	•			s		s	s
Congo (Brazzaville)	•	•	•	•	•			s	s	s
Congo (Dem. Rep. of the, formerly Zaire)	•		•SA	•	•		s	s		s
Cook Islands				•	•	•	•	•	•	
Costa Rica	•	•SA	•SA	s	•	•	•	•		s
Côte d'Ivoire	•		•SA	•	•	s	•	•	s	s
Croatia	•		•SA	•	•		•	•		s
Cuba	•	s	s	•	•		•	s		s
Cyprus	•		•SA	•	•		•	s		s
Czech Rep.	•		•SA	•	•	•	•	•	s	s
Denmark	•		•SA	•	•		•	•		s
Djibouti	•		•	•			•	s		s
Dominica			•SA	•			s			
Dominican Rep.	•		•SA	•	•	•	•	•	s	s
Ecuador	•		•SA	•	•		•	•		s
Egypt	•		•SA	s	s	s	s	s	s	s

State	Geneva Protocol 1925	Antarctic Treaty 1959	PTBT 1963	Treaty of Tlatelolco 1967	NPT 1968	Seabed Treaty 1971	BTWC 1972	CCW Convention 1981	Rarotonga Treaty 1985	CWC 1993	Bangkok Treaty 1995	Pelindaba Treaty 1996	CTBT 1996
El Salvador	s	•	•	• SA	• SA	•	•			•			s
Equatorial Guinea	•	•	•		•		•			s			s
Eritrea	•				•							s	
Estonia	•		s		• SA		•			•			s
Ethiopia	•		s		• SA	•	•		•	•		s	s
Fiji	•		•		• SA	•	•		•	•			•
Finland	•	•	•		• SA	•	•	•		•		s	
France	•	•		• PI, II	• SA	•	•	• PI, II	PI, 2, 3	•		PI, II, III	s
Gabon	•		•		•		s			s		s	
Gambia	•		•		• SA	s	•	•		s		•	s
Georgia	•		•		•		•	•		•			s
Germany	•	•	•		• SA	•	•	•		•		s	s
Ghana	•		•		• SA	•	•			•		s	s
Greece	•	•	•		• SA	•	•	•		•		s	s
Grenada	•			• SA	• SA							s	
Guatemala	•	•	•	• SA	• SA	•	•	•		s		s	s
Guinea	•				•	s	•			s		s	s
Guinea-Bissau	•		•		•	•	•				s	s	
Guyana		•			•		s						s

Country										
Haiti	s	•	•	s			s			s
Holy See	•		•SA				s			s
Honduras	•	•SA	•SA	•			s			s
Hungary	•		•SA	•	•		•			s
Iceland	•		•SA	•	s		s			s
India	•		•	•	•		•	•		
Indonesia	•		•SA	•			s	s		s
Iran	•		•SA	•			s			s
Iraq	•		•SA	•						
Ireland	•		•SA	•	•		•			s
Israel	•			•	•		s			s
Italy	•		•SA	•	•		•			s
Jamaica	•	•SA	•SA	•			s			s
Japan	•		•SA	•	•					s
Jordan	•		•SA	•			s			s
Kazakhstan			•SA				s			s
Kenya	•		•	•			s		s	s
Kiribati	•		•SA	•		•				
Korea, North	•		•SA	•						
Korea, South	•		•SA	•			s			s
Kuwait	•		•	•						s

State	Geneva Protocol 1925	Antarctic Treaty 1959	PTBT 1963	Treaty of Tlatelolco 1967	NPT 1968	Seabed Treaty 1971	BTWC 1972	CCW Convention 1981	Rarotonga Treaty 1985	CWC 1993	Bangkok Treaty 1995	Pelindaba Treaty 1996	CTBT 1996
Kyrgyzstan					•					s			s
Laos	•		•		•	•		•		s	•		s
Latvia	•				• SA	•	•	•		•			
Lebanon	•		•		• SA	s	•	•		s			s
Lesotho	•				• SA	•	•			•		s	s
Liberia	•		•		•	s	s			s		s	s
Libya	•		•		• SA	•	•					s	
Liechtenstein	•				• SA	•	•	•		s			s
Lithuania	•				• SA	•				s			s
Luxembourg	•		•		• SA	•	•	•		s			s
Macedonia (FYROM)					•		•	•					
Madagascar	•		•		• SA	s	s			s			s
Malawi	•		•		• SA	s	s			s		s	s
Malaysia	•		•		• SA	•	•			s	•		
Maldives	•				• SA	•	•			•			
Mali	•		s		•	s	s	•		s		s	s
Malta	•		•		• SA	•	•	•		s			s
Marshall Islands					•					s			s

Country										
Mauritania	•									
Mauritius	•		•SA	•	•	•		s	•	s
Mexico	•	•SA		•	•			•		s
Micronesia			•SA	•	•			s		s
Moldova				•	•			•		
Monaco	•		•SA	•	•	•		•		s
Mongolia	•		•SA	•	•			s		s
Morocco	•		•SA	•	•	s		•	s	s
Mozambique				•				s	s	s
Myanmar (Burma)	•		•SA	s		s		s	•	s
Namibia				•				•	s	
Nauru			•SA	•			•			s
Nepal	•		•SA		s			•		s
Netherlands	•	•PI SA	•SA	•		s		•		
New Zealand	•		•SA	•	•	•		•		s
Nicaragua	•	•SA	•SA	•	s	•		•		s
Niger	•			•	•			•		
Nigeria	•		•SA		s			•	s	s
Niue							•			
Norway	•	•	•SA	•		•		•		s
Oman				•		•				

State	Geneva Protocol 1925	Antarctic Treaty 1959	PTBT 1963	Treaty of Tlatelolco 1967	NPT 1968	Seabed Treaty 1971	BTWC 1972	CCW Convention 1981	Rarotonga Treaty 1985	CWC 1993	Bangkok Treaty 1995	Pelindaba Treaty 1996	CTBT 1996
Pakistan	•	•	•			•	•	•		s			
Palau					•								
Panama	•		•	• SA	•	•				s			s
Papua New Guinea	•	•	•		• SA		•		•	•			s
Paraguay	•	s	s	• SA	• SA	s				•			s
Peru	•	•	•	• SA	• SA		•			•			s
Philippines	•		•		• SA	•	•	•		•	s		s
Poland	•	•	•		• SA	•	•	•					s
Portugal	•		s		• SA	•	•	s		•			s
Qatar	•				•	•	•	•		s			s
Romania	•	•	•		• SA	•	•	•		•			s
Russia	•	•	•	• PII	• SA	•	•	•	• P2, 3	s		s Pl, II	s
Rwanda	•		•		•	•	•			s		s	
Saint Kitts (Christopher) & Nevis	•				• SA		•			s			
Saint Lucia	•			• SA	• SA		•			s			s
Saint Vincent & the Grenadines				•	• SA					s			
Samoa, Western		•			• SA				•	s			s

Country	1	2	3	4	5	6	7	8	9	10	11
San Marino	s			s							•
Sao Tome & Principe	s	s		s			•		•		•
Saudi Arabia				•			•		•		•
Senegal	s	s		s			•	•SA	s		•
Seychelles	s	s		•			•		•		•
Sierra Leone	s	s		s		s	•	•SA	s		•
Singapore			s	s			•	•SA	•		•
Slovakia	s		s	•			•	•SA	•	•	•
Slovenia	s			s		•	•		•		•
Solomon Islands	s				•		•	•SA	•		•
Somalia						s	s		•		s
South Africa	s			•		s	•	•SA	•		•
Spain	s			•		•	•	•SA	•		•
Sri Lanka	s			•		•	•	•SA	•		•
Sudan		s				s	•	•SA	s		•
Suriname							•	•SA	•	•SA	•
Swaziland	s	s		•			•	•SA	•		•
Sweden	s	s		•			•	•SA	•		•
Switzerland				•		•	•	•SA	•		•
Syria	s						s	•SA	s		•

State	Geneva Protocol 1925	Antarctic Treaty 1959	PTBT 1963	Treaty of Tlatelolco 1967	NPT 1968	Seabed Treaty 1971	BTWC 1972	CCW Convention 1981	Rarotonga Treaty 1985	CWC 1993	Bangkok Treaty 1995	Pelindaba Treaty 1996	CTBT 1996
Taiwan			•		•	•	•			•			
Tajikistan													s
Tanzania	•		•		•	s				s		s	s
Thailand	•		•		•SA		•			s	s		s
Togo	•		•		•	•	•	•		s			s
Tonga	•		•		•SA		•		s				
Trinidad & Tobago	•		•	•SA	•SA		•						
Tunisia	•		•		•SA	•	•	•		s		s	s
Turkey	•	•	•		•SA	•	•	s		s		s	s
Turkmenistan					•SA					•			s
Tuvalu					•SA				•				
Uganda	•		•		•	•	•	•		s		s	s
UK	•		•	•PI, II	•SA	•	•	•	s P1, 2, 3	•		s PI, II	s
Ukraine	•	•	•		•SA	•	•	•		s			s
United Arab Emirates					•		s			s			s
Uruguay	•	•	•	•SA	•SA	s	•	•		•			s
USA	•	•	•	•PI SA, II	•SA	•	•	•	s P1, 2, 3	s		s PI, II	s
Uzbekistan			•		•		•			•			s

Vanuatu	•				•			•	s
Venezuela	•	•SA	•SA	•	•		s	s	s
Viet Nam	•	•SA	•SA	•	s	•	s	s	s
Yemen	•	•	•	•	•		s	s	s
Yugoslavia[1]	•	•SA	•SA	•	•	•	s	s	s
Zambia	•	•SA	•SA	•	•		s	s	s
Zimbabwe		•SA	•				s	s	s

[1] The Federal Republic of Yugoslavia split into several separate states in 1991–92. The international legal status of what remains of the former Yugoslavia—Yugoslavia (Serbia and Montenegro)—is ambiguous, but since it considers that it is the same entity, the name 'Yugoslavia' is used in this list. (The former Yugoslav republics of Bosnia and Herzegovina, Croatia, Macedonia and Slovenia have succeeded, as independent states, to several of these agreements.)

Note: The years given in the column headings are those in which the treaties were opened for signature.

6. The United Nations

6.1 Introduction

When the United Nations was created in 1945, its purpose and powers were set out by its founders in the organization's Charter. The opening statement of the Charter reads: 'We the peoples of the United Nations determined to save succeeding generations from the scourge of war . . . and . . . to unite our strength to maintain international peace and security'.

Since its creation in the closing days of World War II, the UN has evolved and changed, as has the international security system as a whole. While its organizational structure remains essentially the same as it was in 1945, the UN in its day-to-day operations is neither the organization its creators imagined nor even the organization it was a decade ago.

An appreciation of the place of the United Nations in the international security system requires an understanding of its major bodies and their responsibilities. At the same time, it must be kept in mind that there are many UN bodies which do not have a direct peace and security function. However, they do play an important role in improving the lives of millions of people around the world in fields such as health, education and agriculture. This work contributes to the UN's peace and security functions in an indirect way.

6.2 The United Nations structure

6.2.1 The General Assembly

All member states of the UN are represented in the General Assembly. Unlike the Security Council, the General Assembly does not have the authority to enforce its decisions. Instead, it considers international problems and expresses its views in the form of resolutions.

The General Assembly's main powers and responsibilities are:

• to consider any issue within the scope of the Charter—including international peace and security issues—and make recommendations to the Security Council, except on issues already before the Council;

• to initiate studies and make recommendations promoting international cooperation, the development and codification of international law, and the implementation of human rights and fundamental freedoms;

• to receive and consider reports from the Security Council and other organs of the UN; and

• to consider and approve the UN budget.

Much of the UN's work is carried out by committees formed by the General Assembly. Some are permanent and are concerned with specific issues, while some are ad hoc, that is, created to deal with particular issues as they arise.

6.2.2 The Security Council

The UN Security Council has 15 member states, five of which are permanent: China, France, Russia, the United Kingdom and the United States. Permanent members have a power of veto. By casting a negative vote, a permanent member can block a Security Council resolution.

The other 10 members of the Council are non-permanent and serve two-year terms. Any member of the UN may be elected as a non-permanent member of the Council. The vote is carried out among all UN members.

Proposals have been put forward to increase the number of members of the Security Council, both the permament and non-permanent members, thereby achieving better representation among the continents in the permanent membership. The question may be brought before the General Assembly for a vote, in which case the UN Charter must be changed.

The Security Council has the authority under the Charter to intervene in international conflicts and to enforce its decisions if necessary. The Council's main powers and responsibilities are the following:

• to maintain international peace and security;
• to investigate threats to international peace or acts of aggression;
• to recommend to the parties concerned how they could settle their dispute;
• to apply non-military measures to support its decisions; and

THE SIX PRINCIPAL ORGANS OF THE UN SYSTEM

General Assembly

Consists of all members of the United Nations.

Security Council

Consists of 15 UN members: 5 permanent members and
10 non-permanent members, 5 of which are elected each year by the
General Assembly for a term of 2 years.

Economic and Social Council (ECOSOC)

Consists of 54 members of the UN elected by the General Assembly.
Eighteen members of the Council are elected each year
for a term of 3 years.

Trusteeship Council

Composed of the permanent members of the Security Council.
The Trusteeship Council suspended operation on 1 November 1994 with
the independence of Palau, the last remaining United Nations trust territory.

International Court of Justice (ICJ)

Composed of 15 judges elected by the General Assembly and
Security Council, voting independently, for 9-year terms. The terms of
five of the judges expire every 3 years.

Secretariat

Comprises the Secretary-General, appointed by the General Assembly
upon the recommendation of the Security Council, for a 5-year term, and
such staff as the organization may require.

General Assembly	Security Council	ECOSOC
Main committees (1st to 6th) Procedural committees Standing committees Subsidiary, ad hoc and other bodies Treaty bodies *The Conference on Disarmament (CD) reports to the General Assembly.*	• Military Staff Committee Standing committees Ad hoc committees Peacekeeping operations Commissions established pursuant to SC Res. 687 International tribunals: • Yugoslav War Crimes Tribunal • Rwanda Genocide Tribunal Other organizations	Subsidiary bodies: Functional commissions Regional economic commissions Standing committees and expert bodies

Specialized agencies and other autonomous bodies

The Administrative Committee on Coordination (ACC), composed of the Secretary-General and the heads of the specialized agencies and the IAEA, ensures full coordination between all branches of the UN system.

• Food and Agricultural Organization (FAO) • International Atomic Energy Agency (IAEA) • International Civil Aviation Organization (ICAO) • International Labour Organization (ILO) • International Maritime Organization (IMO) • International Monetary Fund (IMF) • International Telecommunication Union (ITU) • UN Educational, Scientific and Cultural Organization (UNESCO) • UN Industrial Development Organization (UNIDO) • Universal Postal Union (UPU) • World Health Organization (WHO) • World Intellectual Property Organization (WIPO) • World Meteorological Organization (WMO) • World Tourism Organization (WTO) • World Trade Organization (WTO)

World Bank Group

• International Bank for Reconstruction and Development (IBRD) • International Development Association (IDA) • International Finance Corporation (IFC) • Associated organizations

Other UN bodies and programmes

Administrative Committee on Coordination (ACC) • Basel Convention on the Control of Trans-boundary Movements of Hazardous Wastes and their Disposal • Convention on Biological Diversity (CBD) • Convention on International Trade in Endangered Species of Wild Fauna and Flora (CITES) • Global Environment Facility (GEF) • Information Systems Coordination Committee (ISCC) • Intergovernmental Panel on Climate Change (IPCC) • International Consultative Group on Food Irradiation (ICGFI) • International Fund for Agricultural Development (IFAD) • International Narcotics Control Board (INCB) • International Research and Training Institute for the Advancement of Women (INSTRAW) • International Trade Centre UNCTAD/GATT (ITC) • International Union for the Protection of New Varieties of Plants (UPOV) • Office of the Secretary-General in Afghanistan and Pakistan (OSGAP) • Office of the UN High Commissioner for Human Rights (UNHCHR) • Office of the UN High Commissioner for Refugees (UNHCR) • UN Capital Development Fund (UNCDF) • UN Children's Fund (UNICEF) • UN Conference on Trade and Development (UNCTAD) • UN Convention to Combat Desertification in Countries Experiencing Serious Drought and/or Desertification, especially in Africa • UN Development Fund for Women (UNIFEM) • UN Development Programme (UNDP) • UN Environment Programme (UNEP) • UN Framework Convention on Climate Change (UNFCCC) • UN Institute for Disarmament Research (UNIDIR) • UN Institute for Training and Research (UNITAR) • UN International Drug Control Programme (UNDCP) • UN Interregional Crime and Justice Research Institute (UNICRI) • UN Population Fund (UNFPA) • UN Relief and Works Agency for Palestine Refugees in the Near East (UNRW) • UN Research Institute for Social Development (UNRISD) • UN University (UNU) • UN Volunteers (UNV) • Vienna Convention for the Protection of the Ozone Layer and the Montreal Protocol on Substances that Deplete the Ozone Layer • World Food Council (WFC) • World Food Programme (WFP)

Regional development banks

• African Development Bank • Asian Development Bank • Caribbean Development Bank • Inter-American Development Bank

• to take whatever military action is necessary to maintain or restore international peace and security.

The Security Council acts by adopting decisions in resolutions which it can enforce. According to the Charter, members of the UN are to respect and carry out these decisions.

6.2.3 The Secretariat

The UN has an international civil service which supports its work, called the Secretariat. The head of the Secretariat is the Secretary-General. While the Secretary-General is the head administrator of the UN, he also has the authority to bring the Security Council's attention to any situation he sees as a threat to international peace.

6.2.4 The International Court of Justice

The International Court of Justice (ICJ) was established at the founding conference of the UN in 1945. It is the principal judicial organ of the United Nations. Its Statute is an integral part of the UN Charter.

The Court decides cases submitted to it by states and gives advisory opinions to the General Assembly, the Security Council, and other major organs of the United Nations and specialized agencies. All the UN states are members of the Statute of the Court, but non-UN states may also become members under certain conditions (e.g., currently Nauru and Switzerland).

The authority of the Court to decide in a case is based on the consent of the states involved. The ICJ is composed of 15 members—the President, Vice-President and 13 other judges, no two of whom may be nationals of the same state. They are elected by separate votes in the General Assembly and the Security Council and must receive an absolute majority of votes in each body.

6.2.5 UN criminal tribunals

The creation of the temporary UN criminal tribunals for the former Yugoslavia (in 1993) and Rwanda (in 1995) marked the world's first attempt to prosecute war criminals since the Nuremberg Trials after World War II. The Rwandan tribunal is based in Arusha, Tanzania, and the Yugoslav tribunal in The Hague, the Netherlands. The UN is also discussing the establishment of a permanent International Criminal Court, which the new Secretary-General, Kofi Annan, has cited as a priority reform of the UN. A preparatory commission on the establishment of an International Criminal Court was set up in the autumn of 1994.

6.3   The evolving United Nations

6.3.1   The shadow of the cold war

Because of the veto power of the five permanent members, known as the 'Permanent Five' (P5), the Security Council's ability to act in response to threats or breaches of the peace is dependent upon the agreement of these members. The Security Council's enforcement powers are laid out in Chapter VII of the Charter, 'Action with Respect to Threats to the Peace, Breaches of the Peace, and Acts of Aggression'.

6.3.2   The Military Staff Committee

The Charter describes how member states are to make military contingents available to the Security Council. The Council's use of armed force is to be planned with the assistance of the Military Staff Committee. The Military Staff Committee itself was supposed to be made up of the military Chiefs of Staff of the P5.

The machinery that was designed to give the United Nations its muscle quickly failed because it lacked a vital ingredient: the support of the permanent members of the Security Council. The cold war split between East and West meant that the common sense of purpose that is expressed by the Charter was lost in practice. While the UN did take action in the case of the Korean War in the summer of 1950, by authorizing a military force under US command, this was an exception. The United Nations was able to act only because the Soviet Union was boycotting meetings of the Security Council at the time.

6.3.3   The Uniting for Peace Resolution

In response to the Security Council being undermined by cold war rivalry, the General Assembly passed the Uniting for Peace Resolution in November 1950. With this resolution, the Assembly gave itself the power to act in a case where there appars to be a threat to the peace, breach of the peace or act of aggression and where the Security Council had failed to act because of a veto by one of the P5. This meant that the General Assembly became more active in the consideration of political disputes than would have been expected given a strict interpretation of the Charter.

By means of the Uniting for Peace Resolution, the General Assembly could give moral support or a sense of legitimacy to states which decided collectively to act in support of UN principles. However, because the Assembly can only recommend action, and not intervene to enforce the peace, Uniting for Peace did not change the fact that the security system provided by the UN was not put into full effect.

6.3.4   The Secretary-General

The Secretary-General's role was also quick to change and evolve because of the cold war. Although the Charter made him both an administrator and a diplomat, the Security Council's inaction increased the value and prestige of his office in the service of international peace and security. More than ever, he became a figure of importance in the international community who, with the backing of the General Assembly or the Security Council or on his own initiative, could mediate, negotiate, conduct fact-finding missions and otherwise lend his good offices to deal with international problems.

6.3.5   The Agenda for Peace

With the fall of the Berlin Wall in 1989 and the end of the cold war, many people saw an opportunity for the UN to take centre stage in the international security system, assuming the role that its founders had set for it.

In January 1992 the first ever summit meeting of the Security Council was held, attended by heads of state and government. The Council called upon then Secretary-General Boutros Boutros-Ghali to recommend ways of making the UN stronger in peace-making, peacekeeping and arms control and disarmament. The Secretary-General responded with the Agenda for Peace.[1]

[1] Boutros-Ghali, B., An Agenda for Peace: Preventive Diplomacy, Peacemaking and Peace-keeping, Report of the Secretary-General pursuant to the statement adopted by the

In the Agenda for Peace, the Secretary-General refers on numerous occasions to the UN's lost promise as an instrument of international security. In particular, he notes that finally, with the passing of the cold war, the Security Council 'has emerged as a central instrument for the prevention and resolution of conflicts and for the preservation of peace'.

The Agenda spells out four types of activity for the UN:

1. *Preventive diplomacy* seeks to prevent disputes, prevent them from becoming conflicts, and limit their spread when they do occur. This could be achieved by such things as early warning and the preventive deployment of UN forces.

The Secretary-General, Security Council, General Assembly, other UN organs (or bodies) and regional organizations all have a role to play in preventive diplomacy.

2. *Peacemaking* is action to bring hostile parties to agreement. Mediation, negotiations, sanctions and the use of military force are possible measures. Boutros-Ghali suggested that standing forces could be made permanently available to the Security Council. By having these forces on hand, the Security Council could deter breaches of the peace.

The Agenda also proposes that the UN establish peace-enforcement units, which would be used in cases which fell short of outright aggression. For example, such units could be used in cases where cease-fires have been agreed but not carried out.

3. *Peacekeeping* is the use of UN or other international forces to bring stability to areas of tension, help implement agreements and contribute to settlements.

The Secretary-General noted that civilian political officers, human rights monitors, electoral officials, refugee and humanitarian aid specialists and police have come to play a greater role in UN peace-keeping.

4. *Peace-building* is a post-conflict process. It seeks to tackle the deep causes of conflict by identifying and supporting the structures that will promote peace. The Secretary-General argues that durable peace is only possible with 'sustained, cooperative work to deal with underlying economic, social, cultural and humanitarian problems'.

Summit Meeting of the Security Council on 31 January 1992, UN document A/47/277 (S/2411), 17 June 1992.

Since 1989, the UN has been increasingly confronted by ethnic and civil violence within states, rather than violence between states. The most obvious exception to this development has been the conflict between Iraq and Kuwait, where the Security Council applied numerous measures against Iraq, including military force.

The 1992 Agenda for Peace recognized that the breakdown of peace within states was the hallmark of the post-cold war world. Although the Agenda deals at length with the UN's need to deal with this new reality, the organization has had mixed results to date.

Much of the problem concerns force and how and when it should be used. For example, the international community's desire to protect and provide for the victims of internal conflict has collided head-on with the problem of bringing pressure to bear on or deterring the parties responsible for such suffering in the first place. The UN operations in Somalia (UNOSOM II) and Bosnia and Herzegovina (UNPROFOR) have clearly shown the difficulties of providing humanitarian relief under such circumstances.

There is also the larger question of how to bring the parties to an internal conflict to the negotiating table. When a state has broken down and the lines of authority and control are non-existent and the factions many, how is the international community to respond?

The UN has had to wrestle with more and more cases that involve rethinking traditional approaches to peace and security. To make matters worse, this has been taking place at a time when UN finances are stretched to the limit. Many members continue to owe money to both the peacekeeping and the regular budgets of the UN.[2]

6.4   The United Nations and disarmament

6.4.1   The Security Council

Under Article 26 of the UN Charter, the Security Council is called upon to make plans for the creation of a system for the regulation of armaments. However, it has never been able to follow through on this obligation. In fact, the Security Council has played a minimal role in arms control and disarmament.

---

[2] As of 31 Dec. 1996, unpaid regular assessments of member states of the UN totalled $546 million and unpaid assessments for peacekeeping $1.7 billion.

This cannot be said of the Council's response to Iraq's invasion of Kuwait. In this case, the Security Council made disarmament a key element of its plan to deal with this international crisis. Part C of Security Council Resolution 687 addresses Iraq's weapons of mass destruction, in all their aspects. It established that these weapons must be declared, identified, located and disposed. In addition, a monitoring system was created to ensure that they are not reintroduced into Iraq.

As a subsidiary body of the Security Council, the United Nations Special Commission on Iraq (UNSCOM) was created. Its mandate is to conduct on-site inspection of Iraq's biological, chemical and missile capabilities.[3]

6.4.2   The General Assembly

The UN Charter gives the General Assembly the power to consider the 'principles governing disarmament and the regulation of armaments'. While it cannot negotiate treaties, the Assembly has used its powers to debate issues, establish principles, make recommendations and direct research studies on disarmament. In fact, its first resolution called for the elimination of atomic weapons and other weapons of mass destruction, and the peaceful use of atomic energy. Since this resolution was passed in 1946, the General Assembly has been the source of many other disarmament resolutions and plans.

For example, in 1953, US President Dwight Eisenhower pursued the objective of the peaceful use of atomic energy in his Atoms for Peace plan. His proposal led to the establishment in 1957 of the International Atomic Energy Agency (IAEA). The IAEA was given a broad mandate to foster the peaceful use of nuclear energy as well as design and administer the necessary safeguards to ensure nuclear technology and materials were not diverted for military purposes.

As can be seen in the sections below, the General Assembly plays an important role in arms control and disarmament by providing a high-profile, international stage for discussion of security concerns and launching of new initiatives. Another example was in 1967, when the Ambassador of Malta proposed that the UN declare the deep seabed beyond the reach of national jurisdiction to be 'the common heritage of mankind'. This suggestion sparked a debate which led to the

---

[3] For more on UNSCOM, see chapter 4, section 4.5.

146 SIPRI–UNESCO HANDBOOK

UN member states

The year in which states became members is indicated in brackets.
Permanent members of the Security Council are denoted by an asterisk (*).

Afghanistan (1946); Albania (1955); Algeria (1962); Andorra (1993); Angola (1976); Antigua and Barbuda (1981); Argentina (1945); Armenia (1992); Australia (1945); Austria (1955); Azerbaijan (1992); Bahamas (1973); Bahrain (1971); Bangladesh (1974); Barbados (1966); Belarus (1945); Belgium (1945); Belize (1981); Benin (1960); Bhutan (1971); Bolivia (1945); Bosnia and Herzegovina (1992); Botswana (1966); Brazil (1945); Brunei Darussalam (1984); Bulgaria (1955); Burkina Faso (1960); Burundi (1962); Cambodia (1955); Cameroon (1960); Canada (1945); Cape Verde (1975); Central African Republic (1960); Chad (1960); Chile (1945); China (1945)*; Colombia (1945); Comoros (1975); Congo (Brazzaville) (1960); Congo, Democratic Republic of (formerly Zaire) (1960); Costa Rica (1945); Côte d'Ivoire (1960); Croatia (1992); Cuba (1945); Cyprus (1960); Czech Republic (1993); Denmark (1945); Djibouti (1977); Dominica (1978); Dominican Republic (1945); Ecuador (1945); Egypt (1945); El Salvador (1945); Equatorial Guinea (1968); Eritrea (1993); Estonia (1991); Ethiopia (1945); Fiji (1970); Finland (1955); France (1945)*; Gabon (1960); Gambia (1965); Georgia (1992); Germany (1973); Ghana (1957); Greece (1945); Grenada (1974); Guatemala (1945); Guinea (1958); Guinea-Bissau (1974); Guyana (1966); Haiti (1945); Honduras (1945); Hungary (1955); Iceland (1946); India (1945); Indonesia (1950); Iran (1945); Iraq (1945); Ireland (1955); Israel (1949); Italy (1955); Jamaica (1962); Japan (1956); Jordan (1955); Kazakhstan (1992); Kenya (1963); Korea, North (1991); Korea, South (1991); Kuwait (1963); Kyrgyzstan (1992); Lao People's Democratic Republic (1955); Latvia (1991); Lebanon (1945); Lesotho (1966); Liberia (1945); Libya (1955); Liechtenstein (1990); Lithuania (1991); Luxembourg (1945); Macedonia, Former Yugoslav Republic of (1993); Madagascar (1960); Malawi (1964); Malaysia (1957); Maldives (1965); Mali (1960); Malta (1964); Marshall Islands (1991); Mauritania (1961); Mauritius (1968); Mexico (1945); Micronesia (1991); Moldova (1992); Monaco (1993); Mongolia (1961); Morocco (1956); Mozambique (1975); Myanmar (Burma) (1948); Namibia (1990); Nepal (1955); Netherlands (1945); New Zealand (1945); Nicaragua (1945); Niger (1960); Nigeria (1960); Norway (1945); Oman (1971); Pakistan (1947); Palau (1994); Panama (1945); Papua New Guinea (1975); Paraguay (1945); Peru (1945); Philippines (1945); Poland (1945); Portugal (1955); Qatar (1971); Romania (1955); Russia (1945)*†; Rwanda (1962); Saint Kitts (Christopher) and Nevis (1983); Saint Lucia (1979); Saint Vincent and the Grenadines (1980); Samoa, Western (1976); San Marino (1992); Sao Tome and Principe (1975); Saudi Arabia (1945); Senegal (1960); Seychelles (1976); Sierra Leone (1961); Singapore (1965); Slovakia (1993); Slovenia (1992); Solomon Islands (1978); Somalia (1960); South Africa (1945); Spain (1955); Sri Lanka (1955); Sudan (1956); Suriname (1975); Swaziland (1968); Sweden (1946); Syria (1945); Tajikistan (1992); Tanzania (1961); Thailand (1946); Togo (1960); Trinidad and Tobago (1962); Tunisia (1956); Turkey (1945); Turkmenistan (1992); Uganda (1962); UK (1945)*; Ukraine (1945); United Arab Emirates (1971); Uruguay (1945); USA (1945)*; Uzbekistan (1992); Vanuatu (1981); Venezuela (1945); Viet Nam (1977); Yemen (1947); Yugoslavia (1945)††; Zambia (1964); Zimbabwe (1980)

† In Dec. 1991 Russia informed the UN Secretary-General that it was continuing the membership of the Soviet Union in the Security Council and all other UN bodies.

†† A claim by Yugoslavia (Serbia and Montenegro) in 1992 to continue automatically the membership of the former Yugoslavia was not accepted by the UN General Assembly. It was decided that Yugoslavia should apply for membership, which it had not done by Sep. 1997. It may not participate in the work of the General Assembly, its subsidiary organs or the conferences and meetings it convenes.

Seabed Treaty of 1971. The treaty bars the emplacement of weapons of mass destruction on the ocean floor or its subsoil. It also created an atmosphere that was conducive to negotiating the 1982 UN Convention on the Law of the Sea.

The General Assembly may also decide to encourage international conferences to negotiate certain arms control measures. This is what happened when a special conference met in 1979 to discuss inhumane weapons, leading to the signing in 1981 of the Inhumane Weapons Convention.

A more recent achievement of the General Assembly is the UN Register of Conventional Arms. Many people argue that unexpected or unsuspected build-ups of conventional weapons are a threat to international peace and security. One way of reducing the destabilizing consequences of the conventional arms trade is to make the trade transparent to the world. In December 1991 the UN General Assembly passed a resolution establishing the United Nations Register of Conventional Arms. After operating procedures were developed by a team of experts appointed by the Secretary-General, the Register was implemented in 1992. It covers imports and exports of weapons under seven categories: battle tanks, armoured combat vehicles, large-calibre artillery systems, combat aircraft, attack helicopters, warships, and missiles and missile launchers.

This is a voluntary mechanism and, although many UN members have chosen not to submit reports to the Register, almost all the major arms exporting countries have. States which manufacture their own conventional weapons, as opposed to importing them, have been encouraged to report these holdings to the Register as well.

The following sections describe the ways the General Assembly has organized itself to take action on disarmament issues.

6.4.3   UN Special Sessions on Disarmament

From time to time, the General Assembly may hold a Special Session to devote its attention to a single issue. On three occasions, in 1978, 1982 and 1988, the General Assembly held UN Special Sessions on Disarmament (UNSSODs).

UNSSOD I, held in 1978, produced an ambitious Final Document containing 129 paragraphs, reaffirming the goal of 'general and complete disarmament under effective international control' that had been set out by the General Assembly in 1959. UNSSOD II moved very little beyond the 1978 Final Document, and neither UNSSOD II nor UNSSOD III agreed on a final statement.

One of the features of the UNSSODs has been to give non-governmental organizations, research institutions and academics an opportunity to address the General Assembly on arms control and disarmament issues.

6.4.4   The First Committee

The First Committee is one of the General Assembly's six main committees. Since UNSSOD I, the First Committee's sole task has been questions of disarmament and international security. It recommends draft resolutions which are forwarded to the General Assembly. All members of the UN have a seat on the First Committee, and it decides on the basis of majority vote.

6.4.5   The Disarmament Commission

Established in 1952, the United Nations Disarmament Commission (UNDC)—a deliberative body and subsidiary organ of the UN General Assembly—has not been particularly active over the years. It was given the task of considering and making recommendations on various disarmament problems, as well as following up on UNSSOD decisions. However, the DC has produced few agreed recommendations. At its 1996 session the Commission adopted guidelines for international arms transfers. All UN members have a seat on the UNDC and decisions are usually taken by a vote. Sessions of the Commission often cover the same ground as the debate in the First Committee and the General Assembly itself. It is questionable whether routine annual sessions of the UNDC are needed.

6.4.6   The Conference on Disarmament

The Conference on Disarmament (CD), technically not a UN body, is a negotiating forum that receives its budget from the UN, reports to the General Assembly, but establishes its own agenda.[4]

---

[4] For more on the CD, see also chapter 5, section 5.3.1.

The CD comprises members and observers which represent all the regions of the world. The members include all the permanent members of the Security Council. Its goal is to negotiate disarmament treaties.

6.4.7   The International Atomic Energy Agency

The International Atomic Energy Agency (IAEA) was established in 1957. Its main functions are: to assist research on and the development and practical application of atomic energy for peaceful purposes; to provide for relevant materials, services, equipment and facilities, with due consideration for the needs of the underdeveloped world; to foster and encourage the peaceful uses of atomic energy; to administer safeguards to ensure that atomic materials, equipment and information are not diverted from peaceful to military purposes; and to establish standards of safety to protect health and minimize danger.

The IAEA is involved in the verification of the NPT and the nuclear weapon-free zone treaties and in the activities of the UN Special Commission on Iraq.

7. Regional and subregional security: Europe and Asia

7.1 Introduction

This chapter looks at how two regions of the world—Europe and the Asia–Pacific—address the security issues they face in the 1990s. For some 45 years, security concerns, institutions and approaches in Europe were driven by the cold war and the superpowers of the day: the United States and the Soviet Union. Today, European security is in a transitional stage. Russia is no longer a superpower but remains a nuclear weapon power. The USA, while the only unchallenged superpower, is still defining its new role.

The security environment in Europe will be further shaped by two developments. On the one hand, there is the evolution of the European Union (EU) and the North Atlantic Treaty Organization (NATO). On the other, there is the democratic transformation of the states in Central and Eastern Europe (CEE) and Russia.

As seen in section 7.2, the security organization that is being built in Europe is meant to avoid the harsh dividing lines that were so prominent in the cold war. The ultimate success of this effort will depend in large part on Western Europe being able to build a new partnership with Central and Eastern Europe and Russia.

In contrast, the Asia–Pacific region is only in the early stages of organizing its security structures. Furthermore, the subregions of South-East Asia and North-East Asia are themselves at quite different points in this process. South-East Asia has shown increasing interest in dealing with security concerns on a multilateral basis and already has several forums in place. North-East Asia, on the other hand, still lacks some of the basic ingredients necessary to build multilateral security institutions: a modest amount of trust, mutual confidence and some agreement on the form of cooperation.

Both Europe and the Asia–Pacific region, despite different circumstances, are working to refine and improve their multilateral security institutions. While Europe has significantly more experience in this regard, recent developments in South-East Asia suggest that multilateral approaches are taking hold where previously there were few.

7.2 European security: the intricate web

In December 1989, soon after the Berlin Wall came down, US Secretary of State James Baker spoke about the security challenges facing Europe.[1] He stressed the continuing importance of the established structures, while emphasizing their need to evolve and serve new purposes. These structures must draw the West together, he said, provide an open door to the East, and overcome the division of Europe. These comments are just as relevant today.

Since the time of Baker's speech, the European security environment has changed dramatically. Germany has been unified and Czechoslovakia has split into two states. Both the Soviet and the Yugoslav federations have been dissolved, creating 20 newly formed or re-emerged states. Thanks to the 1990 Treaty on Conventional Armed Forces in Europe (CFE Treaty), heavy weapons have been reduced by over 50 000 items in the Atlantic-to-the-Urals (ATTU) area covered by the treaty.

The North Atlantic Treaty Organization (NATO) and the Warsaw Treaty Organization (WTO, or Warsaw Pact) no longer divide Europe into two hostile blocs. An invisible line between East and West still exists although it is gradually eroding. The West European states are secure and relatively united within NATO and the EU. Meanwhile, the CEE states are seeking greater security through membership of these and other organizations.

A security system is shaped by two factors. The first is threats and perceptions of threats to the peace. The second is the means to deal with those threats. In Europe, multilateral security structures are in place. Indeed, one of Europe's challenges is to sort out the roles and responsibilities of its security institutions. To this end, there has been an ongoing process of institutional change since the end of the cold war. This has been necessary because the security agenda in Europe is now dominated by concerns over actual and potential internal conflicts. The security institutions created during the cold war were not designed to deal with these types of conflict.

Not only has Europe been adapting its institutions but it has also been doing so with conflicts in its midst. Europe was unprepared for coping with conflict in either the Balkans or on the former Soviet ter-

---

[1] A new Europe, a new Atlanticism: architecture for a new era, address by James A. Baker, III, US Secretary of State, to the Berlin Press Club, Berlin, 12 Dec. 1989. See *SIPRI Yearbook 1992*, p. 565.

The overlapping membership of multilateral security structures in Europe, as of May 1997

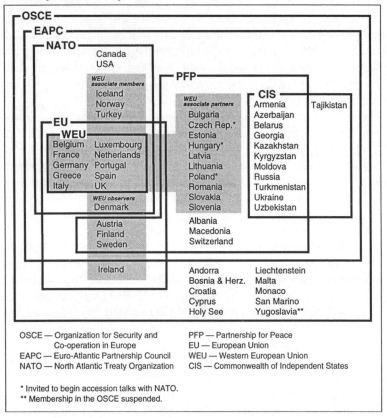

OSCE — Organization for Security and
    Co-operation in Europe
EAPC — Euro-Atlantic Partnership Council
NATO — North Atlantic Treaty Organization

PFP — Partnership for Peace
EU — European Union
WEU — Western European Union
CIS — Commonwealth of Independent States

* Invited to begin accession talks with NATO.
** Membership in the OSCE suspended.

ritories, for instance. As a result, the progress that has been achieved in rethinking and redirecting security institutions understandably seems modest when compared to the realities of bloodshed in Europe.

7.2.1   The North Atlantic Treaty Organization

NATO was created when the North Atlantic Treaty was signed in Washington, DC, in 1949.[2] It was a response to the perceived threat posed by the Soviet Union and its allies in Europe.

[2] It is sometimes referred to as the Washington Treaty. The 12 founding members of NATO were: Belgium, Canada, Denmark, France, Iceland, Italy, Luxembourg, the Nether-

The Atlantic Alliance is a collective defence organization, that is, the members of NATO are committed to come to the defence of each other in the case of an attack against one or more of them. This commitment is found in Article 5 of the North Atlantic Treaty, which reads: 'The Parties agree that an armed attack against one or more of them in Europe or North America shall be considered an attack against them all'.

Since its creation, NATO has been at the centre of the defence and security policies of its members. It has linked the security interests of Western Europe and North America by developing elaborate mechanisms for planning, consultation, military cooperation and coordination.

With the collapse of the Soviet Union and the WTO, NATO had to come to grips with its role in the absence of a clearly defined enemy. Some observers have suggested that it would be best if NATO quietly disbanded and faded from the scene, although this view is much less common now. Others have argued that in a time of transition and uncertainty an alliance with the long history and stability of NATO is needed to stabilize the situation and guide Europe through the post-cold war period.

Enlargement of NATO membership

Much time and thinking in recent years has been consumed by the question of the security needs of the CEE states. In the 1990 London Declaration, NATO leaders noted that in developing new security institutions for Europe 'these institutions should reflect the fact that the newly democratic countries of CEE form part of the political structure of the new Europe'.[3] In 1991 NATO ministers declared that 'any form of coercion or intimidation' of the CEE states would be a matter of 'direct and natural concern' to NATO.

For the CEE states, military security and stability are viewed as a key ingredient in the development of their new democracies and free markets. Accordingly, they have turned to NATO and European structures such as the EU and the Western European Union (WEU) as

lands, Norway, Portugal, the UK and the USA. In 1952 Greece and Turkey acceded to the treaty; in 1955 the Federal Republic of Germany joined the Alliance and in 1982 Spain became a member.

[3] London Declaration on a Transformed North Atlantic Alliance, issued by the heads of state and government participating in the meeting of the North Atlantic Council, London, 5–6 July 1990.

Collective defence, collective security and cooperative security

Collective defence, collective security and cooperative security are terms frequently used in any discussion of 'security architecture', or the way states organize themselves to ensure their security.

Collective defence • States pursue collective defence by forming alliances of like-minded states. Collective defence means that states agree to come to the defence of any other in their alliance if they are attacked.

Collective security • In its ideal form, this is a system in which all states join together to punish any state that carries out an aggressive act. The United Nations is the closest example of a collective security mechanism although a pure collective security mechanism does not exist.

Cooperative security • Cooperative security can be pursued by individual states or alliances. It involves adopting mutual, cooperative measures that when carried out by each side improve the security of each side. It is designed to ensure that organized aggression cannot start or be carried out on any large scale. It seeks to devise agreed measures to prevent war (i.e., on-site monitoring, observation of military manoeuvres, and so on).

anchors during this transition. Joining Western security organizations is seen as something of a natural conclusion to the process that began in 1989–90 with the disintegration of the Eastern bloc.

A deep-seated concern is Russia. In particular, having been released from the grip of the Soviet Union, the CEE states have no desire to be treated as a buffer zone or a sphere of Russian influence.

Within NATO itself, there have been three schools of thought on enlargement of its membership. These are opposition; support; and postponement of the decision or adoption of gradual, step-by-step solutions.

Opponents of NATO enlargement to the East are concerned about how Russia would interpret such a move. In their view, many Russians would see this as designed to encircle and isolate Russia. It is argued that democratic reform and development in Russia are very fragile. NATO enlargement would provide the enemies of reform ideal ammunition to attack the West and all the values and changes associated with it. There is also scepticism about whether there is suf-

ficient public support in the NATO countries for assuming the costs
and responsibilities of extending NATO defence guarantees eastward.
Some fear that this might risk involving the Alliance in national and
ethnic conflicts between or within CEE nations.

Those who support extending NATO membership to the East point
out that the process of the CEE states' accession to NATO has facili-
tated reconciliation, for example, between Poland and its neighbours
(Germany, Lithuania and Ukraine), Hungary and Romania, Ukraine
and Romania, the Czech Republic and Germany, and so on. In addition, it will guarantee the existing borders of the CEE states and
thereby reduce ethnic tension and national rivalry. It is also argued
that NATO membership will strengthen the forces of stability and
progress in the CEE states by promoting the rule of law and political
pluralism, respect for democratic freedoms and human rights, civilian
control over the military and the development of market economies.

NATO ministers, in launching the Partnership for Peace (PFP) programme in January 1994 (see section 7.2.3), reaffirmed that their
alliance remained open to other European states 'in a position to further the principles of the Treaty and to contribute to the security of the
North Atlantic area'.[4] In December 1994 NATO made it clear that
enlargement was an option.

This approach was reaffirmed by the 1995 'Study on NATO
Enlargement'. It concluded that enlargement will take place on a case-
by-case basis, with some nations attaining membership before others.
Another important point was the Atlantic Alliance's commitment to
develop its relationship with Russia 'in rough parallel with NATO
enlargement'.[5] The Founding Act on Mutual Relations, Cooperation
and Security between Russia and NATO, signed in Paris on 27 May
1997, demonstrated the political will of the Alliance to base its relations with Russia on the principles of cooperativeness and inclusiveness instead of deterrence and exclusiveness, as was the case in the
cold war period.

At the July 1997 Madrid NATO summit meeting, the first group of
new members—the Czech Republic, Hungary and Poland—was
invited to begin accession talks. These talks were initiated in September and completed in November. Their accession protocols are to be

---

[4] For the full text see *SIPRI Yearbook 1994*, p. 272.
[5] Statement by Secretary General Willy Claes at a press conference at NATO Headquarters, Brussels, 28 Sep. 1995, reprinted in *NATO Review*, no. 6 (Nov. 1995), p. 10.

signed in December, before the ratification process is conducted in 1998. Their accession to NATO will be completed in 1999.

NATO has also created and used the PFP programme and the North Atlantic Cooperation Council (NACC) as mechanisms to explore greater cooperation with the CEE states and Russia and possibly lay the groundwork for an evolutionary enlargement. Finally, agreement was reached in December 1996 on the establishment of a Euro-Atlantic Partnership Council to engage non-members in both an expanded political dimension of partnership with NATO and practical cooperation under the PFP (see section 7.2.2).

Russia and NATO enlargement

Russia's view on NATO enlargement to the East has shifted and changed in emphasis on various occasions. It is safe to say, however, that Russia is not enthusiastic about an enlarged NATO. In Russia's view, even after the signing of the NATO–Russian Founding Act in 1997, the extension of the Alliance to the East is 'the most fateful error' of the West in the entire post-cold war era.

In August 1993, as the enlargement idea heated up, President Boris Yeltsin expressed some understanding for states such as Poland that wished to join NATO. He quickly abandoned this position, however, and suggested that Russia and NATO should jointly guarantee the security of the CEE states. Russia returned to this theme in early 1994, as it considered its involvement in the PFP programme.

In a paper outlining how Russia viewed its participation in the Partnership, the Russian Defence Minister suggested a complete transformation of European security. Russia called for the Conference on Security and Co-operation in Europe (CSCE, from 1995 the OSCE) to play a central role, with NACC acting as its military arm. Its strategy was 'a long-term system of collective security and stability in Europe under the aegis of the OSCE'.[6] The OSCE would become something of a European United Nations.[7]

On occasion, there have been harsh statements from Russian officials about NATO enlargement. Some have gone so far as to suggest that Russia might respond with a new military bloc and even aim

---

[6] ITAR-TASS World Service in Russian, 25 May 1994. See *SIPRI Yearbook 1995*, p. 276.

[7] Under this scheme, the CSCE would coordinate the activities of not only NATO but also the European Union, the Council of Europe, the WEU and even the CIS. It was put forward by Russian Foreign Minister Andrei Kozyrev in *NATO Review*, vol. 42, no. 4 (Aug. 1994), p. 5. See also *SIPRI Yearbook 1995*, p. 277, note 50.

some of its nuclear weapons at former allies such as Poland and the Czech Republic. In his letter of July 1996 to the US President, leaked to the Russian press, President Yeltsin warned that extending NATO membership to the Baltic states 'is categorically unacceptable for Russia'. This opposition was interpreted as Russia reconciling itself to the possibility of a limited group of CEE states being admitted to the Alliance.

By late 1996 Russia seemed to settle on three conditions that would have to be met before its objections could be overcome: (*a*) that NATO extension be limited to some former WTO member states but not former Soviet republics; (*b*) that a treaty establishing special relations between NATO and Russia be concluded; and (*c*) that NATO promise not to place nuclear or conventional weapons on the territories of any new CEE member states. In response NATO declared that the Alliance has 'no intention, no plan and no reason to deploy nuclear weapons on the territory of new members nor any need to change any aspect of NATO's nuclear posture or nuclear policy—and [does] not foresee any future need to do so'.[8] It later also announced that it does not envisage a build-up of its permanently stationed combat forces close to Russia.

The 1997 Founding Act and the decision to invite three CEE states to join reflect the new political philosophy of cooperativeness and inclusiveness. These decisions were meant as the foundation for a truly cooperative European security structure.

The Founding Act also established the NATO–Russia Permanent Joint Council as a mechanism for consultation and cooperation at the level of foreign ministers. The council first met in September 1997 in New York, focusing on confidence building, peacekeeping (particularly in Bosnia), international terrorism, military strategy and nuclear doctrine.

7.2.2   The North Atlantic Cooperation Council and the Euro-Atlantic Partnership Council

The North Atlantic Cooperation Council (NACC) was proposed by the NATO Rome summit meeting in 1991, and it met for the first time in Brussels in December. NACC, as a multilateral forum, was primar-

---

[8] NATO Final Communiqué, Ministerial meeting of the North Atlantic Council, Brussels, 9–10 Dec. 1996.

ily meant for political consultation. It was created to manage the evolving political and military situation in the wake of the collapse of the Soviet Union and to assist in implementing the CFE Treaty. Cooperation within NACC has been based on a combination of common documents and individual bilateral arrangements.

In 1992 NACC decided to focus on cooperation in the following areas: military strategies, defence management, the legal framework for military forces, harmonization of defence planning and arms control, exercises and training, defence education, reserve forces, environmental protection, air traffic control, search and rescue, humanitarian aid and military medicine, and peacekeeping. In practice, peacekeeping has been the main focus of discussions and activities.

At the NATO meeting of foreign ministers in December 1996, a decision was taken to merge the activities of NACC and the PFP in the Euro-Atlantic Partnership Council (EAPC). The intention was to unite the positive experience of NACC and the PFP by 'providing the overarching framework for political and security-related consultations and for enhanced cooperation under PfP, whose basic elements will remain valid'.[9] Cooperative arrangements with former members of the WTO, including Russia, opened the way for a new stage of politico-military relations among the NATO countries and former enemies from the East.

7.2.3 The Partnership for Peace programme

The PFP programme was proposed at a meeting of NATO defence ministers in 1993. It was then brought forward and agreed upon at a NATO summit meeting in January 1994. The PFP is based on bilateral relationships between NATO and its 27 partner states. Each partner state develops an Individual Partnership Programme (IPP) with NATO. As a result, each PFP relationship is unique and reflects different levels of cooperation.

The aim of the PFP is to engage its partners in cooperative military activities. These include peacekeeping, search and rescue, and humanitarian operations. The PFP also promotes transparency and democratic control of defence ministries and armed forces.

---

[9] The decision was announced in May 1997; see Final Communiqué of the Ministerial Meeting of the North Atlantic Council in Sintra, Portugal, 29 May 1997. As a result of this decision, NACC no longer exists.

The PFP is open to all European states outside NATO. It does not provide security guarantees to states which become active participants, but the PFP Invitation document does promise that 'NATO will consult with any active participant in the Partnership if that partner perceives a direct threat to its territorial integrity, political independence, or security'.

Participants in the PFP are invited to send permanent liaison officers to NATO headquarters as well as to a separate Partnership Coordination Cell which plans the implementation of Partnership programmes.

7.2.4   The European Union and the Western European Union

The WEU was established in the 1954 Protocols to the 1948 Brussels Treaty of Economic, Social and Cultural Collaboration and Collective Self-Defence among Western European States. The Brussels Treaty established a defence arrangement between Belgium, France, Luxembourg, the Netherlands and the UK. With the creation of NATO in 1949, the Brussels Treaty was quickly eclipsed. In 1954 the WEU emerged when the treaty was amended to include Italy and what was then West Germany.

The WEU was rejuvenated when members of the European Community agreed in December 1991 to the Treaty on European Union (the Maastricht Treaty), which established the European Union. The Maastricht Treaty and the June 1992 Petersberg Declaration established the WEU as the defence dimension of European integration and the European pillar of NATO.[10]

Further progress was made in June 1996, when the Combined Joint Task Forces (CJTF) were created between NATO and the WEU. Under this arrangement NATO provides logistical support and resources to operations led by the WEU. This allows NATO to support WEU efforts to resolve regional conflicts without itself taking on a central role. These decisions, taken at the June 1996 Ministerial Meeting of the North Atlantic Council, offered practical meaning to the new WEU commitments.

Under the Maastricht Treaty, the member states of the EU are committed to defining and implementing a Common Foreign and Security Policy (CFSP). When the EU makes decisions with defence

---

[10] The so-called Petersberg tasks emanate from the declaration. See chapter 9, section 9.1.

implications, they are to be fleshed out and acted upon by the WEU. At the same time, those decisions have to respect obligations undertaken by EU member states under the North Atlantic Treaty. This mechanism ensures that EU and NATO defence and security initiatives do not stray far from each other. The objectives of the CFSP were defined as follows:

• to safeguard the common values, fundamental interests and independence of the European Union;
• to strengthen the security of the EU and its member states in all ways;
• to preserve peace and strengthen international security, in accordance with the principles of the United Nations Charter as well as the principles of the 1975 Helsinki Final Act and the objectives of the 1990 Charter of Paris for a New Europe (Paris Charter);
• to promote international cooperation; and
• to develop and consolidate democracy, the rule of law and respect for human rights and fundamental freedoms.

To date, the WEU's activities have focused largely on the EU's humanitarian and peacekeeping assistance. For example, from 1992 to 1996 it coordinated the European naval forces which helped enforce the UN sanctions against Serbia.

Members of the WEU allocate forces for specific purposes, such as enforcement of sanctions, as noted above. The WEU maintains lists of these forces, recommends command, control and communications arrangements, and prepares contingency plans for the use of WEU forces.

7.2.5   The Organization for Security and Co-operation in Europe

The Organization for Security and Co-operation in Europe (OSCE) began as the Conference on Security and Co-operation in Europe (CSCE). The CSCE first met in 1973 in Helsinki, Finland. It involved all the states of Europe (except Albania), as well as Canada and the USA. The purpose of the CSCE was to overcome the mistrust, suspicion and tension between East and West and to take measures to avoid confrontation and build confidence. In 1997 the OSCE comprises 55 participating states from the region stretching from Vancouver, Canada, to Vladivostok, Russia.

OSCE structures and institutions

Summit meetings • Meetings of Heads of State or Government set the priorities and direction of the OSCE at the highest political level.

Senior Council • The Senior Council is responsible for the overview, management and coordination of OSCE activities. It meets at least twice a year.

Ministerial Council • The Foreign Ministers of the OSCE member states form the Ministerial Council, the central decision-making and governing body of the OSCE. It meets at least once a year.

Permanent Council • The Permanent Council is responsible for day-to-day operational tasks. It is the regular body for political consultation and decision making.

Forum for Security Co-operation (FSC) • The FSC meets weekly and consults on concrete measures aimed at strengthening security and stability throughout Europe.

Chairman-in-Office (CIO) • The CIO has overall responsibility for executive action. The term in office is normally one calendar year.

Secretary General • The Secretary General is appointed for three years and acts as the representative of the Chairman-in-Office. The Secretary General is also the OSCE's chief Administrative Officer.

Secretariat • The Secretariat provides administrative support for the OSCE, under the direction of the Secretary General. The Conflict Prevention Center functions within the Secretariat.

High Commissioner on National Minorities (HCNM) • The HCNM provides early warning and early action to prevent tensions involving national minority issues from developing into a conflict.

Office for Democratic Institutions and Human Rights (ODIHR) • The ODIHR is responsible for furthering human rights, democracy and the rule of law.

The 1975 Helsinki Final Act became the foundation of the CSCE. In it, the member states of the CSCE agreed to provisions in three areas or 'baskets':

• security and dialogue on principles guiding the relations between states;
• economic, environmental, and science and technology issues; and
• human contacts, information, culture and education.

Particularly important to the Eastern bloc, the CSCE adopted the principles of the inviolability of frontiers, territorial integrity and non-intervention in domestic affairs.[11] In essence, one-party rule in the East would not be challenged. However, at the same time the 'Basket 3' issues of human contacts, free flows of information and respect for human rights gave the West a powerful tool to encourage more respect for human rights and individual freedoms.

Since 1975, the CSCE/OSCE has held six follow-up and review meetings to consider its progress and other issues of importance.[12]

The CSCE process can be divided into three broad phases. From 1975 to 1985, the focus was on human rights, political liberties and Basket 3 issues. From 1986 to 1992, it was on military security and confidence-building measures. There were several important achievements. The 1986 Stockholm Document and the three Vienna Documents (1990, 1992 and 1994) established a set of political and military confidence- and security-building measures (CSBMs). The CFE Treaty placed limits on five categories of heavy conventional weapons in Europe. Lastly, the 1992 Open Skies Treaty (which is not yet in force) provides for short-notice overflights to aid in confidence building and arms control verification.[13]

During the third phase, beginning in 1992, a transformed CSCE—now the OSCE—has been preoccupied with promoting common values as defined by the Paris Charter, conflict prevention and crisis management. It has also been working to promote and develop cooperative security, including the strengthening of OSCE mechanisms such as instruments of preventive diplomacy.

The Paris Charter announced new principles for the post-cold war European system. It also marked the beginning of the transformation of the CSCE from a series of conferences to an institution. In 1995 it was renamed the Organization for Security and Co-operation in Europe to reflect this change. The Paris Charter reads, in part: 'The era of confrontation and division of Europe is ended . . . Ours is a time for fulfilling the hopes and expectations our peoples have cher-

[11] The principle of the inviolability of borders meant that the new borders established in Europe after World War II were accepted by the CSCE members as legitimate and beyond dispute.
[12] Follow-up and review meetings were held in Belgrade (1977–78), Madrid (1980–83) and Vienna (1986–89) as well as before the summit meetings in Helsinki (1992), Budapest (1994) and Lisbon (1996) (the review meeting held prior to the Lisbon summit meeting was held in Vienna).
[13] For more on the CFE Treaty and the Open Skies Treaty, see chapter 5, section 5.3.2.

ished for decades: steadfast commitment to democracy based on human rights and fundamental freedoms; prosperity through economic liberty and social justice; and equal security for all our countries.'

These words capture not only the high expectations that followed the end of the cold war but also the significant new directions that the CSCE would follow. First, no longer would it be preoccupied with bridging the gap between well-entrenched, fundamentally different social, economic and political systems. In fact, the Charter proclaimed the triumph of common values and freedoms.

Second, the old CSCE process had been careful to focus on the international relations between European states, generally avoiding domestic issues. The Paris Charter was clear that international peace and security could not be separated from the principles and norms guiding the domestic affairs of states.

The January 1992 meeting of the CSCE Council of Foreign Ministers in Prague marked another important development. The meeting was attended by representatives of such organizations as NATO and the WEU. Before this, all CSCE conferences and meetings were held without official representatives of military alliances. The results of the Prague meeting included rules on cooperation between the CSCE and other bodies.[14] Moreover, all former Soviet republics were welcomed as participating CSCE states.

At the Helsinki II summit meeting in July 1992, the summit leaders declared the CSCE to be a regional security arrangement as described by Chapter VIII of the United Nations Charter. This chapter sets out the right of states to create regional security organizations, provided their activities are consistent with UN principles. With this declaration, the CSCE created an important link with the UN. In October 1993 the UN General Assembly unanimously adopted a resolution inviting the CSCE to participate in the Assembly sessions and work.

The Helsinki II summit meeting also established the post of High Commissioner on National Minorities (HCNM). The purpose of the HCNM is to provide early warning and early action to prevent tensions involving national minority issues from developing into a con-

---

[14] In particular, the CSCE decided to pursue relationships with the following European and transatlantic organizations: the Council of Europe, the UN Economic Commission for Europe, NATO, the WEU, the Organisation for Economic Co-operation and Development (OECD), the European Bank for Reconstruction and Development (EBRD), the European Investment Bank, and any others the CSCE saw fit.

flict. The Forum for Security Co-operation (FSC) was another creation. The FSC is a permanent negotiating body on arms control, CSBMs and other security-related issues.

By 1994 it was clear that the CSCE was assuming a central role in the management of change in Europe. At their Budapest Review Conference and Summit Meeting in December 1994, the CSCE leaders declared the new Organization to be the prime instrument for early warning, conflict prevention and crisis management in Europe. In 1997 the OSCE has had 10 long-duration conflict-prevention missions in the field as well as the Assistance Group to Chechnya and the Presence in Albania. For a limited period a number of Sanctions Assistance Missions were also established to monitor compliance with UN-imposed sanctions against the Federal Republic of Yugoslavia. The latter were launched to advise the authorities of the host countries on the implementation of the sanctions. In addition, the HCNM had become very active in tackling minority rights issues in Europe.

A year later, the OSCE was assigned several important tasks as part of the Dayton Agreement for Bosnia and Herzegovina. In particular, the OSCE is to play a key role in the post-conflict settlement and in the rebuilding of civil society in Bosnia and Herzegovina. The OSCE was given responsibility to prepare, conduct and monitor elections after first certifying when conditions will permit elections; to monitor human rights; and to assist the parties in their negotiations on sub-regional arms control[15] and CSBMs. The OSCE Presence in Albania was established in 1997 to assist the Personal Representative of the Chairman-in-Office, Dr Franz Vranitzky, in coordinating international assistance to Albania in a number of areas, including the rule of law, police reforms, military restructuring and economic reform.

Towards a new security agenda

The main result of the December 1996 OSCE Lisbon Summit was agreement to hold negotiations in early 1997 with the aim of adapting the CFE Treaty to the changing security environment in Europe. Another decision was reflected in the Lisbon Declaration on a Common and Comprehensive Security Model for Europe for the Twenty-First Century. Both decisions are seen as initiatives aimed at defusing Russian fears about NATO enlargement.

---

[15] These negotiations resulted in the 1996 Florence Agreement; see chapter 5, section 5.3.2.

The Lisbon Declaration identified the common elements for shaping a cooperative security system in Europe as being respect for human rights, fundamental freedoms and the rule of law, market economy and social justice. This also implies mutual confidence and peaceful settlement of disputes and excludes any quest for domination. The new political commitments undertaken in the Lisbon Security Model Declaration can be summarized as follows: 'to act in solidarity' to promote full implementation of the principles and norms adopted in different basic documents of the Helsinki process; to consult promptly with a participating state whose security is threatened and to consider 'jointly actions that may have to be undertaken in defence of our common values'; not to support those who are acting 'in violation of international law against the territorial integrity or political independence of any participating State'; and to attach importance to the security concerns of all participating states 'irrespective of whether they belong to military structures or arrangements'.

Of all the regions in the world, Europe has achieved the highest degree of institutionalized security cooperation. However, the focus is too often on organizational and procedural matters. The real problems, which call for a common approach, are often relegated to second place.

No single organization can assume all the responsibilities of the new European security architecture. The issue at stake is not so much how to enlarge membership but how to establish an efficient new system in Europe which will correspond to the new international security environment. The focus should therefore be more on the cooperation between the organizations and institutions than on their structures and procedures.

The process of unifying Europe should be based on accepting common democratic values and building security networks that can help prevent conflicts and find solutions to both common and individual security problems. In this regard, the Council of Europe is an important organization, whose activities in the field of human rights and fundamental freedoms and commitment to the promotion of democratic security in Europe[16] contribute to creating stability and security for individuals and states in the region.

---

[16] The Council first expressed this commitment at its first summit meeting, held in Vienna in Oct. 1993.

7.3   Asia–Pacific security: the emerging dialogue

Unlike Europe, the Asia–Pacific region does not have a tradition of regional institutions to address security concerns.[17] Instead, such issues have usually been dealt with by the parties immediately concerned or in global forums such as the United Nations.

In the early 1990s, however, the situation began to change, in large part because of the growing importance and influence of the states of South-East Asia. Their prosperity and peaceful international relations have provided the foundation for a broader Asia–Pacific dialogue.

The next section looks at the role played by South-East Asia in this process, before turning to the more difficult security situation of North-East Asia in section 7.3.2. Here, the divided nations of China and Korea present Asia's greatest security concerns.

7.3.1   South-East Asia

Several factors have led the nations of South-East Asia to be increasingly interested in a regional mechanism to discuss and resolve security issues. One of these factors is the changing role of the USA.

No longer facing the Soviet Union in the region, the USA has taken the opportunity to reduce its military presence in the Western Pacific. For example, the USA closed its military bases at Subic Bay and Clark Field in the Philippines in late 1992. The USA might have stayed but was asked to leave by the Philippine Government. The volcanic eruption of Mt Pinatubo in 1992, which damaged Clark Field, provided further impetus. There have also been closures in South Korea and Japan, and certain domestic constituencies in those countries question the justification for a continued US presence in the wake of the cold war.

Ever since the end of World War II, US military power, and in particular naval power, has been the dominant factor in the security equation of the Asia–Pacific. Indeed, during the cold war, the USA was the protector of much of the region's security interests. Because

---

[17] For the purposes of this discussion, the Asia–Pacific region includes South-East Asia—Brunei, Cambodia, Indonesia, Laos, Malaysia, Myanmar, the Philippines, Singapore, Thailand and Viet Nam—and North-East Asia—China (including Hong Kong), Japan, North Korea, South Korea, Macao, Mongolia, Russia and Taiwan) plus Australia, Canada, New Zealand, Papua New Guinea, Russia, the United States and the island states of the South Pacific.

of this, US force reductions, even gradual ones, have raised some fears of a power vacuum.

A second factor is internal stability. Armed communist and secessionist rebellions were long a feature of the politics of much of South-East Asia. Today, only the communist insurgency in the Philippines is notable. While there are still internal ethnic and religious conflicts, they are less destabilizing than communist insurgencies, which had broader, cold war implications.

This greater domestic stability has allowed governments in South-East Asia to focus on a third set of factors shaping multilateral approaches to security in the region: external issues which may be a source of regional conflict. For example, there are a number of territorial questions that deserve attention. The most serious of these is the Spratly Islands in the South China Sea.

The Spratly Islands are poorly delineated geographically, uninhabited, generally barren islets, rocks and coral reefs. Some of them are under water. None the less, seven governments lay claim to all or parts of the Spratlys. The reason for this competition is that there may be major deposits of energy resources—oil and gas—under the islands. In addition, numerous other territorial issues remain unresolved in South-East Asia.[18]

Fourth, South-East Asia's tremendous economic growth is an additional factor pushing along the security dialogue. The region has spent a great amount of energy in the past two decades on internal economic growth and nation-building. This has led to impressive economic expansion and increasing prosperity. Ironically, however, the same growth in economic prosperity has also led to increased military spending, creating fears of an arms race in the subregion.

With economic success in hand, governments in the region realized the value of developing economically oriented regional organizations to nurture and promote continued prosperity. In turn, this has paved the way for a regional security dialogue. Two forums have been particularly important in the evolution of this dialogue. They are the Association of South-East Asian Nations (ASEAN) and the Asia–Pacific Economic Co-operation (APEC).

---

[18] See Swinnerton, R., 'Strategic environment and arms acquisitions in South-East Asia', eds B. Gill and J. N. Mak, *Arms, Transparency and Security and South-East Asia*, SIPRI Research Report no. 13 (Oxford University Press; Oxford, 1997), table 3.1, p. 26.

Map of South-East Asia

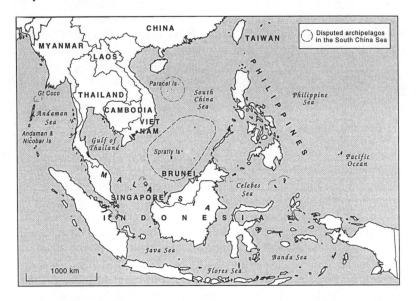

The Association of South-East Asian Nations

ASEAN was founded by the 1967 Bangkok Declaration by Indonesia, Malaysia, the Philippines, Singapore and Thailand. Brunei joined the organization in 1984 followed by Viet Nam in 1995, and Laos and Myanmar in 1997. The expected admission of Cambodia was post-poned owing to the violent leadership struggle taking place in the country.

One of ASEAN's original purposes was to promote the close-knit economic integration of its members. This achievement has been slow in coming, and only recently has the Association agreed on the goal of an ASEAN free trade area by the year 2007. None the less, ASEAN's existence and activities have given South-East Asia a political coher-ence that the Asia–Pacific region as a whole lacks. As a side benefit, by organizing themselves, the ASEAN member states gained political clout they would not have individually. This has given ASEAN a sig-nificant voice in the debate on Asia–Pacific security issues.

While one of its fundamental goals is peace and stability in the sub-region, ASEAN specifically excluded security issues from its agenda in 1976. In 1979, however, ASEAN opened the door to a greater security role when it established the ASEAN Post Ministerial Conference (ASEAN–PMC) with a number of 'dialogue partners': Australia, Canada, Japan, South Korea, New Zealand, the USA and the European Community (now the European Union).

The ASEAN–PMC allowed ASEAN members to discuss with its dialogue partners multilateral political and security issues of ASEAN's choosing. ASEAN went a step further in 1991 when it allowed China and Russia to have separate consultations during the ASEAN–PMC, although these two could not observe the actual PMC meetings.

After the creation of the ASEAN–PMC, the momentum grew for ASEAN to engage in broader regional security dialogue. Much of the enthusiasm for this initially came from outside the Association. For example, Japan sought an enhanced dialogue, in part so that it could play a political role in Asia that was more in line with its economic might. The USA had traditionally frowned on the idea of regional security structures in Asia, arguing that such a development would hamper the ability of the USA to pursue its interests. None the less, having reduced its military presence in the Pacific, the USA began to view an Asian regional security dialogue in a different light. In 1993 US policy shifted and it called for the development of 'new mechanisms to manage or prevent' emerging regional problems.[19] The USA thereby removed a significant barrier to states in the region taking a more active role in managing their security interests.

Later in 1993, the ASEAN Ministerial Meeting surprised observers when it decided to establish the ASEAN Regional Forum (ARF) as a forum for discussion of regional political and security issues and development of cooperative measures. The first ARF meeting was held in 1994, and membership now stands at 21 (see chapter 9, section 9.3). Sensing the growing interest in a regional security dialogue, ASEAN saw the advantage of leading it and providing its foundation.

[19] *SIPRI Yearbook 1994*, p. 141.

The Asia–Pacific Economic Co-operation

The economic growth of the Asia–Pacific has resulted not only from its trade with North America and Europe but also from intra-Asian trade. Trade within Asia has led to strong economic interdependencies and a sense of economic regionalism. Non-governmental and mixed government and non-governmental trade bodies have played a role in fostering greater economic cooperation in the region. Not until 1989, however, was a strictly government-level body set up to promote regional trade. At the suggestion of Australia, APEC was created.

Made up of Asia–Pacific 'participating economies' instead of states, APEC promotes economic trade and growth in the region.[20] Its member economies are Australia, Brunei, Canada, Chile, China, Hong Kong (China), Indonesia, Japan, South Korea, Malaysia, Mexico, New Zealand, Papua New Guinea, the Philippines, Singapore, 'Chinese Taipei' (Taiwan), Thailand and the USA. APEC holds annual ministerial meetings and has a Secretariat in Singapore.

In 1993 APEC met for the first time at the level of heads of government. The APEC members held an 'informal leadership conference' in Seattle, Washington, following the fifth APEC Annual Ministerial Meeting. This was the largest gathering of Asia–Pacific heads of government in some 30 years. Subsequent APEC summit meetings have been held in 1994 (Bogor, Indonesia), 1995 (Osaka, Japan), 1996 (Manila, the Philippines) and 1997 (Vancouver, Canada).

Over time, it is likely that APEC will add more members, although its role will probably remain limited to economics and trade. The presence of both Taiwan and China will effectively keep APEC away from sensitive political and security issues.

The South-East Asia nuclear weapon-free zone

The South-East Asian states had for many years proclaimed their intention to establish a regional nuclear weapon-free zone. It was, however, only with the end of the cold war and the withdrawal of US bases from the Philippines that movement on the issue was possible. Following surprisingly rapid negotiations, on 15 December 1995 the

---

[20] By making 'economies' members instead of states, APEC convinced China, Hong Kong and Taiwan to join. The political significance of this development will be better understood after reading section 7.3.2.

Southeast Asia Nuclear-Weapon-Free Zone Treaty, also known as the Treaty of Bangkok, was opened for signature. This treaty prohibits the development, manufacture, acquisition or testing of nuclear weapons inside or outside the zone area as well as the stationing and transport of nuclear weapons. The parties should conclude agreements to apply IAEA safeaguards to their peaceful nuclear activities. The treaty entered into force in March 1997. However, none of the five declared nuclear weapon states had, by November, signed the protocol to the treaty. This protocol would oblige them to undertake not to use or threaten to use nuclear weapons against any state party to the treaty or within the zone.

7.3.2   North-East Asia

Supporters of multilateral approaches to security have reason to be optimistic about overall developments in the Asia–Pacific region in the 1990s. However, the subregion of North-East Asia remains hostage to the legacy of the cold war.

In particular, strained relations between mainland China and Taiwan and between North and South Korea remain a threat to peace and stability. While there have been some modest multilateral efforts to improve dialogue between these governments, it is their bilateral relations which dominate the security politics of North-East Asia.

Multilateral security institutions, as they have developed in Europe and on an international level, tend to be highly public, universalist in membership and egalitarian—that is, all members have a seat and a role to play. In contrast, in the tradition of Asia, political talks are better conducted in a private, informal setting in which hierarchy is important. Within the Asia–Pacific as a whole, and in North-East Asia in particular, Western approaches to multilateral security are not widely accepted.

North-East Asia has had a long history of upheaval and conflict which has meant that 'normal' international relations have only recently begun to take hold. Patterns of cooperation, peaceful dialogue and exchange are not yet deeply rooted. It must be remembered that in this century millions of lives were lost in the Chinese Civil War and in the wars in Korea and Viet Nam. In addition, there are still many bitter memories of Japan's treatment of its neighbours during World War II.

Map of North-East Asia

The security pattern established by the USSR and the USA after World War II must also be considered. The USA developed strong bilateral relationships, especially with Japan and South Korea. The Soviet Union was also a major influence in the region, particularly in North Korea and North Viet Nam.

During the cold war, the superpowers held considerable sway over the debate on security in North-East Asia. They defined the issues and developed bilateral security structures and relationships. This drew client states close to their superpower but also helped to keep them apart from other states in the region.

Today, in the absence of this superpower rivalry, security issues are much more fluid. In the 1990s, North-East Asia has greater latitude to define its own security interests but at the same time lacks a clear framework or set of guidelines.

Domestic considerations

Throughout North-East Asia, domestic politics have also played a part in the slow development of regional security institutions. In China, the domestic scene was in early 1997 dominated by the question of what course it would take and which person or faction would emerge to lead China following the death of Deng Xiaoping in February. Under the new leader, Jiang Zemin, many issues were clarified at the 15th Chinese Party Congress in September, but the vexing longer-term questions of political and social reform will remain.

Taiwan has undergone a process of reform and democratization. This has led to open political divisions within President Lee Teng-hui's Nationalist Party (Kuomintang or KMT) and within the popula-tion of Taiwan at large. The increasingly public political debate in Taiwan has revealed a growing split between Taiwanese who believe that unification with mainland China remains desirable and those who think that Taiwan should abandon this long-held policy. Even with President Lee's 1996 victory in the first direct presidential election in Taiwan, he must carefully balance the political scene on the island.

The delicate relations between North and South Korea were com-plicated by the death in 1994 of North Korean President Kim Il Sung, who had firmly ruled the country for over four decades. Although the late president groomed his son Kim Jong Il to take his place, it remains uncertain how firm a grip the younger Kim has on power. The newly developed democracy in South Korea has grown stronger in the mid-1990s but continues to face numerous challenges.

These kinds of domestic uncertainty have delayed the evolution of multilateralism in North-East Asia.

Emerging multilateralism in North-East Asia

During the cold war, the Soviet Union had made numerous declara-tions of support for such arrangements in the Asia–Pacific region as a whole, but the USA and other key countries were lukewarm to the idea.

In 1992 South Korean President Roh Tae Woo reiterated a proposal he first made in 1988. He called for a Consultative Conference for Peace in North-East Asia. Later that same year Russian President Boris Yeltsin expressed support for President Roh's idea. None the less, it did not come to pass.

The modest progress to date in building institutions has not been the result of government proposals but of non-governmental initiatives.

The Council for Security and Co-operation in the Asia–Pacific (CSCAP), the North Pacific Co-operative Security Dialogue (NPCSD) and a third, 'quasi-official', 'track two' dialogue, the North-East Asia Cooperation Dialogue (NEACD), have brought together scholars and regional officials acting in their private capacities only.

CSCAP was officially launched in June 1993 by 10 non-governmental research institutes in Australia, Canada, Indonesia, Japan, South Korea, Malaysia, the Philippines, Singapore, Thailand and the USA. Since then, China, North Korea, Mongolia, New Zealand, Russia and Viet Nam have joined. The European Union and India have joined as associate members. It was created to provide a process for regional confidence building and security cooperation among the countries and territories in the Asia–Pacific.

The NPCSD programme, funded by Canada, brought together scholars and officials from Canada, China, Japan, North Korea, South Korea, Russia and the USA for workshops and conferences. After its meetings, the NPCSD generated a series of follow-on studies.

However, the bilateral relations between North and South Korea and between China and Taiwan present considerable hurdles to creating government-level security institutions in North-East Asia.

North and South Korea

In 1953 the Korean Armistice Agreement between North Korea and the United Nations ended the Korean War. A peace treaty never followed. Technically, a state of war still exists. South Korea (the Republic of Korea) and North Korea (the Democratic People's Republic of Korea) are separated by a demilitarized zone (DMZ) and share the distinction of having the world's most heavily militarized border. Their respective forces are constantly prepared for battle and the animosities left from the war are still an obstacle to peaceful reunification. None the less, there has been some progress.

Almost 20 years after the end of the Korean War, North and South Korea signalled a thaw in their relations when they published a seven-point communiqué in 1972, agreeing to end hostility and work together for peaceful reunification. This official channel of dialogue was used only sparingly until 1991, when the two sides agreed on new formal accords.[21] A preliminary series of discussions was initiated in August 1997 among China, North Korea, South Korea and the United States. The discussions were intended to set the agenda for the proposed 'Four Party Talks' among these countries which, among other objectives, would negotiate a formal peace treaty to conclude the Korean War.

There were no official trade ties between the two Korean states before 1989. Since then, trade has grown steadily. North Korea is not a major customer for the South, but South Korea is the North's third largest trading partner after Japan and China. Trade relations took a considerable step forward in November 1994, when South Korea ended a ban on direct business investment in the North. This policy shift resulted in joint ventures between the two countries. It has been humanitarian issues, however, that have resulted in the most contacts between North Korea and its neighbours to the south and the rest of the world.

A grain shortage and widespread flooding in North Korea in 1995 forced the North Korean Government to turn to the outside world for assistance. Estimates of the extent of the food shortage ranged between 25 and 38 per cent of North Korea's annual requirements, particularly in rice. In June 1995 talks began in Beijing, China, between North and South Korea. Agreement was quickly reached that South Korea would ship 150 000 tonnes of rice free of charge, but when North Korean authorities seized a South Korean vessel carrying rice, the talks were suspended. South Korea has said that it will not continue to provide food aid until the North agrees to a North–South dialogue on peace and the political future of the peninsula. A typhoon in 1997 exacerbated an increasingly desperate situation for the North.

---

[21] In Dec. 1991 North and South Korea signed the Agreement on Reconciliation, Non-aggression, Exchange and Co-operation and announced that they had signed a Joint Declaration on the Denuclearization of the Korean Peninsula, formally issued in Jan. 1992. Both agreements entered into force in Feb. 1992.

The US–South Korean security relationship

When the Korean War broke out in 1950, it was the USA which pushed the United Nations to respond, and US troops made up the bulk of the forces serving under the UN flag in Korea. Since then, the USA and South Korea have maintained a very close security relationship, formalized by a mutual security pact. Today, some 37 000 US forces are stationed in South Korea. Their presence has often generated heated rhetoric from North Korea, and their removal would be a major demand of the North Koreans in any peace settlement.

Nuclear proliferation on the Korean Peninsula

In 1992 North and South Korea issued the North–South Joint Declaration on the Denuclearization of the Korean Peninsula. The two sides agreed not to 'test, manufacture, receive, possess, store, deploy or use nuclear weapons'. However, they did not take steps to formally implement the Denuclearization Declaration.

Despite this declaration, the nuclear issue created a serious crisis in the early 1990s. Because it was suspected that North Korea may have had sufficient fissile material to build a nuclear weapon or might already have done so, the international community became involved.

In the 1980s North Korea had built a nuclear research reactor that produced plutonium as a by-product. Plutonium is a key ingredient in nuclear weapons. In 1985 North Korea became a party to the Non-Proliferation Treaty (NPT) but did not conclude a safeguards agreement with the International Atomic Energy Agency (IAEA) until 1992.[22] In its initial examination of the reactor's activities, the IAEA raised concerns that North Korea had produced and stored more plutonium than it was willing to admit.

This was the beginning of a serious nuclear proliferation crisis. In March 1993 North Korea announced that it would withdraw from the NPT as from 12 June. On 11 June, however, it suspended its withdrawal, after the UN Security Council had called on North Korea to honour its obligations and allow IAEA inspectors to complete their work.

---

[22] The NPT requires non-nuclear weapon states parties to conclude safeguards agreements with the IAEA which must enter into force not later than 18 months after the date of initiation of negotiations.

There were also incidents in 1994 in which North Korea resisted IAEA efforts and was reported to be in non-compliance with its NPT safeguards obligations. On 13 June 1994, North Korea renounced its IAEA membership, which took effect in September.

The USA undertook intense diplomatic efforts in 1994 to resolve the crises, adopting a two-track approach. On the one hand, it provided air-defence missiles to South Korea and boosted its naval presence off Korean shores. On the other hand, it launched direct negotiations with North Korea, which followed a mediation effort by former US President Jimmy Carter.

This strategy resulted in the Agreed Framework signed by the USA and North Korea in October 1994. In the Agreed Framework, North Korea agreed to take steps to implement the 1992 Joint Declaration on the Denuclearization of the Korean Peninsula and close the nuclear facilities it had built, to remain a party to the NPT and eventually to allow the IAEA to apply full safeguards to its nuclear facilities. In return, the agreement stipulated that the USA must lead a project to build two light-water nuclear reactors (LWRs) for North Korea and supply fuel oil to help it meet its energy needs.

To build the LWRs, an international consortium was formed by Japan, the USA and South Korea—the Korean Peninsula Energy Development Organization (KEDO). KEDO was necessary because of the political sensitivities of the North Koreans who did not want to see South Korea playing the lead role in the LWR project. None the less, South Korea will make the largest financial and material contribution to the Agreed Framework and the construction of the LWRs. Implementing the Framework will further develop North–South ties and a long-term channel for official discussions on nuclear-related issues. Ground was officially broken for the construction project in August 1997, and the total cost is estimated at approximately $5.5 billion.

The China–Taiwan dialogue

As the Chinese civil war drew to a close in 1949 and it was clear that the Communist Party would prevail, the Nationalist leaders and their supporters fled to the island of Taiwan, across the Taiwan Strait from mainland China. Since then, Taiwan's political status has proved a difficult point in North-East Asian politics and has also been troublesome for other states in their relations with China and Taiwan.

The People's Republic of China (mainland China) maintains that Taiwan is an integral and subordinate part of the People's Republic—or, 'one China, two systems'. On the other hand, the government on Taiwan (which uses the term Republic of China) agrees that Taiwan is part of China, but holds that Taiwan possesses a separate identity as a 'political entity' that is equal to that of the mainland—or, 'one China, two equal political entities'.

Since the civil war, the Communist Party has ruled China and the Nationalist Party (or KMT) has ruled Taiwan. Each has pursued its own political and economic system, with Taiwan becoming particularly prosperous and relatively well developed. In the mid- to late 1980s the communist leadership in China began to loosen its grip on the Chinese economy while firmly controlling the political system. Today, the economy of mainland China is one of the fastest growing in the world.

In the 1990s there have been several initiatives to improve economic relations and other contacts across the Taiwan Strait. What remains unchanged, however, is the gulf between the two parties' views of the political status of Taiwan.

To handle ties with the mainland, the unofficial Straits Exchange Foundation (SEF) was established in Taiwan in March 1991. In December of that year, China set up the Association for Relations Across the Taiwan Straits (ARATS). These bodies are a channel for semi-official dialogue between the two sides. The chairmen of the two organizations first met for talks in April 1993, and by the end of 1996 a total of 11 rounds of meetings between ARATS and the SEF had taken place. These discussions generated some modest results, but the fragile nature of the entire exercise became clear in June 1995.

In June the ARATS and SEF talks were suspended by China. The Chinese were angered by the decision of the USA to allow President Lee Teng-hui to visit the USA. Tensions increased when China decided to hold military exercises and missile tests in waters north of Taiwan. These were designed to pressure Taiwan as it approached its first democratic presidential elections in March 1996. By the end of 1996, the ARATS–SEF channel was still in place but had not been reactivated.

Not until November 1987 did Taiwan allow a partial lifting of its ban on travel to China. In September 1990 the respective Red Cross societies of Taiwan and China signed an agreement on returning illegal immigrants. Before June 1993 there was no direct mail delivery between Taiwan and China. These are just a few examples of the small forward moves in people-to-people contacts that have taken place in recent years.

On the economic front, the two sides have experienced considerable growth in their relations. Taiwan's exports and investments in China have grown steadily in the 1990s and by 1995 China was its second-largest export market, despite the fact that official Taiwan policy prohibits direct transport and trade ties (trade between China and Taiwan typically passes through Hong Kong).

Both the Chinese and the Taiwanese leadership have made economic exchange and promotion of Chinese culture key elements of their reunification proposals. These contacts can help build mutual confidence and trust. Even so, the competing political, social and economic systems of the two sides continue to make progress towards reconciliation and reunification extremely slow and tense. With the reversion of Hong Kong to Chinese sovereignty in July 1997, China and Taiwan will be carefully watching the successes and failures of the former colony under the auspices of 'one country, two systems'. With Macao scheduled to revert to Chinese sovereignty in 1999, increasing political pressure will mount on both sides of the Straits— both for and against—on the issue of Taiwan's reunification with the mainland.

8. Chronology of major events related to peace, security and conflict prevention, 1992–96

1992

16 Jan.   The Salvadoran Government and the Farabundo Marti National Liberation Front (FMLN) sign a peace agreement to officially end the 11-year civil war. The UN Observer Mission in El Salvador (ONUSAL) is to monitor the disarmament of the FMLN forces and supervise a 50% reduction of the Salvadoran Army.

20 Jan.   North and South Korea issue a Joint Declaration on the Denuclearization of the Korean Peninsula.

28 Jan.   US President George Bush announces deeper cuts in US strategic weapons than those required by the 1991 Strategic Arms Reduction Treaty (START).

29 Jan.   Russian President Boris Yeltsin proposes to the USA that each side should reduce its nuclear warheads to 2000–2500.

30 Jan.   North Korea signs a safeguards agreement with the International Atomic Energy Agency (IAEA), allowing inspection of all its nuclear facilities.

30–31 Jan.   The Conference on Security and Co-operation in Europe (CSCE) admits all the nations of the Commonwealth of Independent States (CIS) as member states.

31 Jan.   The heads of state and government of the member states of the UN Security Council adopt a joint statement, asking the UN Secretary-General to recommend how the Council can take a more active and positive role in preserving peace and averting crises. This is the first UN Security Council summit meeting since the UN was founded.

7 Feb.   The Treaty on European Union (Maastricht Treaty) is signed.

21 Feb.   The UN Security Council adopts Resolution 743, establishing a UN Protection Force (UNPROFOR) to create the conditions of peace and security required for settlement of the Yugoslav crises.

28 Feb.   The UN Security Council adopts Resolution 745, authorizing the establishment of a UN Transitional Authority in Cambodia (UNTAC) to oversee the country's transition to a new administration after multi-party elections.

29 Feb.– *1 Mar.*	Over 99% of the voters in Bosnia and Herzegovina vote in favour of independence. A great majority of the Serb population boycotts the referendum. On *3 Mar.* Bosnia and Herzegovina declares independence.
9 Mar.	China accedes to the 1968 Non-Proliferation Treaty (NPT).
24 Mar.	The Treaty on Open Skies, providing for a system of unarmed reconnaissance flights over the entire territory of each of the parties, is signed by the NATO member states, as well as Belarus, Bulgaria, Czechoslovakia, Georgia, Hungary, Poland, Romania, Russia and Ukraine.
25 Mar.	The International Atomic Energy Agency (IAEA) announces its decision to destroy Iraqi facilities and equipment designed for producing nuclear devices. The demolition takes place on *13 Apr.*
8 Apr.	The French Prime Minister announces that France will stop nuclear testing until the end of 1992.
24 Apr.	The UN Security Council adopts Resolution 751, establishing a UN Operation in Somalia (UNOSOM).
27 Apr.	Serbia and Montenegro announce the formation of a new state: the Federal Republic of Yugoslavia (FRY).
15 May	Meeting in Tashkent, Armenia, Azerbaijan, Belarus, Georgia, Kazakhstan, Moldova, Russia and Ukraine agree on how to implement the 1990 Treaty on Conventional Armed Forces in Europe (CFE Treaty).
23 May	Meeting in Lisbon, the US Secretary of State and the Foreign Ministers of Belarus, Kazakhstan, Russia and Ukraine sign the Lisbon Protocol to facilitate the implementation of the 1991 START I Treaty. Belarus, Kazakhstan, Russia and Ukraine agree to assume the obligations of the USSR under START I.
30 May	The UN Security Council adopts Resolution 757, imposing sanctions, including a trade embargo, on Yugoslavia (Serbia and Montenegro).
3–14 June	The UN Conference on Environment and Development (UNCED, or the 'Earth Summit') is held in Rio de Janeiro. It adopts the Rio Declaration, which includes a principle stating that, in times of armed conflict, states should respect international law providing protection for the environment.
19 June	The WEU Council of Ministers, meeting in Petersberg, Germany, decides to empower the WEU with military forces drawn from its members to engage in different kinds of mission and to ensure the collective defence of all NATO member states.
2 July	President Bush announces that all US ground-launched and naval tactical nuclear weapons abroad have been withdrawn.

1992 contd

10 July	The Concluding Act of the Negotiation on Personnel Strength of Conventional Armed Forces in Europe (CFE-1A Agreement), which places politically binding limits on military personnel in the Atlantic-to-the-Urals (ATTU) zone, is signed in Helsinki by the NATO states and Armenia, Azerbaijan, Belarus, Bulgaria, Czechoslovakia, Georgia, Hungary, Kazakhstan, Moldova, Poland, Romania, Russia and Ukraine.
3 Aug.	France accedes to the 1968 Non-Proliferation Treaty (NPT).
13 Aug.	The UN Security Council adopts Resolution 770, authorizing the use of force, if necessary, to ensure the delivery of humanitarian aid to Bosnia and Herzegovina.
17 Aug.	The UN Security Council adopts Resolution 772, authorizing the Secretary-General to deploy a UN Observer Mission to South Africa (UNOMSA).
19 Aug.	In a Joint Declaration on the complete prohibition of chemical weapons, India and Pakistan undertake not to use, develop, produce or otherwise acquire chemical weapons or encourage anyone to engage in such activities.
28 Aug.	The UN Security Council adopts Resolution 775, endorsing the Secretary-General's request for 3500 security troops to be sent to Somalia.
19 Sep.	The UN Security Council adopts Resolution 777, recommending that Yugoslavia (Serbia and Montenegro) should not participate in the General Assembly and that it should apply for membership in the UN. On *22 Sep.* the General Assembly adopts Resolution 47/1 to the same effect.
2 Oct.	President Bush signs a bill containing provisions for a nine-month moratorium on nuclear testing and a three-year period of regulated testing, culminating in a complete ban on all US nuclear testing from *1 Oct. 1996,* provided no other state tests after that date. The moratorium is extended by US President Clinton on *3 July 1993* and *30 Jan. 1995.*
4 Oct.	The President of Mozambique and the leader of the Mozambique National Resistance (MNR) sign a General Peace Agreement ending the country's 16-year civil war.
9 Nov.	The 1990 Treaty on Conventional Armed Forces in Europe (CFE Treaty) enters into force.
3 Dec.	The UN Security Council adopts Resolution 794, authorizing a major multinational military force to use all necessary means to secure the delivery of humanitarian aid to Somalia. On *4 Dec.* the USA announces that it has offered to lead this military force.

16 Dec.   The UN Security Council adopts Resolution 797, establishing a UN Operation in Mozambique (ONUMOZ).

1993

1 Jan.   The Czechoslovak Federation splits into the Czech Republic and Slovakia.

3 Jan.   Presidents Bush and Yeltsin sign the START II Treaty.

7 Jan.   Iraq declares it will not allow the UN to transport its personnel into Iraq using UN aircraft. In response, US and British air forces attack military targets in Iraq on *13 Jan.* On *17 Jan.* US warships launch 40 cruise missiles at military targets outside Baghdad. Iraq agrees to allow UN flights into Iraq on a case-by-case basis and offers a cease-fire on *19 Jan.*

13 Jan.   The Convention on the Prohibition of the Development, Production, Stockpiling and Use of Chemical Weapons and on their Destruction (Chemical Weapons Convention, or CWC) is signed in Paris.

15 Jan.   For the first time, NATO says that it is willing to carry out military operations outside its area, in support of UN operations in Bosnia and Herzegovina.

18 Feb.   Russia and the USA sign the Highly Enriched Uranium (HEU) Agreement in Washington, DC. It commits the USA to purchasing Russian HEU from dismantled nuclear warheads.

22 Feb.   The UN Security Council adopts Resolution 808, establishing an international tribunal for the prosecution of persons responsible for serious violations of international humanitarian law committed in the former Yugoslavia.

7 Mar.   A Peace Accord is signed by the President of Afghanistan, the leader of one faction of the Hizp-e-Islami and six Mujahideen leaders.

12 Mar.   North Korea announces it will withdraw from the Non-Proliferation Treaty (NPT) on *12 June 1993*. It considers International Atomic Energy Agency (IAEA) requests to inspect two military installations to be interference with its internal affairs and a hostile act.

24 Mar.   South Africa discloses that it developed and produced nuclear weapons in the late 1970s. The weapons were dismantled and destroyed before South Africa acceded to the Non-Proliferation Treaty (NPT) in 1991.

1993 contd

26 Mar.   The UN Security Council adopts Resolution 814, approving a new UN Peacekeeping Operation for Somalia (UNOSOM II) that will have the authority to use force, if necessary, to disarm factions and ensure the delivery of humanitarian aid. UNOSOM II will replace the multinational force headed by the USA.

1 Apr.   The International Atomic Energy Agency (IAEA) reports to the UN that North Korea is in non-compliance with its nuclear safeguards obligations under the Non-Proliferation Treaty (NPT).

13 May   The USA announces that the Strategic Defense Initiative Organization (SDIO) has been renamed the Ballistic Missile Defense Organization, and its emphasis will shift from strategic to theatre defences against ballistic missiles.

23–28 May   The UN Transitional Authority in Cambodia (UNTAC) conducts elections in Cambodia as provided under the 1991 Paris Peace Accords.

11 June   After talks with the USA, North Korea suspends its withdrawal from the Non-Proliferation Treaty (NPT). The USA and North Korea agree on the principles of assurances against the threat and use of force, including nuclear weapons, and on peace and security in a nuclear-free Korean Peninsula, including full-scope nuclear safeguards.

16 June   The UN Security Council adopts Resolution 841, authorizing a world-wide oil and arms embargo against Haiti. Unless sufficient progress has been made to return Haiti's deposed President Aristide to power by 23 June, the sanctions will take effect. They were suspended on *16 June.*

3 July   A peace agreement mediated by the UN and the Organization of American States (OAS) is signed by the exiled Haitian President and the leader of the coup of Sep. 1991.

25 July   A peace agreement is signed to end the civil war raging since 1990 in Liberia. On *22 Sep.* the UN Security Council decides to establish a UN Observer Mission in Liberia (UNOMIL) to monitor the peace accord.

27 July   A cease-fire agreement, mediated by Russia, is signed by the President of Georgia and the Abkhazian leader. On *24 Aug.* the UN Security Council adopts Resolution 858, establishing a UN Observer Mission in Georgia (UNOMIG) to verify compliance with the agreement. However, the Abkhazian offensive resumes on *16 Sep.*

4 Aug.	A peace agreement is signed between the Rwandan Government and the Patriotic Front. The two parties call for a UN mission to implement the peace. On *6 Apr.* fighting breaks out after the president is killed in an air crash.
30 Aug.	After 14 months of secret talks, sponsored by Norway, Israeli and Palestine Liberation Organization (PLO) officials agree to a Declaration of Principles (the Oslo Agreement).
7 Sep.	India and China sign an Agreement on the Maintenance of Peace and Tranquillity along their border areas.
13 Sep.	The Declaration of Principles is signed by the Israeli and PLO Foreign Ministers. According to the Declaration Israel will, during a five-year period, withdraw from the Gaza Strip and from the West Bank town of Jericho. A permanent Palestine settlement, based on Security Council Resolution 242 (1967) and Resolution 338 (1973), will be established in the area. The accord is also signed by the US Secretary of State and the Russian Foreign Minister.
14 Sep.	Israel and Jordan sign the Israel and Jordan Initial and Common Agenda, pledging to start negotiations on a comprehensive peace treaty, based on UN Security Council Resolutions 242 and 338.
21 Sep.	President Yeltsin, claiming that it has blocked economic and constitutional reform, issues a decree declaring the suspension of the Russian Parliament.
23–24 Sep.	The Russian Parliament votes to impeach President Yeltsin. The Parliament building is sealed off by the president's troops. On *4 Oct.* President Yeltsin's opponents, under siege in the parliament building, are forced to surrender.
5 Oct.	The UN Security Council adopts Resolution 872, establishing the UN Assistance Mission for Rwanda (UNAMIR).
8 Oct.	The UN General Assembly adopts Resolution 48/1, lifting the economic sanctions imposed on South Africa in 1962.
20–21 Oct.	The US Defense Secretary proposes a Partnership for Peace (PFP) allowing the Central and East European countries to establish defence-related cooperation agreements with NATO. The PFP is later launched at the NATO summit meeting in *Jan. 1994.*
1 Nov.	The Treaty on European Union (Maastricht Treaty) enters into force.
9 Nov.	The Russian and Chinese defence ministers sign a five-year military cooperation agreement.
17 Nov.	The South African Government and the African National Congress (ANC) sign an agreement on an interim constitution to end white minority rule in South Africa.

1993 contd

15 Dec.   The British and Irish prime ministers sign a declaration (the Downing Street Declaration) setting out general principles for holding peace talks on Northern Ireland.

1994

14 Jan.   The US, Russian and Ukrainian Presidents announce agreement on the transfer of all Ukrainian nuclear weapons to Russia for dismantlement. The USA will provide technical and financial assistance.

14 Jan.   The US and Russian Presidents agree that by *30 May* the USA and Russia will no longer target each other's strategic nuclear missiles.

12 Feb.   The final consignment of highly enriched uranium (HEU) is removed from Iraq, in accordance with UN Security Council Resolution 687 (1991). This resolution called for the complete removal of declared stocks of nuclear weapon-grade material from Iraq.

28 Feb.   NATO aircraft shoot down four Serbian fighter-bombers which were in violation of the UN prohibition against unauthorized flights in the airspace of Bosnia and Herzegovina. This is the first NATO military action since the alliance was created in 1949.

20 Mar.   Under supervision of the UN, the first round of free elections for the presidency and the legislative assembly is held in El Salvador.

10 Apr.   In response to the continued bombing by Bosnian Serbs of the Muslim enclave of Gorazde, NATO conducts its first air strike against Bosnian Serb positions.

26–29 Apr.   Nelson Mandela is elected President of South Africa in that country's first democratic election.

4 May   The Palestine Liberation Organization (PLO) and Israel sign an agreement providing for Palestinian self-rule in the Gaza Strip and Jericho, as stipulated under the 1993 Israel–PLO Declaration of Principles.

14 May   An Agreement on a Cease-fire and Separation of Forces is signed in Moscow by Georgian and Abkhazian representatives.

17 May   The UN Security Council adopts Resolution 918B, declaring an arms embargo against the parties to the conflict in Rwanda.

25 May   The UN Security Council lifts the 1977 embargo on the sale of arms to South Africa and the 1984 ban on the purchase of arms from South Africa.

13 June   Following an International Atomic Energy Agency (IAEA) resolution withdrawing technical aid to North Korea, North Korea announces its withdrawal from the IAEA.

22 *June*	Russia signs the NATO Partnership for Peace (PFP) Framework Document.
22 *June*	The UN Security Council adopts Resolution 929, supporting the plan for a French-led force to move into Rwanda with the mandate to use all necessary means to protect civilians and humanitarian aid operations.
25 *July*	Jordanian King Hussein and Israeli Prime Minister Rabin sign a Declaration pledging to end hostilities and to settle conflicts between the two states by peaceful means in the future.
27 *July*	The defence ministers of Armenia and Azerbaijan and the military commander of Nagorno-Karabakh sign an agreement formalizing a cease-fire.
31 *July*	The UN Security Council adopts Resolution 940 authorizing a Multinational Force (MNF) under unified command to use all necessary means to restore the Aristide government to power in Haiti.
31 *Aug.*	The Irish Republican Army (IRA) announces a cease-fire.
31 *Aug.*	The last former Soviet troops leave eastern Germany, Estonia and Latvia.
5–7 *Sep.*	The first combined international peacekeeping training exercise with US and Russian troops is held in Totskoe, Russia.
8 *Sep.*	The last US, British and French troops leave Berlin.
12–16 *Sep.*	The first training exercise under NATO's Partnership for Peace (PFP) programme is held in Poland.
26 *Sep.*	President Clinton addresses the UN General Assembly and calls for a UN global regime to eventually eliminate all the world's land-mines.
13 *Oct.*	Protestant groups in Northern Ireland announce a cease-fire.
21 *Oct.*	North Korea and the USA sign the Agreed Framework in which North Korea agrees to close one nuclear reactor and to stop building two others which could produce weapon-grade plutonium. North Korea agrees to abide by the Non-Proliferation Treaty (NPT) and accept full-scope International Atomic Energy Agency (IAEA) safeguards. The USA will contribute to the financing of two light-water reactors in North Korea. The USA and North Korea agree to low-level diplomatic relations.
26 *Oct.*	Jordanian King Hussein and Israeli Prime Minister Rabin sign a peace agreement.
27–29 *Oct.*	Under UN supervision, free elections are held in Mozambique for the first time.
13 *Nov.*	Iraq informs the UN Security Council that it recognizes the sovereignty, territorial integrity and political independence of Kuwait.

1994 contd

16 Nov.   The 1982 UN Convention on the Law of the Sea (UNCLOS) enters into force.

20 Nov.   A Protocol, brokered by the UN, is signed by the Government of Angola and the National Union for the Total Independence of Angola (UNITA). A cease-fire is proclaimed as of *22 Nov.*

29 Nov.   President Yeltsin issues an ultimatum demanding the disarmament of 'illegal armed formations' in Chechnya. (Chechnya declared itself an independent state in 1991.)

5 Dec.   The 1991 START I Treaty enters into force.

9 Dec.   President Yeltsin authorizes the Russian military to use force in Chechnya.

21 Dec.   After the breakdown of the peace agreement of July 1993, a new peace agreement is signed by the warring parties in Liberia.

1995

8 Feb.   The UN Security Council authorizes the establishment of the UN Angola Verification Mission (UNAVEM III) to implement the Nov. 1994 Lusaka Protocol between the warring parties in Angola.

20–21 Mar.   In Paris, the Pact on Stability in Europe (a French proposal from 1993) is adopted by over 50 states, for inclusion in the EU Common Foreign and Security Policy. The instruments and procedures are handed over to the Organization for Security and Co-operation in Europe (OSCE).

31 Mar.   The UN Mission in Haiti (UNMIH) takes over responsibility for Haiti from the US-led Multinational Force (MNF).

31 Mar.   The failed UN Operation in Somalia (UNOSOM II) ends. The withdrawal is assisted by a seven-nation operation ('United Shield').

6 Apr.   At the Conference on Disarmament (CD) the five declared nuclear weapon states each pledges that it will not use nuclear weapons against non-nuclear weapon states parties to the Non-Proliferation Treaty (NPT) and will come to the assistance of a non-nuclear weapon state attacked with, or threatened by the use of, nuclear weapons.

11 Apr.   In advance of the Non-Proliferation Treaty (NPT) Review and Extension Conference, the UN Security Council adopts a resolution taking note of the security assurances given by nuclear weapon states not to use nuclear weapons against non-nuclear weapon states parties to the NPT.

17 Apr.– *12 May*	The Non-Proliferation Treaty (NPT) Review and Extension Conference is held in New York. Without a formal vote, the delegates endorse an indefinite extension of the NPT. A Declaration of Principles and Objectives for Nuclear Proliferation and Disarmament, as well as a decision on strengthening the review process, are also adopted.
13 June	French President Chirac announces that France will end its nuclear testing moratorium and carry out eight underground explosions in French Polynesia between Sep. 1995 and May 1996, and that France will halt all tests by May 1996 and sign a comprehensive test ban treaty (CTBT). (Five tests are conducted in 1995 and one in 1996.)
17 Aug.	At a meeting of the UN Special Commission on Iraq (UNSCOM) in Baghdad, Iraq discloses for the first time that it has a full-scale programme for biological weapon development.
8 Sep.	The foreign ministers of Bosnia and Herzegovina, Croatia and Yugoslavia (Serbia and Montenegro), meeting in Geneva with representatives of the Contact Group (France, Germany, Russia the UK and the USA), sign an agreement covering the basic principles of a peace accord. The Principles for a Comprehensive Peace Settlement in Bosnia and Herzegovina include the continued existence of Bosnia within its present international borders.
25 Sep.	At the Review Conference of the 1981 Convention on Prohibitions or Restrictions on the Use of Certain Conventional Weapons Which May Be Deemed to be Excessively Injurious or to Have Indiscriminate Effects (Certain Conventional Weapons Convention, or CCW Convention), a new Protocol IV, restricting the use of blinding laser weapons, is agreed.
26 Sep.	NATO presents to Russia a draft proposal for a political framework for NATO–Russian relations beyond the Partnership for Peace (PFP).
28 Sep.	Israeli Prime Minister Rabin and Palestine Liberation Organization (PLO) Chairman Arafat, meeting in Washington, DC, sign, in the presence of President Clinton, the King of Jordan and Egyptian President Mubarak, an agreement on extended PLO government on the West Bank.
28 Sep.	NATO presents a study to the North Atlantic Co-operation Council (NACC) and the Partnership for Peace (PFP) states on possible enlargement of NATO membership. The 'Study on NATO Enlargement' explains the goals and principles of enlargement and the conditions that candidate countries must fulfil.

1995 contd

5 Oct.   President Clinton announces a 60-day cease-fire in Bosnia and Herzegovina to allow for peace talks. The cease-fire becomes effective on *12 Oct.*

24 Oct.   The largest gathering of the world's leaders in history, on the occasion of the 50th Anniversary of the UN, adopts at UN headquarters in New York a Declaration urging the redirection of the UN to greater service to humankind.

16 Nov.   China issues a policy document on arms control, expressing its opposition to the US proposal to deploy ballistic missile defence systems in Asia to protect Japan and US military forces.

21 Nov.   The General Framework Agreement for Peace in Bosnia and Herzegovina (the Dayton Agreement, negotiated in Dayton, Ohio) is initialled by Serbian President Milosevic, Croatian President Tudjman and Bosnian President Izetbegovic. The agreement includes a new constitution for Bosnia and Herzegovina. An Implementation Force (IFOR), consisting mostly of NATO forces, is established to stay in the area for one year.

22 Nov.   The UN Security Council unanimously adopts Resolution 1021 on conditional suspension of general sanctions against Yugoslavia (Serbia and Monetnegro). Russia abstains from voting.

14 Dec.   The General Framework Agreement for Peace in Bosnia and Herzegovina is signed in Paris by Serbian President Milosevic, Croatian President Tudjman and Bosnian President Izetbegovic.

15 Dec.   At a summit meeting of the Association of South-East Asian Nations (ASEAN), the Southeast Asia Nuclear-Weapon-Free Zone Treaty (Treaty of Bangkok) is signed.

16 Dec.   North Korea and the Korean Peninsula Energy Development Organization (KEDO) sign an agreement implementing the North Korean–US Agreed Framework signed in Oct. 1994. Under the agreement, KEDO will provide North Korea with two light-water reactors to replace its existing graphite-based models.

20 Dec.   The UN Protection Force (UNPROFOR) in the former Yugoslavia is formally replaced by IFOR, under the command of NATO.

1996

26 Jan.   The US Senate ratifies the 1993 START II Treaty.

26 Jan.   Representatives of Bosnia and Herzegovina, the Bosnian–Croat Federation and the Bosnian Serbs sign an agreement on confidence- and security-building measures (CSBMs) largely based on the Vienna Document 1994 on Confidence- and Security-Building Measures and adapted to subregional conditions.

29 Jan.   President Chirac announces the end of France's nuclear tests.

9 Feb.   The Irish Republican Army (IRA) explodes a large device in London's Docklands area, ending its 17-month cease-fire.

22 Feb.   President Chirac announces that all short-range Hadès missiles will be dismantled, the Plateau d'Albion missile site will be closed and the 18 S3D medium-range ballistic missiles based there will be dismantled. The military uranium enrichment facility in southern France will be closed and no further weapon-grade uranium produced.

29 Feb.   A group of states led by Denmark urges the UN Secretary-General to form a Multinational UN Stand-by Forces High Readiness Brigade (SHIRBRIG) for deployment in peacekeeping operations for a maximum of six months until replaced by a regular UN peacekeeping force.

13 Mar.   Following the withdrawal of the Bosnian Serb forces from the zones of separation, the embargo on deliveries of weapons and military equipment to the republics of the former Yugoslavia, imposed in 1991 by UN Security Council Resolution 713, is terminated, except for deliveries of heavy weapons.

25 Mar.   France, the UK and the USA sign the three protocols to the 1985 South Pacific Nuclear Free Zone Treaty (Treaty of Rarotonga) in Suva, Fiji, pledging not to station or test nuclear weapons in the area and not to use or threaten to use nuclear weapons against the parties to the treaty.

29 Mar.   The European Union (EU) Intergovernmental Conference (IGC) opens in Turin, Italy. The EU heads of government entrust the conference with the task of implementing a common foreign and security policy, including the eventual framing of a common defence policy.

2 Apr.   Russian President Yeltsin and Belarussian President Lukashenko, meeting in Moscow, sign a treaty establishing the foundation for deepening political, economic and military cooperation between the two states.

1996 contd

11 Apr.   The African Nuclear-Weapon-Free Zone Treaty (Treaty of Pelind-aba) is signed in Cairo by 43 African states. By *11 May* all the five nuclear weapon states had signed Protocols I and II, pledging not to attack parties to the treaty with nuclear weapons and renouncing the stationing or testing of nuclear weapons in the region. France signs Protocol III, undertaking to apply the provisions of the treaty with respect to its territories in the region.

19–20 Apr.   A summit meeting of the G7 states, Russia and Ukraine on nuclear safety and security issues is held in Moscow. A declaration is adopted which includes a statement on the safe storage and disposal of fissile material removed from dismantled nuclear weapons.

25 Apr.   Russian President Yeltsin and Chinese President Jiang Zemin, meeting in Beijing, issue a joint statement on a Russian–Chinese strategic partnership. As a symbol, a telephone 'hot line' will be established between Beijing and Moscow.

26 Apr.   The heads of state and government of China, Russia, Kazakhstan, Kyrgyzstan and Tajikistan sign an agreement in Shanghai, China, on confidence building in the military field in border areas.

3 May   An amended Protocol II to the Convention on Certain Conventional Weapons (CCW Convention) on prohibitions or restrictions on the use of mines, booby-traps and other devices, including further restrictions on the use, production and transfer of anti-personnel land-mines, is adopted in Geneva by the CCW Convention Review Conference.

7 May   The foreign and defence ministers of the Western European Union (WEU), meeting in Birmingham, UK, declare that the WEU will establish closer links with the EU, to implement EU decisions and actions which have defence implications, and with NATO, to be able to use NATO assets and capabilities, in particular through Combined Joint Task Forces (CJTF), for European operations in the framework of the Petersberg tasks (agreed in 1992).

15–31 May   The first Review Conference of the 1990 Treaty on Conventional Armed Forces in Europe (CFE Treaty) is held in Vienna. The parties agree on a numerical and geographical reorganization of the flank areas, including a contraction of the areas, which allows Russia and Ukraine to deploy more treaty-limited equipment (TLE) along their respective borders.

1 June   Ukrainian President Kuchma announces that the last of the strategic nuclear warheads based on Ukraine's territory have been transferred to Russia for dismantlement.

3 June	NATO foreign ministers, meeting in Berlin, declare that NATO will build up a European Security and Defence Identity (ESDI) and a Combined Joint Task Forces (CJTF) concept.
10 June	Russian Nationalities Minister Mikhailov and Chechen Chief of Staff Maskhadov sign in Nazran (the capital of the neighbouring Ingush republic) two protocols: one on Russian troop withdrawal from Chechnya by the end of August and the second on the release of all hostages and prisoners of war.
14 June	An Agreement on Subregional Arms Control, negotiated under the mandate of the 1995 Dayton Agreement and under the auspices of the Organization for Security and Co-operation in Europe (OSCE), is signed at Florence, Italy, at the Ministerial Meeting of the Peace Implementation Council by Croatia, Bosnia and Herzegovina and its two entities—the Muslim–Croat Federation of Bosnia and Herzegovina and the Bosnian–Serb Republika Srpska—and Yugo-slavia (Serbia and Montenegro). On *18 June* the UN Security Council votes to formally end the heavy-arms embargo against the states of the former Yugoslavia.
16 June	The first democratic presidential elections are held in Russia. No candidate receives the necessary '50 per cent plus one' margin. In a second round, on *3 July*, President Yeltsin receives 53.82% of the vote.
17 June	The Conference on Disarmament (CD) formally admits 23 new member states.
8 July	Replying to a request made by the UN General Assembly in Dec. 1994 to rule on the legality of nuclear weapons, the International Court of Justice (ICJ) hands down an advisory opinion, stating that while the use of or threat to use nuclear weapons might be legal in an extreme circumstance of self-defence, this would 'generally be contrary to the rules of international law applicable in armed conflict and in particular the principles and rules of humanitarian law'.
12 July	Thirty states, meeting in Vienna, agree on the initial elements of the Wassenaar Arrangement on Export Controls for Conventional Arms and Dual-use Goods and Technologies.
16 July	The Belarussian Parliament puts forth an initiative to create a nuclear weapon-free zone from Ukraine to the Nordic countries.
21 July	A peace agreement, mediated by the UN, is signed in Ashkhabad by the Tajik Government and opposition parties. (See also *23 Dec.*)
29 July	After having conducted its second nuclear test in 1996, China declares that it will abide by a moratorium on nuclear testing, effective from *30 July*.

1996 contd

14 Aug. The Canberra Commission on the Elimination of Nuclear Weapons, established in 1995, issues a report, identifying a series of steps and practical measures to bring about a nuclear weapon-free world.

23 Aug. Croatia and Yugoslavia (Serbia and Montenegro) sign an Agreement on Normalization of the Relations between the two states.

30 Aug. Following the cease-fire agreements of 27 May and 22 Aug. and an agreement on troop withdrawal of *27 Aug.*, Secretary of the Russian Security Council Lebed and Chechen Chief of Staff Maskhadov sign a peace agreement in Khasaviurt, Dagestan, that finally ends the war in Chechnya. Definition of Chechnya's future political status is postponed until *31 Dec. 2001.*

2 Sep. The Philippine Government and the Moro National Liberation Front (MNLF), the largest Muslim opposition faction, sign a peace agreement, ending 24 years of conflict between the two sides on the southern island of Mindanao.

10 Sep. By a vote of 158 to 3, with 5 abstentions, the UN General Assembly adopts the Comprehensive Nuclear Test-Ban Treaty (CTBT) as negotiated at the CD. (The treaty is opened for signature on *24 Sep.* at UN Headquarters, New York. The five nuclear weapon states together with 66 other states sign the treaty on the first day.)

1 Oct. The UN Security Council unanimously adopts Resolution 1074, terminating all sanctions imposed on Yugoslavia (Serbia and Montenegro).

3–5 Oct. An international conference on land-mines is held in Ottawa. The states represented at the conference agree to enhance cooperation and coordinate efforts to ensure an international ban on anti-personnel land-mines at the earliest possible date and to secure reductions in new deployments of anti-personnel land-mines.

4 Nov. On behalf of 84 states, the USA introduces a UN resolution to pursue vigorously an effective, legally binding ban on the use, stockpiling, production and transfer of anti-personnel land-mines. (The resolution is adopted by the General Assembly on *10 Dec.*)

9 Nov. France, Italy, Portugal and Spain create, in Florence, a European multinational force, which will have the task of acting in peacekeeping missions within the Western European Union (WEU), NATO and the UN.

27 Nov. Belarus announces that the last Soviet nuclear missiles based on its territory have been withdrawn to Russia. (On *23 Nov.* the associated nuclear warheads had been transferred to Russia for dismantlement.)

30 Nov.   A peace agreement is signed in Abidjan, Côte d'Ivoire, by the President of Sierra Leone and the Revolutionary United Front (RUF).

2 Dec.   The Organization for Security and Co-operation in Europe (OSCE) heads of state and government, meeting in Lisbon, approve the Lisbon Declaration on a Common and Comprehensive Security Model for Europe for the Twenty-first Century. The participants also give the OSCE the mandate to begin negotiations to adapt the Treaty on Conventional Armed Forces in Europe (CFE Treaty) to the new security environment in Europe.

10 Dec.   The NATO foreign ministers, meeting in Brussels, recommend that the NATO summit meeting scheduled for 8–9 July 1997 invite one or more of the countries that have expressed interest in joining the Alliance to begin accession negotiations. The ministers confirm that 'NATO countries have no intention, no plan and no reason to deploy nuclear weapons on the territory of new members' nor any need to change any aspect of their nuclear policy. They agree to merge the activities of the North Atlantic Cooperation Council (NACC) and the Partnership for Peace (PFP) in a new cooperative forum, later called the Euro-Atlantic Partnership Council (EAPC). They also approve the operational plan for the Stabilization Force (SFOR) which will replace IFOR in Bosnia and be led by NATO for 18 months.

20 Dec.   A new NATO-led multinational Stabilization Force (SFOR) takes over from IFOR in the former Yugoslavia.

29 Dec.   A peace agreement is signed in Guatemala City by the commanders of the Guatemalan National Revolutionary Unity (URNG) guerrillas and the President of Guatemala, formally ending 36 years of civil wars.

31 Dec.   The last Russian combat troops leave Grozny, Chechnya.

9. Glossary

Terms, acronyms and membership of international organizations

The glossary is not exhaustive but provides a description or definition of the major terms, acronyms and organizations discussed in the book. It also includes some terms that are not discussed in the book; they are presented to enhance the reader's general knowledge of the field of international peace and security.

9.1 Terms and organizations

Anti-ballistic missile (ABM) system

See Ballistic missile defence.

Arab League

Established in 1945, the principal objective of the League of Arab States, known as the Arab League, is to form closer union among Arab states and foster political and economic cooperation. The seat of the Secretary-General is in Cairo. An agreement for collective defence and economic cooperation was signed in 1950. *See* the list of members in section 9.3.

Association of South-East Asian Nations (ASEAN)

ASEAN was established in 1967 to promote economic, social and cultural development as well as regional peace and security in South-East Asia. The seat of the ASEAN Secretariat is in Jakarta. The ASEAN Regional Forum (ARF) was established in 1993 to address security issues in a multilateral forum, with an official and a non-official programme. The ASEAN Post Ministerial Conference (ASEAN–PMC) was established in 1979 as a forum for discussions of political and security issues with dialogue partners. *See* the list of members in section 9.3.

Atlantic-to-the-Urals (ATTU) zone

Zone of the 1990 CFE Treaty and the 1992 CFE-1A Agreement, stretching from the Atlantic Ocean to the Ural Mountains in Russia. It covers the entire land territory of the European NATO states, the CEE states and the CIS states.

Australia Group

Group of states, formed in 1985, which meets informally each year to monitor the proliferation of chemical and biological products and to discuss chemicals which should be subject to various national regulatory measures. The name of the group is derived from its first formal meeting, held at the Australian Embassy in Paris. *See* the list of members in section 9.3.

Ballistic missile Missile which follows a ballistic trajectory (part of which may be outside the earth's atmosphere) when thrust is terminated.

Ballistic missile defence (BMD) Weapon system designed to defend against a ballistic missile attack by intercepting and destroying ballistic missiles or their warheads in flight.

Baltic Council Established in 1990 for the promotion of democracy and development of cooperation between the three Baltic states. *See* the list of members in section 9.3.

Binary chemical weapon A shell or other device filled with two chemicals of relatively low toxicity which mix and react while the device is being delivered to the target, the reaction product being a super-toxic chemical warfare agent, such as a nerve agent.

Biological weapon (BW) Weapon containing living organisms, whatever their nature, or infective material derived from them, when used or intended to cause disease or death in humans, animals or plants. The effect of this weapon depends on its means of delivery, as well as the organism multiplying in the person, animal or plant attacked.

Central and Eastern Europe (CEE) Bulgaria, the Czech Republic, Hungary, Poland, Romania and Slovakia. The term is sometimes also taken to include the European former Soviet republics—Armenia, Azerbaijan, Belarus, Georgia, Moldova, the European part of Russia and Ukraine—and sometimes also the Baltic states.

Chemical weapon (CW) Chemical substances—whether gaseous, liquid or solid—when used or intended for use as weapons, because of their direct toxic effects on humans, animals or plants, as well as their means of delivery.

Combined Joint Task Forces (CJTF) Concept declared at the June 1996 Berlin meeting of NATO foreign ministers to facilitate NATO contingency operations, including the use of 'separable but not separate' military capabilities in operations led by the Western European Union, with the participation of states outside the NATO Alliance.

Common Foreign and Security Policy (CFSP) Institutional framework, established by the 1992 Maastricht Treaty, for consultation and development of common positions and joint action on European foreign and security policy. It constitutes the second of the three European Union 'pillars'.

Commonwealth of Independent States (CIS)	Established in 1991, the CIS is an organization of 12 former Soviet republics, for political and economic cooperation. *See* the list of members in section 9.3.
Conference on Disarmament (CD)	A multilateral arms control negotiating body, based in Geneva, composed of states representing all the regions of the world, and including the permanent members of the UN Security Council. The CD reports to the UN General Assembly. *See* the list of members in section 9.3.
Conference on Security and Co-operation in Europe (CSCE)	*See* Organization for Security and Co-operation in Europe.
Confidence- and security-building measure (CSBM)	Measure to promote confidence and security undertaken by a state. A CSBM is militarily significant, politically binding and verifiable.
Confidence-building measure (CBM)	Measure undertaken by a state to help reduce the danger of armed conflict and of misunderstanding or miscalculation of military activities.
Conventional weapon	Weapon not having mass destruction effects. *See also* Weapon of mass destruction.
Conversion	Term used to describe the shift in resources from military to civilian use. It usually refers to the conversion of industry from military to civilian production.
Cooperative Threat Reduction (CTR)	Programme established to facilitate bilateral cooperation between the USA and the former Soviet republics with nuclear weapons on their territories (Belarus, Kazakhstan, Russia and Ukraine), primarily for US assistance in the safe and environmentally responsible storage, transportation, dismantlement and destruction of former Soviet nuclear weapons. The programme also provides assistance for the destruction of chemical weapons in Russia.
Council for Security Cooperation in the Asia Pacific (CSCAP)	Established in 1993, CSCAP is an informal, non-governmental, process for regional confidence building and security cooperation through dialogue, consultation and cooperation. *See* the list of members in section 9.3.
Council of Europe	Established in 1949, with its seat in Strasbourg, the Council is open to all European states which accept the principle of the rule of law and guarantee their citizens human rights and fundamental freedoms. Its main aims are defined in the 1950 European Convention on Human Rights and the 1953 Convention for the Protection of Human Rights and Fundamental Freedoms. Among its organs is the European Court of Human Rights. *See* the list of members in section 9.3.

Council of Baltic Sea States (CBSS)	Organization comprising the states bordering on the Baltic Sea plus Iceland and Norway, established in 1992 to promote common strategies for political and economic cooperation and development. *See* the list of members in section 9.3.
Dayton Agreement	The accord struck in 1995 in Dayton, Ohio, to establish peace in Bosnia and Herzegovina. It consists of the General Framework Agreement for Peace and 11 annexes.
Dual-capable	Term that refers to a weapon system or platform that can carry either conventional or non-conventional explosives.
Dual-use technology	Dual-use technology can be used for both civilian and military applications.
Economic Community of West African States (ECOWAS)	A regional organization established in 1975, with a secretariat in Abuja, Nigeria, to promote cooperation and development in economic activity, improve relations among its member countries and contribute to development in Africa. In 1981 it adopted the Protocol on Mutual Assistance in Defence Matters. In 1990 it established the ECOWAS Cease-fire Monitoring Group (ECOMOG) in Liberia. *See* the list of members in section 9.3.
Euro-Atlantic Partnership Council (EAPC)	The new council, established in 1997, which merges the activities of NACC and the PFP in a single forum, replacing NACC. The EAPC provides the overarching framework for practical cooperation between NATO and PFP partners, with an expanded political dimension. The current NACC members and PFP countries automatically become EAPC members if they so wish. It is also open to accession by other OSCE participating states. New members may join by approving the PFP Framework Document and stating their acceptance of the EAPC. *See* the list of members in section 9.3.
European Atomic Energy Community (Euratom)	Based on a treaty signed in Rome in 1957 at the same time as the treaty establishing the European Economic Community, Euratom aims to integrate the programmes of the EU member states for the peaceful uses of atomic energy. Euratom is located in Brussels.
European Security and Defence Identity (ESDI)	Concept aimed at strengthening the European pillar of NATO while reinforcing the transatlantic link by creating militarily coherent and effective forces capable of conducting operations under the control of the Western European Union.

European Union (EU)   Organization of 15 West European states. The Treaty on European Union (Maastricht Treaty), which created the EU, was signed in 1992 and entered into force in 1993. The 1997 Amsterdam Treaty strengthens the political dimension of the EU and prepares the EU for enlargement. It also contains a provision that the EU will avail itself of the WEU to elaborate and implement those decisions and actions of the EU which have defence implications. The operational responsibilities will remain within the WEU. The EU Council and Commission are in Brussels. *See* the list of members in section 9.3.

Fissile material   Material composed of atoms which can be split by either fast or slow (thermal) neutrons. Uranium-235 and plutonium-239 are the most common examples of fissile material.

Group of Seven (G7)   Group of leading industrialized nations which have met informally, at the level of heads of state or government, since the late 1970s. At the Summit of the Eight held in Denver, Colorado, in June 1997, Russia participated for the first time as a full member. *See* the list of members in section 9.3.

Group of 21 (G-21)   Originally 21, now 30, non-aligned CD member states which act together in the CD on proposals of common interest. *See* the list of members in section 9.3.

Intercontinental ballistic missile (ICBM)   Ground-launched ballistic missile with a range greater than 5500 km.

Intermediate-range nuclear forces (INF)   Theatre nuclear forces with a range of from 1000 km up to and including 5500 km.

International Atomic Energy Agency (IAEA)   An independent, intergovernmental organization within the UN system, with headquarters in Vienna. The IAEA is endowed by its Statute, which entered into force in 1957, to promote the peaceful uses of atomic energy and ensure that nuclear activities are not used to further any military purpose. It is involved in verification of the NPT and the nuclear weapon-free zone treaties and in the activities of the UN Special Commission on Iraq (UNSCOM). *See* the list of members in section 9.3.

International Court of Justice (ICJ)   The main judicial body of the UN, set up in 1945 and located in The Hague. Its Statute forms an integral part of the UN Charter.

International Criminal Tribunal for the Former Yugoslavia   The international tribunal whose task it is to prosecute those who committed war crimes during the conflict in the former Yugoslavia.

Kiloton (kt)	Measure of the explosive yield of a nuclear weapon equivalent to 1000 tonnes of trinitrotoluene (TNT) high explosive. The bomb detonated at Hiroshima in World War II had a yield of about 12–15 kilotons.
Megaton (Mt)	Measure of the explosive yield of a nuclear weapon equivalent to 1 million tonnes of trinitrotoluene (TNT) high explosive.
Minsk Group	Group of states acting together in the OSCE for political settlement of the conflict in the Armenian enclave of Nagorno-Karabakh in Azerbaijan (also known as the Minsk Process or Minsk Conference). *See* the list of members in section 9.3.
Missile Technology Control Regime (MTCR)	An informal military-related export control regime, established in 1987, which produced the Guidelines for Sensitive Missile-Relevant Transfers. Its goal is to limit the spread of weapons of mass destruction by controlling their delivery systems. *See* the list of members in section 9.3.
Multiple independently targetable re-entry vehicles (MIRVs)	Re-entry vehicles, carried by a single ballistic missile, which can be directed to separate targets along separate trajectories. A missile can carry two or more re-entry vehicles.
National technical means (of verification) (NTM)	Technical intelligence means, under the national control of a state, which are used to monitor compliance with an arms control treaty to which the state is a party.
NATO–Russia Permanent Joint Council	The Permanent Joint Council was established in the 1997 Founding Act on Mutual Relations, Cooperation and Security for consultation and cooperation. The first meeting, at the level of foreign ministers, was held in New York in September 1997; it defined a detailed work programme and discussed *inter alia* peacekeeping issues.
Non-Aligned Movement (NAM)	Group of countries established at Belgrade in 1961, sometimes referred to as the Movement of Non-Aligned Countries. NAM is a forum for consultations and coordination of positions on political and economic issues. The Coordinating Bureau of the Non-Aligned Countries (also called the Conference of Non-Aligned Countries) is the forum in which NAM coordinates its actions within the UN. *See* the list of members in section 9.3.
Non-strategic nuclear forces	*See* Theatre nuclear forces.
Nordic Council	Political advisory organ for cooperation between the parliaments of the Nordic states, founded in 1952. The Plenary Assembly is the highest political organ. The Nor-

dic Council of Ministers, established in 1971, is an organ for cooperation between the governments of the Nordic countries and between these governments and the Nordic Council. *See* the list of members in section 9.3.

North Atlantic
Cooperation Council
(NACC)

The NATO institution created in 1991 for consultation and cooperation on political and security issues between NATO and the former WTO states and former Soviet republics. NACC ceased to exist when the Euro-Atlantic Partnership Council was launched in May 1997. *See* the list of members in section 9.3.

North Atlantic Treaty
Organization (NATO)

A political and military defence alliance established in 1949 by the North Atlantic Treaty. It has 16 members and its headquarters are in Brussels. In July 1997 the Czech Republic, Hungary and Poland were invited to begin NATO accession talks, held in September–November 1997. *See* the list of members in section 9.3.

Nuclear Suppliers
Group (NSG)

Also known as the London Club, the NSG coordinates multilateral export controls on nuclear materials. In 1977 it agreed on the Guidelines for Nuclear Transfers (London Guidelines), revised in 1993. The Guidelines contain a 'trigger list' of materials which should trigger IAEA safeguards when exported for peaceful purposes to any non-nuclear weapon state. In 1992 the NSG agreed the Guidelines for Transfers of Nuclear-Related Dual-Use Equipment, Material and Related Technology (Warsaw Guidelines, subsequently revised). *See* the list of members in section 9.3.

Organisation for
Economic Co-operation
and Development
(OECD)

Established in 1961 to replace the Organization for European Economic Cooperation, the OECD's objectives are to promote economic and social welfare by coordinating policies. Its headquarters are in Paris. *See* the list of members in section 9.3.

Organisation for the
Prohibition of Chemical
Weapons (OPCW)

Forum established by the Chemical Weapons Convention to resolve questions of compliance with the convention. Its seat is in The Hague.

Organization for
Security and
Co-operation in Europe
(OSCE)

Since 1995 the Conference on Security and Co-operation in Europe (CSCE) has been called the OSCE. The CSCE opened in 1973, with the participation of European states plus the USA and Canada. It adopted its Final Act in 1975. Through follow-up meetings, summits and the creation of numerous institutions, the CSCE, and now the OSCE, has sought to enhance security and cooperation in Europe. *See* the list of members in section 9.3.

Organization of African Unity (OAU)	Established in 1963, the OAU is a union of African states with the principal objective of promoting cooperation among the states in the region. The seat of the OAU Secretary-General is in Addis Ababa. *See* the list of members in section 9.3.
Organization of American States (OAS)	Group of states in the Americas, established in 1890, which also has member states and permanent observers from other continents. Its principal objective is to strengthen peace and security in the western hemisphere. The General Secretariat is in Washington, DC. *See* the list of members in section 9.3.
Organization of the Islamic Conference (OIC)	Initiated in 1969 and established in 1971 by Islamic states to promote cooperation among the member states and to support peace, security and the struggle of the people of Palestine and all Muslim people. The Secretariat of the organization is in Jedda, Saudi Arabia. *See* the list of members in section 9.3.
Ottawa Group	A group of states which first met in Ottawa in October 1996 to negotiate a global ban on anti-personnel landmines. By September 1997 over 100 states participated in the work of the group—including France, the UK and the USA—and 89 states adopted the text of the Convention on the Prohibition of the Use, Stockpiling, Production and Transfer of Anti-Personnel Mines and on their Destruction. The treaty was opened for signature in December 1997.
Pact on Stability in Europe	French proposal presented in 1993 for inclusion in the framework of the EU Common Foreign and Security Policy (CFSP). The objective is to contribute to stability by preventing tension and potential conflicts connected with border and minorities issues. The Pact was adopted in 1995 and the instruments and procedures were handed over to the OSCE.
Partnership for Peace (PFP)	The NATO programme, launched in 1994, for cooperation with NACC and other OSCE states in such areas as military planning, budgeting and training, under the authority of the North Atlantic Council. It provides for enhanced cooperation to prepare for and undertake multilateral crisis-management activities such as peacekeeping. In May 1997 the activities of the PFP and NACC were merged in the EAPC. *See* the list of members in section 9.3.

Peaceful nuclear explosion (PNE)	A nuclear explosion for non-military purposes, such as digging canals or harbours or creating underground cavities. The USA terminated its PNE programme in 1973. The USSR conducted its last PNE in 1988.
Petersberg tasks	The Petersberg tasks emanate from the 1992 meeting of the WEU Council at Petersberg, Germany. WEU members will engage in humanitarian and rescue tasks, peace-keeping operations, and tasks of combat forces in crisis management, including peacemaking. NATO will also engage in these tasks.
Re-entry vehicle (RV)	The part of a ballistic missile which carries a nuclear warhead and penetration aids to the target. It re-enters the earth's atmosphere and is destroyed in the final phase of the missile's trajectory. A missile can have one or several RVs and each RV contains a warhead.
Safeguards agreements	Under the NPT and the nuclear weapon-free zone treaties, non-nuclear weapon states must accept IAEA safeguards to demonstrate the fulfilment of their obligation not to manufacture nuclear weapons.
Short-range nuclear forces (SNF)	Nuclear weapons, including artillery, mines, missiles, etc., with ranges of up to 500 km.
South Pacific Forum	Group of South Pacific states created in 1971 which *inter alia* proposed the South Pacific Nuclear Free Zone, embodied in the 1985 Treaty of Rarotonga. The Secretariat of the organization is in Suva, Fiji. *See* the list of members in section 9.3.
Strategic nuclear weapons	ICBMs and SLBMs with a range usually of over 5500 km, as well as bombs and missiles carried on aircraft of intercontinental range.
Submarine-launched ballistic missile (SLBM)	A ballistic missile launched from a submarine, usually with a range in excess of 5500 km.
Tactical nuclear weapon	A short-range nuclear weapon which is deployed with general-purpose forces along with conventional weapons.
Theatre missile defence (TMD)	Weapon systems designed to defend against non-strategic nuclear missiles by intercepting and destroying them in flight.
Theatre nuclear forces (TNF)	Nuclear weapons with ranges up to and including 5500 km.
Throw-weight	Sum of the weight of a ballistic missile's re-entry vehicle(s), dispensing mechanisms, penetration aids, and targeting and separation devices.

Toxins	Poisonous substances which are products of organisms but are not living or capable of reproducing themselves, as well as chemically created variants of such substances. Some toxins may also be produced by chemical processes.
Treaty-limited equipment (TLE)	Five categories of equipment on which numerical limits are established in the CFE Treaty: battle tanks, armoured combat vehicles, artillery, combat aircraft and attack helicopters.
United Nations Register of Conventional Arms	A voluntary reporting mechanism set up in 1992 for member states of the United Nations to report imports and exports of 5 categories of weapons or systems: aircraft, armour and artillery, guidance and radar systems, missiles, and warships.
Warhead	The part of a weapon which contains the explosive or other material intended to inflict damage.
Warsaw Treaty Organization (WTO)	The WTO, or Warsaw Pact, was established in 1955 by the Treaty of Friendship, Cooperation and Mutual Assistance between eight countries: Albania (withdrew in 1968), Bulgaria, Czechoslovakia, the German Democratic Republic, Hungary, Poland, Romania and the USSR. The WTO was dissolved in 1991.
Wassenaar Arrangement	The Wassenaar Arrangement on Export Controls for Conventional Arms and Dual-Use Goods and Technologies was formally established in 1996. It aims to prevent the acquisition of armaments and sensitive dual-use goods and technologies for military uses by states whose behaviour is cause for concern to the Wassenaar members. *See* the list of members in section 9.3.
Weapon of mass destruction	Nuclear weapon and any other weapon which may produce comparable effects, such as chemical and biological weapons.
Western European Union (WEU)	Established in the 1954 Protocols to the 1948 Brussels Treaty of Economic, Social and Cultural Collaboration and Collective Self-Defence among Western European States. The seat of the WEU is in Brussels. Within the EU Common Foreign and Security Policy (CFSP) and at the request of the EU, the WEU is to elaborate and implement EU decisions and actions which have defence implications. The Western European Armaments Group (WEAG) is the WEU armaments cooperation authority. *See* the list of members in section 9.3.

Yield	Released nuclear explosive energy expressed as the equivalent of the energy produced by a given number of tonnes of trinitrotoluene (TNT) high explosive.
Zangger Committee	The Nuclear Exporters Committee, called the Zangger Committee after its first chairman, is a group of nuclear supplier countries that meets informally twice a year to coordinate export controls on nuclear materials. *See* the list of members in section 9.3.

9.2 Acronyms

Note that acronyms for the names of observer, peacekeeping and electoral operations can be found in chapter 2.

ABM	Anti-ballistic missile
ACM	Advanced cruise missile
ADM	Atomic demolition munition
ALCM	Air-launched cruise missile
ANC	African National Congress
APEC	Asia–Pacific Economic Co-operation
ARATS	Association for Relations Across the Taiwan Straits
ARF	ASEAN Regional Forum
ASEAN	Association of South-East Asian Nations
ASEAN–PMC	ASEAN Post Ministerial Conference
ASLCM	Advanced sea-launched cruise missile
ASMP	Air-sol moyenne portée
ATTU	Atlantic-to-the-Urals (zone)
BMD	Ballistic missile defence
BTWC	Biological Weapons Convention
BW	Biological and toxin weapon/warfare
CBM	Confidence-building measure
CBSS	Council of Baltic Sea States
CBW	Chemical and biological weapon/warfare
CCW	Certain Conventional Weapons (Convention)
CD	Conference on Disarmament
CEE	Central and Eastern Europe
CFE	Conventional forces in Europe
CFSP	Common Foreign and Security Policy
CIO	Chairman-in-Office
CIS	Commonwealth of Independent States
CJTF	Combined Joint Task Forces
CPI	Consumer price index
CSBM	Confidence- and security-building measure
CSCAP	Council for Security and Co-operation in the Asia–Pacific
CSCE	Conference on Security and Co-operation in Europe
CTBT	Comprehensive Nuclear Test-Ban Treaty
CTBTO	Comprehensive Nuclear Test-Ban Treaty Organization
CTR	Cooperative Threat Reduction
CW	Chemical weapon/warfare
CWC	Chemical Weapons Convention
DMZ	Demilitarized zone
DOD	Department of Defense
EAPC	Euro-Atlantic Partnership Council
EBRD	European Bank for Reconstruction and Development
EC	European Community

ECOWAS	Economic Community of West African States
EMU	Economic and Monetary Union
Enmod	Environmental modification
EPU	European Political Union
ESDI	European Security and Defence Identity
EU	European Union
Euratom	European Atomic Energy Community
FMLN	Farabundo Marti National Liberation Front
FRY	Federal Republic of Yugoslavia (Serbia and Montenegro)
FSC	Forum for Security Co-operation
FYROM	Former Yugoslav Republic of Macedonia
G7	Group of Seven (leading industrialized nations)
G-21	Group of 21
GLCM	Ground-launched cruise missile
HCNM	High Commissioner on National Minorities
HEU	Highly enriched uranium
IAEA	International Atomic Energy Agency
ICBM	Intercontinental ballistic missile
ICJ	International Court of Justice
IFOR	Implementation Force
IMF	International Monetary Fund
INF	Intermediate-range nuclear forces
IRA	Irish Republican Army
IRBM	Intermediate-range ballistic missile
JACO	Joint Armaments Cooperation Organization
KEDO	Korean Peninsula Energy Development Organization
LDC	Least developed country
LEU	Low-enriched uranium
LWR	Light-water reactor
MAD	Mutual assured destruction
MIRV	Multiple independently targetable re-entry vehicle
MLPA	Popular Movement for the Liberation of Angola
MNF	Multinational Force
MNR	Mozambican National Resistance (Renamo)
MPLA–PT	Popular Liberation Movement of Angola–Worker's Party
MTCR	Missile Technology Control Regime
NACC	North Atlantic Cooperation Council
NAM	Non-Aligned Movement
NATO	North Atlantic Treaty Organization
NBC	Nuclear, biological and chemical weapons
NEACD	North-East Asia Cooperation Dialogue
NGO	Non-governmental organization
NPCSD	North Pacific Co-operative Security Dialogue
NPT	Non-Proliferation Treaty
NSG	Nuclear Suppliers Group
NTM	National technical means (of verification)

NWFZ	Nuclear weapon-free zone
NWS	Nuclear weapon state
OAS	Organization of American States
OAU	Organization of African Unity
ODIHR	Office of Democratic Institutions and Human Rights
OECD	Organisation for Economic Co-operation and Development
OIC	Organization of the Islamic Conference
OPCW	Organisation for the Prohibition of Chemical Weapons
OSCE	Organization for Security and Co-operation in Europe
PFP	Partnership for Peace
PLO	Palestine Liberation Organization
PNE	Peaceful nuclear explosion
PNET	Peaceful Nuclear Explosions Treaty
PTBT	Partial Test Ban Treaty
RV	Re-entry vehicle
SALT	Strategic Arms Limitation Talks/Treaty
SCC	Standing Consultative Committee
SEF	Straits Exchange Foundation
SFOR	Stabilization Force
SHIRBRIG	Stand-by Forces High Readiness Brigade
SLBM	Submarine-launched ballistic missile
SLCM	Sea-launched cruise missile
SNF	Short-range nuclear forces
SSBN	Nuclear-powered, ballistic-missile submarine
SSD	Safe and Secure Dismantlement (Talks)
SSN	Nuclear-powered attack submarine
START	Strategic Arms Reduction Talks/Treaty
TLE	Treaty-limited equipment
TMD	Theatre missile defence
TTBT	Threshold Test Ban Treaty
UAE	United Arab Emirates
UNCED	United Nations Conference on Environment and Development
UNCLOS	United Nations Convention on the Law of the Sea
UNDC	United Nations Disarmament Commission
UNITA	National Union for the Total Independence of Angola
UNSCOM	United Nations Special Commission on Iraq
UNSSOD	United Nations Special Session on Disarmament
USEC	United States Enrichment Corporation
VEREX	Ad Hoc Group of Governmental Experts to Identify and Examine Potential Verification Measures from a Scientific and Technical Standpoint
WEAG	Western European Armaments Group
WEU	Western European Union
WTO	Warsaw Treaty Organization (Warsaw Pact)
YNA	Yugoslav National Army

9.3   Membership of international organizations

For membership of the United Nations, see the panel in chapter 6. Membership of organizations in this list is as of 1 January 1997, unless otherwise indicated.

Arab League

Members: Algeria, Bahrain, Comoros, Djibouti, Egypt, Iraq, Jordan, Kuwait, Lebanon, Libya, Mauritania, Morocco, Oman, Palestine, Qatar, Saudi Arabia, Somalia, Sudan, Syria, Tunisia, United Arab Emirates, Yemen

Association of South-East Asian Nations (ASEAN)

Members: Brunei, Indonesia, Malaysia, Philippines, Singapore, Thailand, Viet Nam
Note: Laos and Myanmar (Burma) were admitted in July 1997.

ASEAN Regional Forum (ARF)

Members: The ASEAN states plus Australia, Cambodia, Canada, China, European Union (EU), India, Japan, Korea (South), New Zealand, Papua New Guinea, Russia, USA

ASEAN Post Ministerial Conference (ASEAN–PMC)

Members: The ASEAN states plus Australia, Canada, European Union (EU), Japan, South Korea, New Zealand, USA

Australia Group

Members: Argentina, Australia, Austria, Belgium, Canada, Czech Republic, Denmark, Finland, France, Germany, Greece, Hungary, Iceland, Ireland, Italy, Japan, Korea (South), Luxembourg, Netherlands, New Zealand, Norway, Poland, Portugal, Romania, Slovakia, Spain, Sweden, Switzerland, UK, USA
Observer: European Commission

Baltic Council

Members: Estonia, Latvia, Lithuania

Commonwealth of Independent States (CIS)

Members: Armenia, Azerbaijan, Belarus, Georgia, Kazakhstan, Kyrgyzstan, Moldova, Russia, Tajikistan, Turkmenistan, Ukraine, Uzbekistan

Conference on Disarmament (CD)

Members: Algeria, Argentina, Australia, Austria, Bangladesh, Belarus, Belgium, Brazil, Bulgaria, Cameroon, Canada, Chile, China, Colombia, Cuba, Egypt, Ethiopia, Finland, France, Germany, Hungary, India, Indonesia, Iran, Iraq, Israel, Italy, Japan, Kenya, Korea (North), Korea (South), Mexico, Mongolia, Morocco, Myanmar (Burma), Netherlands, New Zealand, Nigeria, Norway, Pakistan, Peru, Poland, Romania, Russia, Senegal, Slovakia, South Africa, Spain, Sri Lanka, Sweden, Switzerland, Syria, Turkey, UK, Ukraine, USA, Venezuela, Viet Nam, Yugoslavia,* Zaire, Zimbabwe

* Yugoslavia (Serbia and Montenegro) has been suspended since 1992.

Council for Security Cooperation in the Asia Pacific (CSCAP)

Members: Australia, Canada, China, Indonesia, Japan, Korea (North), Korea (South), Malaysia, Mongolia, New Zealand, Philippines, Russia, Singapore, Thailand, USA, Viet Nam

Council of Europe

Members: Albania, Andorra, Austria, Belgium, Bulgaria, Croatia, Cyprus, Czech Republic, Denmark, Estonia, Finland, France, Germany, Greece, Hungary, Iceland, Ireland, Italy, Latvia, Liechtenstein, Lithuania, Luxembourg, Macedonia (Former Yugoslav Republic of), Malta, Moldova, Netherlands, Norway, Poland, Portugal, Romania, Russia, San Marino, Slovakia, Slovenia, Spain, Sweden, Switzerland, Turkey, UK, Ukraine

Observers: Canada, Holy See, Japan, USA

Council of Baltic Sea States (CBSS)

Members: Denmark, Estonia, European Union (EU), Finland, Germany, Iceland, Latvia, Lithuania, Norway, Poland, Russia, Sweden

Economic Community of West African States (ECOWAS)

Members: Benin, Burkina Faso, Cape Verde, Côte d'Ivoire, Gambia, Ghana, Guinea, Guinea-Bissau, Liberia, Mali, Mauritania, Niger, Nigeria, Senegal, Sierra Leone, Togo

European Union (EU)

Members: Austria, Belgium, Denmark, Finland, France, Germany, Greece, Ireland, Italy, Luxembourg, Netherlands, Portugal, Spain, Sweden, UK

Group of Seven (G7)

Members: Canada, France, Germany, Italy, Japan, UK, USA

Note: Russia became a member at the Summit of the Eight in 1997.

International Atomic Energy Agency (IAEA)

Members: Afghanistan, Albania, Algeria, Argentina, Armenia, Australia, Austria, Bangladesh, Belarus, Belgium, Bolivia, Bosnia and Herzegovina, Brazil, Bulgaria, Cambodia, Cameroon, Canada, Chile, China, Colombia, Costa Rica, Côte d'Ivoire, Croatia, Cuba, Cyprus, Czech Republic, Denmark, Dominican Republic, Ecuador, Egypt, El Salvador, Estonia, Ethiopia, Finland, France, Gabon, Georgia, Germany, Ghana, Greece, Guatemala, Haiti, Holy See, Hungary, Iceland, India, Indonesia, Iran, Iraq, Ireland, Israel, Italy, Jamaica, Japan, Jordan, Kazakhstan, Kenya, Korea (South), Kuwait, Lebanon, Liberia, Libya, Liechtenstein, Lithuania, Luxembourg, Macedonia (Former Yugoslav Republic of), Madagascar, Malaysia, Mali, Marshall Islands, Mauritius, Mexico, Monaco, Mongolia, Morocco, Myanmar (Burma), Namibia, Netherlands, New Zealand, Nicaragua, Niger, Nigeria, Norway, Pakistan, Panama, Paraguay, Peru, Philippines, Poland, Portugal, Qatar, Romania, Russia, Saudi Arabia, Senegal, Sierra Leone, Singapore, Slovakia, Slovenia, South Africa, Spain, Sri Lanka, Sudan, Sweden, Switzerland, Syria, Tanzania, Thailand, Tunisia, Turkey, Uganda, UK, Ukraine, United Arab Emirates, Uruguay, USA, Uzbekistan, Venezuela, Viet Nam, Yemen, Yugoslavia,* Zaire, Zambia, Zimbabwe

* Yugoslavia (Serbia and Montenegro) has been suspended since 1992. It is deprived of the right to participate in the IAEA General Conference and the Board of Governors' meetings but is assessed for its contribution to the budget of the IAEA.

Note: North Korea was a member of the IAEA until Sep. 1994.

Missile Technology Control Regime (MTCR)

MTCR partners: Argentina, Australia, Austria, Belgium, Brazil, Canada, Denmark, Finland, France, Germany, Greece, Hungary, Iceland, Ireland, Italy, Japan, Luxembourg, Netherlands, New Zealand, Norway, Portugal, Russia, South Africa, Spain, Sweden, Switzerland, UK, USA

Non-Aligned Movement (NAM)

Members: Afghanistan, Algeria, Angola, Bahamas, Bahrain, Bangladesh, Barbados, Belize, Benin, Bhutan, Bolivia, Botswana, Brunei, Burkina Faso, Burundi, Cambodia, Cameroon, Cape Verde, Central African Republic, Chad, Chile, Colombia, Comoros, Congo (Brazzaville), Congo, Democratic Republic of (formerly Zaire), Côte d'Ivoire, Cuba, Cyprus, Djibouti, Ecuador, Egypt, Equatorial Guinea, Eritrea, Ethiopia, Gabon, Gambia, Ghana, Grenada, Guatemala, Guinea, Guinea-Bissau, Guyana, Honduras, India, Indonesia, Iran, Iraq, Jamaica, Jordan, Kenya, Korea (North), Kuwait, Laos, Lebanon, Lesotho, Liberia, Libya, Madagascar, Malawi, Malaysia, Maldives, Mali, Malta, Mauritania, Mauritius, Mongolia, Morocco, Mozambique, Myanmar (Burma), Namibia, Nepal, Nicaragua, Niger, Nigeria, Oman, Pakistan, Palestine, Panama, Papua New Guinea, Peru, Philippines, Qatar, Rwanda, Saint Lucia, Sao Tome and Principe, Saudi Arabia, Senegal, Seychelles, Sierra Leone, Singapore, Somalia, South Africa, Sri Lanka, Sudan, Suriname, Swaziland, Syria, Tanzania, Thailand, Togo, Trinidad and Tobago, Tunisia, Turkmenistan, Uganda, United Arab Emirates, Uzbekistan, Vanuatu, Venezuela, Viet Nam, Yemen, Yugoslavia,* Zambia, Zimbabwe

* Yugoslavia (Serbia and Montenegro) has not been permitted to participate in NAM activities since 1992.

Nordic Council

Members: Denmark (including the Faroe Islands and Greenland), Finland (including Åland), Iceland, Norway, Sweden

North Atlantic Treaty Organization (NATO)

Members: Belgium, Canada, Denmark, France,* Germany, Greece, Iceland, Italy, Luxembourg, Netherlands, Norway, Portugal, Spain,* Turkey, UK, USA

* France and Spain are not in the integrated military structures of NATO.

Note: In July 1997 the Czech Republic, Hungary and Poland were invited to begin NATO accession talks.

NATO North Atlantic Cooperation Council (NACC)

Members: Albania, Armenia, Azerbaijan, Belarus, Belgium, Bulgaria, Canada, Czech Republic, Denmark, Estonia, France, Georgia, Germany, Greece, Hungary, Iceland, Italy, Kazakhstan, Kyrgyzstan, Latvia, Lithuania, Luxembourg, Macedonia (Former Yugoslav Republic of), Moldova, Netherlands, Norway, Poland, Portugal, Romania, Russia, Slovakia, Slovenia, Spain, Tajikistan, Turkey, Turkmenistan, UK, Ukraine, USA, Uzbekistan

Observers: Austria, Finland, Sweden and Switzerland have observer status, as participants in the Partnership for Peace.

Note: NACC ceased to exist in May 1997.

Partnership for Peace (PFP)

Partner states with approved PFP Framework Documents: Albania, Armenia, Austria, Azerbaijan, Belarus, Bulgaria, Czech Republic, Estonia, Finland, Georgia, Hungary, Kazakhstan, Kyrgyzstan, Latvia, Lithuania, Macedonia (Former Yugoslav Republic of), Moldova, Poland, Romania, Russia, Slovakia, Slovenia, Sweden, Switzerland, Turkmenistan, Ukraine, Uzbekistan

Partner states with approved PFP Presentation Documents: Albania, Armenia, Austria, Azerbaijan, Belarus, Bulgaria, Czech Republic, Estonia, Finland, Georgia, Hungary, Kazakhstan, Kyrgyzstan, Latvia, Lithuania, Macedonia (Former Yugoslav Republic of), Moldova, Poland, Romania, Russia, Slovakia, Slovenia, Sweden, Switzerland, Turkmenistan, Ukraine, Uzbekistan

Partner states with approved PFP Individual Partnership Programmes (IPP): Albania, Armenia, Austria, Azerbaijan, Bulgaria, Czech Republic, Estonia, Finland, Georgia, Hungary, Kazakhstan, Kyrgyzstan, Latvia, Lithuania, Macedonia (Former Yugoslav Republic of), Moldova, Poland, Romania, Slovakia, Slovenia, Sweden, Switzerland, Ukraine, Uzbekistan

Euro-Atlantic Partnership Council (EAPC)

Members: The NACC members and states which have signed the PFP Framework Document, as of July 1997.

Nuclear Suppliers Group (NSG)

Members: Argentina, Australia, Austria, Belgium, Brazil, Bulgaria, Canada, Czech Republic, Denmark, Finland, France, Germany, Greece, Hungary, Ireland, Italy, Japan, Korea (South), Luxembourg, Netherlands, New Zealand, Norway, Poland, Portugal, Romania, Russia, Slovakia, South Africa, Spain, Sweden, Switzerland, UK, Ukraine, USA

Organisation for Economic Co-operation and Development (OECD)

Members: Australia, Austria, Belgium, Canada, Czech Republic, Denmark, Finland, France, Germany, Greece, Hungary, Iceland, Ireland, Italy, Japan, Korea (South), Luxembourg, Mexico, Netherlands, New Zealand, Norway, Poland, Portugal, Spain, Sweden, Switzerland, Turkey, UK, USA

The European Commission participates in the work of the OECD.

Organization for Security and Co-operation in Europe (OSCE)

Members: Albania, Andorra, Armenia, Austria, Azerbaijan, Belarus, Belgium, Bosnia and Herzegovina, Bulgaria, Canada, Croatia, Cyprus, Czech Republic, Denmark, Estonia, Finland, France, Georgia, Germany, Greece, Holy See, Hungary, Iceland, Ireland, Italy, Kazakhstan, Kyrgyzstan, Latvia, Liechtenstein, Lithuania, Luxembourg, Macedonia (Former Yugoslav Republic of), Malta, Moldova, Monaco, Netherlands, Norway, Poland, Portugal, Romania, Russia, San Marino, Slovakia, Slovenia, Spain, Sweden, Switzerland, Tajikistan, Turkey, Turkmenistan, UK, Ukraine, USA, Uzbekistan, Yugoslavia*

* Yugoslavia (Serbia and Montenegro) has been suspended since 1992.

Members of the Minsk Group: Belarus, Finland, France, Germany, Hungary, Italy, Russia, Sweden, Switzerland, Turkey and USA, plus Armenia and Azerbaijan

Organization of African Unity (OAU)

Members: Algeria, Angola, Benin, Botswana, Burkina Faso, Burundi, Cameroon, Cape Verde, Central African Republic, Chad, Comoros, Congo (Brazzaville), Congo, Democratic Republic of (formerly Zaire), Côte d'Ivoire, Djibouti, Egypt, Equatorial Guinea, Eritrea, Ethiopia, Gabon, Gambia, Ghana, Guinea, Guinea-Bissau, Kenya, Lesotho, Liberia, Libya, Madagascar, Malawi, Mali, Mauritania, Mauritius, Mozambique, Namibia, Niger, Nigeria, Rwanda, Western Sahara (Saharawi Arab Democratic Republic, SADR*), Sao Tome and Principe, Senegal, Seychelles, Sierra Leone, Somalia, South Africa, Sudan, Swaziland, Tanzania, Togo, Tunisia, Uganda, Zambia, Zimbabwe

* The Western Sahara was admitted in 1982. Its membership was disputed by Morocco and other states. Morocco withdrew from the OAU in 1985.

Organization of American States (OAS)

Members: Antigua and Barbuda, Argentina, Bahamas, Barbados, Belize, Bolivia, Brazil, Canada, Chile, Colombia, Costa Rica, Cuba,* Dominica, Dominican Republic, Ecuador, El Salvador, Grenada, Guatemala, Guyana, Haiti, Honduras, Jamaica, Mexico, Nicaragua, Panama, Paraguay, Peru, Saint Kitts (Christopher) and Nevis, Saint Lucia, Saint Vincent and the Grenadines, Suriname, Trinidad and Tobago, Uruguay, USA, Venezuela

* Cuba has been excluded from participation since 1962.

Permanent observers: Algeria, Angola, Austria, Belgium, Cyprus, Egypt, Equatorial Guinea, European Union, Finland, France, Germany, Greece, Holy See, Hungary, India, Israel, Italy, Japan, Korea (South), Lebanon, Morocco, Netherlands, Pakistan, Poland, Portugal, Romania, Russia, Saudi Arabia, Spain, Switzerland, Tunisia, Ukraine

Organization of the Islamic Conference (OIC)

Members: Afghanistan, Albania, Algeria, Azerbaijan, Bahrain, Bangladesh, Benin, Brunei, Burkina Faso, Cameroon, Chad, Comoros, Djibouti, Egypt, Gabon, Gambia, Guinea, Guinea-Bissau, Indonesia, Iran, Iraq, Jordan, Kazakhstan, Kuwait, Kyrgyzstan, Lebanon, Libya, Malaysia, Maldives, Mali, Mauritania, Morocco, Mozambique, Niger, Nigeria, Oman, Pakistan, Palestine, Qatar, Saudi Arabia, Senegal, Sierra Leone, Somalia, Sudan, Syria, Tajikistan, Tunisia, Turkey, Turkmenistan, Uganda, United Arab Emirates, Yemen

South Pacific Forum

Members: Australia, Cook Islands, Fiji, Kiribati, Marshall Islands, Micronesia, Nauru, New Zealand, Niue, Palau, Papua New Guinea, Samoa (Western), Solomon Islands, Tonga, Tuvalu, Vanuatu

Wassenaar Arrangement

Members: Argentina, Australia, Austria, Belgium, Bulgaria, Canada, Czech Republic, Denmark, Finland, France, Germany, Greece, Hungary, Ireland, Italy, Japan, Korea (South), Luxembourg, Netherlands, New Zealand, Norway, Poland, Portugal, Romania, Russia, Slovakia, Spain, Sweden, Switzerland, Turkey, UK, Ukraine, USA

Western European Union (WEU)

Members: Belgium, France, Germany, Greece, Italy, Luxembourg, Netherlands, Portugal, Spain, UK

Associate Members: Iceland, Norway, Turkey

Observers: Austria, Denmark, Finland, Ireland, Sweden

Associate Partners: Bulgaria, Czech Republic, Estonia, Hungary, Latvia, Lithuania, Poland, Romania, Slovakia, Slovenia

Members of WEAG: Belgium, Denmark, France, Germany, Greece, Italy, Luxembourg, Netherlands, Norway, Portugal, Spain, Turkey, UK

Zangger Committee

Members: Argentina, Australia, Austria, Belgium, Bulgaria, Canada, Czech Republic, Denmark, Finland, France, Germany, Greece, Hungary, Ireland, Italy, Japan, Luxembourg, Netherlands, Norway, Poland, Portugal, Romania, Russia, Slovakia, South Africa, Spain, Sweden, Switzerland, UK, USA

Index

USA and 172
USSR and 172
see also under names of countries
North-East Asia Cooperation
  Dialogue 174
Northern Ireland 186, 187 *see also*
  IRA
North Pacific Co-operative Security
  Dialogue 174
North Sea 96
Norway 185
NPT (Non-Proliferation Treaty,
  1968) 86, 87, 108, 119, 125–35
NPT Review Conferences 91–92,
  188, 189
nuclear deterrence 1 *see also* MAD
Nuclear Suppliers Group 113, 114,
  115–16, 202, 213
nuclear weapon-free zones 111–12
nuclear weapons:
  categorization 86
  declared possessor states 87
  legal status 90, 193
  marginalization of 1
  non-use pledges 188
  numbers of 87, 88
  proliferation 1
  undeclared possessor states 87–91
  *see also under names of treaties
    controlling*
Nunn–Lugar programme 105–106

OAS (Organization of American
  States) 184, 203, 209, 214
OAU (Organization of African
  Unity):
  Burundi Mission 49
  Conflict Prevention, Management
    and Resolution Mechanism 52
  description 203
  members 214

peacekeeping 52
UN and 51
Oceania: military expenditure 67
OECD (Organisation for Economic
  Co-operation and Development)
  72, 80, 202, 213
Open Skies Treaty (1992) 110, 122,
  162, 181
Operation Uphold Democracy 49
Organisation for the Prohibition of
  Chemical Weapons (OPCW) 108,
  202
Organization for Security and
  Co-operation in Europe (OSCE):
  arms control and 110–11
  description 202
  established 52, 162
  EU and 188
  evolution of 52, 160–65
  Forum for Security Co-operation
    111, 164
  High Commissioner for National
    Minorities (HCNM) 53, 163
  institutions 161
  Lisbon Declaration (1996)
    164–65, 195
  Lisbon Summit 164
  members 213
  peacekeeping operations 47–48,
    53, 164
  structures 161
  see also Conference on Security
    and Co-operation in Europe
    (CSCE) *and under names of
    countries*
Organization of the Islamic
  Conference 203, 214
Oslo Agreement (1993) 185
Ottawa Group 112, 113, 203
Outer Space Treaty (1967) 112, 118
Owen, Lord 31, 32